The Art of War
and
The Prince

Niccolo Machiavelli
Translated by William K. Marriott

For information regarding special discounts for bulk purchases, please contact BN Publishing at info@bnpublishing.com

©Copyright 2007 – BN Publishing
www.bnpublishing.com

ALL RIGHTS RESERVED
Printed in the U.S.A.

Table of Contents

The Seven Books on the Art of War
PREFACE

Many, Lorenzo, have held and still hold the opinion, that there is nothing which has less in common with another, and that is so dissimilar, as civilian life is from the military. Whence it is often observed, if anyone designs to avail himself of an enlistment in the army, that he soon changes, not only his clothes, but also his customs, his habits, his voice, and in the presence of any civilian custom, he goes to pieces; for I do not believe that any man can dress in civilian clothes who wants to be quick and ready for any violence; nor can that man have civilian customs and habits, who judges those customs to be effeminate and those habits not conducive to his actions; nor does it seem right to him to maintain his ordinary appearance and voice who, with his beard and cursing, wants to make other men afraid: which makes such an opinion in these times to be very true. But if they should consider the ancient institutions, they would not find matter more united, more in conformity, and which, of necessity, should be like to each other as much as these (civilian and military); for in all the arts that are established in a society for the sake of the common good of men, all those institutions created to (make people) live in fear of the laws and of God would be in vain, if their defense had not been provided for and which, if well arranged, will maintain not only these, but also those that are not well established. And so (on the contrary), good institutions without the help of the military are not much differently disordered than the habitation of a superb and regal palace, which, even though adorned with jewels and gold, if it is not roofed over will not have anything to protect it from the rain. And, if in any other institutions of a City and of a Republic every diligence is employed in keeping men loyal, peaceful, and full of the fear of God, it is doubled in the military; for in what man ought the country look for greater loyalty than in that man who has to promise to die for her? In whom ought there to be a greater love of peace, than in him who can only be injured by war? In whom ought there to be a greater fear of God than in him who, undergoing infinite dangers every day, has more need for His aid? If these necessities in forming the life of the soldier are well considered, they are found to be praised by those who gave the laws to the Commanders and by those who were put in charge of military training, and followed and imitated with all diligence by others.

But because military institutions have become completely corrupt and far removed from the ancient ways, these sinister opinions have arisen which make the military hated and intercourse with those who train them avoided. And I, judging, by what I have seen and read, that it is not impossible to restore its ancient ways and return some form of past virtue to it, have decided not to let this leisure time of mine pass without doing something, to write what I know of the art of war, to the satisfaction of those who are lovers of the ancient deeds. And although it requires courage to treat of those matters of which others have made a profession, none the less, I do not believe that it is a mistake to occupy a position with words, which may, with greater presumption, have been occupied with deeds; for the errors which I should make in writing can be corrected without injury to anyone, but those which are made with deeds cannot be found out except by the ruin of the Commanders.

You, Lorenzo, will therefore consider the quality of these efforts of mine, and will give in your judgement of them that censure or praise which will appear to you to be merited. I send you these, as much as to show myself grateful for all the benefits I have received from you, although I will not include in them the (review) of this work of mine, as well as also, because being accustomed to honor similar works of those who shine because of their nobility, wealth, genius, and liberality, I know you do not have many equals in wealth and nobility, few in ingenuity, and no one in liberality.

FIRST BOOK

As I believe that it is possible for one to praise, without concern, any man after he is dead since every reason and supervision for adulation is lacking, I am not apprehensive in praising our own Cosimo Ruccelai, whose name is never remembered by me without tears, as I have recognized in him those parts which can be desired in a good friend among friends and in a citizen of his country. For I do not know what pertained to him more than to spend himself willingly, not excepting that courage of his, for his friends, and I do not know of any enterprise that dismayed him when he knew it was for the good of his country. And I confess freely not to have met among so many men whom I have known and worked with, a man in whom there was a mind more fired with great and magnificent things. Nor does one grieve with the friends of another of his death, except for his having been born to die young, unhonored within his own home, without having been able to benefit anyone with that mind of his, for one would know that no one could speak of him, except (to say) that a good friend had died. It does not remain for us, however, or for anyone else who, like us, knew him, to be able because of this to keep the faith (since deeds do not seem to) to his laudable qualities. It is true however, that fortune was not so unfriendly to him that it did not leave some brief memory of the dexterity of his genius, as was demonstrated by some of his writings and compositions of amorous verses, in which (as he was not in love) he (employed as an) exercise in order not to use his time uselessly in his juvenile years, in order that fortune might lead him to higher thoughts. Here, it can be clearly comprehended, that if his objective was exercise, how very happily he described his ideas, and how much he was honored in his poetry. Fortune, however, having deprived us of the use of so great a friend, it appears to me it is not possible to find any other better remedy than for us to seek to benefit from his memory, and recover from it any matter that was either keenly observed or wisely discussed. And as there is nothing of his more recent than the discussions which the Lord Fabrizio Colonna had with him in his gardens, where matters pertaining to war were discussed at length by that Lord, with (questions) keenly and prudently asked by Cosimo, it seemed proper to me having been present with other friends of ours, to recall him to memory, so that reading it, the friends of Cosimo who met there will renew in their minds the memory of his virtue, and another part grieving for not having been there, will learn in part of many things discussed wisely by a most sagacious man useful not only to the military way of life, but to the civilian as well. I will relate, therefore, how Fabrizio Colonna, when he returned from Lombardy where he had fought a long time gloriously for the Catholic King, decided to pass through Florence to rest several days in that City in order to visit His Excellency the Duke, and see again several gentlemen with whom he had been familiar in the past. Whence it appeared proper to Cosimo to invite him to a banquet in his gardens, not so much to show his generosity as to have reason to talk to him at length, and to learn and understand several things from him, according as one can hope to from such a man, for it appeared to him to give him an opportunity to spend a day discussing such matters as would satisfy his mind.

Fabrizio, therefore, came as planned, and was received by Cosimo together with several other loyal friends of his, among whom were Zanobi Buondelmonti, Battista Della Palla, and Luigi Alamanni, young men most ardent in the same studies and loved by him, whose good qualities, because they were also praised daily by himself, we will omit. Fabrizio, therefore, was honored according to the times and the place with all the highest honors they could give him. As soon as the convivial pleasures were past and the table cleared and every arrangement of feasting finished, which, in the presence of great men and those who have their minds turned to honorable thoughts is soon accomplished, and because the day was long and the heat intense, Cosimo, in order to satisfy their desire better, judged it would be well to take the opportunity to escape the heat by leading them to the more secret and shadowy part of his garden: when they arrived there and chairs brought out, some sat on the grass which was most fresh in the place, some sat on chairs placed in those parts under the shadow of very high trees; Fabrizio praised the place as most delightful, and looking especially at the trees, he did not recognize one of them, and looked puzzled. Cosimo, becoming aware of this said: Perhaps you have no knowledge of some of these trees, but do not wonder about them, because here are some which were more widely known by the ancients than are those commonly seen today. And giving him the name of some and telling him that Bernardo, his grandfather, had worked hard in their culture, Fabrizio replied: I was thinking that it was what you said I was, and this place and this study make me remember several Princes of the Kingdom, who delighted in their ancient culture and the shadow they cast. And stopping speaking of this, and somewhat upon himself as though in suspense, he added: If I did not think I would offend you, I would give you my opinion: but I do not believe in talking and discussing things with friends in this manner that I insult them. How much better would they have done (it is said with peace to everyone) to seek to imitate the ancients in the strong and rugged things, not in the soft and delicate, and in the things they did under the sun, not in the shadows, to adopt the honest and perfect ways of antiquity, not the false and corrupt; for while these practices were pleasing to my Romans, my country (without them) was ruined. To which Cosimo replied (but to avoid the necessity of having to repeat so many times who is speaking, and what the other adds, only the names of those speaking will be noted, without repeating the others). Cosimo, therefore, said: You have opened the way for a discussion which I desired, and I pray you to speak without regard, for I will question you without regard; and if, in questioning or in replying, I accuse or excuse anyone, it will not be for accusing or excusing, but to understand the truth from you.

FABRIZIO: And I will be much content to tell you what I know of all that you ask me; whether it be true or not, I will leave to your judgment. And I will be grateful if you ask me, for I am about to learn as much from what you ask me, as you will from me replying to you, because many times a wise questioner causes one to consider many things and understand many others which, without having been asked, would never have been understood.

COSIMO: I want to return to what you first were saying, that my grandfather and those of yours had more wisely imitated the ancients in rugged things than in delicate ones, and I want to excuse my side because I will let you excuse the other (your side). I do not believe that in your time there was a man who disliked living as softly as he, and that he was so much a lover of that rugged life which you praise: none the less he recognized he could not practice it in his personal life, nor in that of his sons, having been born in so corrupted an age, where anyone who wanted to depart from the common usage would be deformed and despised by everyone. For if anyone in a naked state should thrash upon the sand under the highest sun, or upon the snow in the most icy months of winter, as did Diogenes, he would be considered mad. If anyone (like the Spartan) should raise his children on a farm, make them sleep in the open, go with head and feet bare, bathe in cold water in order to harden them to endure vicissitudes, so that they then might love life less and fear death less, he would be praised by few and followed by none. So that dismayed at these ways of living, he presently leaves the ways of the ancients, and in imitating antiquity, does only that which he can with little wonderment.

FABRIZIO: You have excused him strongly in this part, and certainly you speak the truth: but I did not speak so much of these rugged ways of living, as of those other more human ways which have a greater conformity to the ways of living today, which I do not believe should have been difficult to introduce by one who is numbered among the Princes of a City. I will never forego my examples of my Romans. If their way of living should be examined, and the institutions in their Republic, there will be observed in her many things not impossible to introduce in a Society where there yet might be something of good.

COSIMO: What are those things similar to the ancients that you would introduce?

FABRIZIO: To honor and reward virtue, not to have contempt for poverty, to esteem the modes and orders of military discipline, to constrain citizens to love one another, to live without factions, to esteem less the private than the public good, and other such things which could easily be added in these times. It is not difficult to persuade (people) to these ways, when one considers these at length and approaches them in the usual manner, for the truth will appear in such (examinations) that every common talent is capable of undertaking them. Anyone can arrange these things; (for example), one plants trees under the shadow of which he lives more happily and merrily than if he had not (planted them).

COSIMO: I do not want to reply to anything of what you have spoken, but I do want leave to give a judgment on these, which can be easily judged, and I shall address myself to you who accuse those who in serious and important actions are not imitators of the ancients, thinking that in this way I can more easily carry out my intentions. I should want, therefore, to know from you whence it arises that, on the one hand you condemn those who do not imitate the ancients in their actions, on the other hand, in matters of war which is your profession and in which you are judged to be excellent, it is not observed that you have employed any of the ancient methods, or those which have some similarity.

FABRIZIO: You have come to the point where I expected you to, for what I said did not merit any other question, nor did I wish for any other. And although I am able to save myself with a simple excuse, nonetheless I want, for your greater satisfaction and mine, since the season (weather) allows it, to enter into a much longer discussion. Men who want to do something, ought first to prepare themselves with all industry, in order (when the opportunity is seen) to be prepared to achieve that which they have proposed. And whenever the preparations are undertaken cautiously, unknown to anyone, no none can be accused of negligence unless he is first discovered by the occasion; in which if it is not then successful, it is seen that either he has not sufficiently prepared himself, or that he has not in some part given thought to it. And as the opportunity has not come to me to be able to show the preparations I would make to bring the military to your ancient organization, and it I have not done so, I cannot be blamed either by you or by others. I believe this excuse is enough to respond to your accusation.

COSIMO: It would be enough if I was certain that the opportunity did not present itself.

FABRIZIO: But because I know you could doubt whether this opportunity had come about or not, I want to discuss at length (if you will listen to me with patience) which preparations are necessary to be made first, what occasion needs to arise, what difficulty impedes the preparations from becoming beneficial and the occasion from arriving, and that this is (which appears a paradox) most difficult and most easy to do.

COSIMO: You cannot do anything more pleasing for me and for the others than this. But if it is not painful for you to speak, it will never be painful for us to listen. But at this discussion may be long, I want help from these, my friends, and with your permission, and they and I pray you one thing, that you do not become annoyed if we sometimes interrupt you with some opportune question.

FABRIZIO: I am most content that you, Cosimo, with these other young people here, should question me, for I believe that young men will become more familiar with military matters, and will more easily understand what I have to say. The others, whose hair (head) is white and whose blood is icy, in part are enemies of war and in part incorrigible, as those who believe that the times and not the evil ways constrain men to live in such a fashion. So ask anything of me, with assurance and without regard; I desire this, as much because it will afford me a little rest, as because it will give me pleasure not to leave any doubts in your minds. I want to begin from your words, where you said to me that in war (which is my profession) I have not employed any of the ancient methods. Upon this I say, that this being a profession by which men of every time were not able to live honestly, it cannot be employed as a profession except by a Republic or a Kingdom; and both of these, if well established, will never allow any of their citizens or subjects to employ it as a profession: for he who practices it will never be judged to be good, as to gain some usefulness from it at any time he must be rapacious, deceitful, violent, and have many qualities, which of necessity, do not make him good: nor can men who employ this as a profession, the great as well as the least, be made otherwise, for this profession does not provide for them in peace. Whence they are obliged, either to hope that there will be no peace or to gain so much for themselves in times of war, that they can provide for themselves in times of peace. And wherever one of these two thoughts exists, it does not occur in a good man; for, from the desire to provide for oneself in every circumstance, robberies, violence and assassinations result, which such soldiers do to friends as well as to enemies: and from not desiring peace, there arises those deceptions which Captains perpetrate upon those whom they lead, because war hardens them: and even if peace occurs frequently, it happens that the leaders, being deprived of their stipends and of their licentious mode of living, raise a flag of piracy, and without any mercy sack a province.

Do you not have within the memory of events of your time, many soldiers in Italy, finding themselves without employment because of the termination of wars, gathered themselves into very troublesome gangs, calling themselves companies, and went about levying tribute on the towns and sacking the country, without there being any remedy able to be applied? Have you not read how the Carthaginian soldiers, when the first war they engaged in with the Romans under Matus and Spendius was ended, tumultuously chose two leaders, and waged a more dangerous war against the Carthaginians than that which they had just concluded with the Romans? And in the time of our fathers, Francesco Sforza, in order to be able to live honorably (comfortably) in times of peace, not only deceived the Milanese, in whose pay he was, but took away their liberty and became their Prince. All the other soldiers of Italy, who have employed the military as their particular profession, have been like this man; and if, through their malignity, they have not become Dukes of Milan, so much more do they merit to be censured; for without such a return (if their lives were to be examined), they all have the same cares. Sforza, father of Francesco, constrained Queen Giovanna to throw herself into the arms of the King of Aragon, having abandoned her suddenly, and left her disarmed amid her enemies, only in order to satisfy his ambition of either levying tribute or taking the Kingdom. Braccio, with the same industry, sought to occupy the Kingdom of Naples, and would have succeeded, had he not been routed and killed at Aquilla. Such evils do not result from anything else other than the existence of men who employ the practice of soldiering as their own profession. Do you not have a proverb which strengthens my argument, which says: War makes robbers, and peace hangs them? For those who do not know how to live by another practice, and not finding any one who will support them in that, and not having so much virtue that they know how to come and live together honorably, are forced by necessity to roam the streets, and justice is forced to extinguish them.

COSIMO: You have made me turn this profession (art) of soldiering back almost to nothing, and I had supposed it to be the most excellent and most honorable of any: so that if you do not clarify this better, I will not be satisfied; for if it is as you say, I do not know whence arises the glory of Caesar, Pompey, Scipio, Marcellus, and of so many Roman Captains who are celebrated for their fame as the Gods.

FABRIZIO: I have not yet finished discussing all that I proposed, which included two things: the one, that a good man was not able to undertake this practice because of his profession: the other, that a well established Republic or Kingdom would never permit its subjects or citizens to employ it for their profession. Concerning the first, I have spoken as much as has occurred to me: it remains for me to talk of the second, where I shall reply to this last question of yours, and I say that Pompey and Caesar, and almost all those Captains who were in Rome after the last Carthaginian war, acquired fame as valiant men, not as good men: but those who had lived before them acquired glory as valiant and good men: which results from the fact that these latter did not take up the practice of war as their profession; and those whom I named first as those who employed it as their profession. And while the Republic lived immaculately, no great citizen ever presumed by means of such a practice to enrich himself during (periods of) peace by breaking laws, despoiling the provinces, usurping and tyrannizing the country, and imposing himself in every way; nor did anyone of the lowest fortune think of violating the sacred agreement, adhere himself to any private individual, not fearing the

Senate, or to perform any disgraceful act of tyranny in order to live at all times by the profession of war. But those who were Captains, being content with the triumph, returned with a desire for the private life; and those who were members (of the army) returned with a desire to lay down the arms they had taken up; and everyone returned to the art (trade or profession) by which they ordinarily lived; nor was there ever anyone who hoped to provide for himself by plunder and by means of these arts. A clear and evident example of this as it applies to great citizens can be found in the Regent Attilio, who, when he was captain of the Roman armies in Africa, and having almost defeated the Carthaginians, asked the Senate for permission to return to his house to look after his farms which were being spoiled by his laborers. Whence it is clearer than the sun, that if that man had practiced war as his profession, and by means of it thought to obtain some advantage for himself, having so many provinces which (he could) plunder, he would not have asked permission to return to take care of his fields, as each day he could have obtained more than the value of all his possessions. But as these good men, who do not practice war as their profession, do not expect to gain anything from it except hard work, danger, and glory, as soon as they are sufficiently glorious, desire to return to their homes and live from the practice of their own profession. As to men of lower status and gregarious soldiers, it is also true that every one voluntarily withdrew from such a practice, for when he was not fighting would have desired to fight, but when he was fighting wanted to be dismissed. Which illustrates the many ways, and especially in seeing that it was among the first privileges, that the Roman people gave to one of its Citizens, that he should not be constrained unwillingly to fight. Rome, therefore, while she was well organized (which it was up to the time of the Gracchi) did not have one soldier who had to take up this practice as a profession, and therefore had few bad ones, and these were severely punished. A well ordered City, therefore, ought to desire that this training for war ought to be employed in times of peace as an exercise, and in times of war as a necessity and for glory, and allow the public only to use it as a profession, as Rome did. And any citizen who has other aims in (using) such exercises is not good, and any City which governs itself otherwise, is not well ordered.

COSIMO: I am very much content and satisfied with what you have said up to now, and this conclusion which you have made pleases me greatly: and I believe it will be true when expected from a Republic, but as to Kings, I do not yet know why I should believe that a King would not want particularly to have around him those who take up such a practice as their profession.

FABRIZIO: A well ordered Kingdom ought so much the more avoid such artifices, for these only are the things which corrupt the King and all the Ministers in a Tyranny. And do not, on the other side, tell me of some present Kingdom, for I will not admit them to be all well ordered Kingdoms; for Kingdoms that are well ordered do not give absolute (power to) Rule to their Kings, except in the armies, for only there is a quick decision necessary, and, therefore, he who (rules) there must have this unique power: in other matters, he cannot do anything without counsel, and those who counsel him have to fear those whom he may have near him who, in times of peace, desire war because they are unable to live without it. But I want to dwell a little longer on this subject, and look for a Kingdom totally good, but similar to those that exist today, where those who take up the profession of war for themselves still ought to be feared by the King, for the sinews of armies without any doubt are the infantry. So that if a King does not organize himself in such a way that his infantry in time of peace are content to return to their homes and live from the practice of their own professions, it must happen of necessity that he will be ruined; for there is not to be found a more dangerous infantry than that which is composed of those who make the waging of war their profession; for you are forced to make war always, or pay them always, or to risk the danger that they take away the Kingdom from you. To make war always is not possible: (and) one cannot pay always; and, hence, that danger is run of losing the State. My Romans (as I have said), as long as they were wise and good, never permitted that their citizens should take up this practice as their profession, notwithstanding that they were able to raise them at all times, for they made war at all times: but in order to avoid the harm which this continuous practice of theirs could do to them, since the times did not change, they changed the men, and kept turning men over in their legions so that every fifteen years they always completely re-manned them: and thus they desired men in the flower of their age, which is from eighteen to thirty five years, during which time their legs, their hands, and their eyes, worked together, nor did they expect that their strength should decrease in them, or that malice should grow in them, as they did in corrupt times.

Ottavianus first, and then Tiberius, thinking more of their own power than the public usefulness, in order to rule over the Roman people more easily, begun to disarm them and to keep the same armies continually at the frontiers of the Empire. And because they did not think it sufficient to hold the Roman People and the Senate in check, they instituted an army called the Praetorian (Guard), which was kept near the walls of Rome in a fort adjacent to that City. And as they now begun freely to permit men assigned to the army to practice military matters as their profession, there soon resulted that these men became insolent, and they became formidable to the Senate and damaging to the Emperor. Whence there resulted that many men were killed because of their insolence, for they gave the Empire and took it away from anyone they wished, and it often occurred that at one time there were many Emperors created by the several armies. From which state of affairs proceeded first the division of the Empire and finally its ruin. Kings ought, therefore, if they want to live securely, have their infantry composed of men, who, when it is necessary for him to wage war, will willingly go forth to it for love of him, and afterwards when peace comes, more willingly return to their homes; which will always happen if he selects men who know how to live by a profession other than this. And thus he ought to desire, with the coming of peace, that his Princes return to governing their people, gentlemen to the cultivation of their possessions, and the infantry to their particular arts (trades or professions); and everyone of these will willingly make war in order to have peace, and will not seek to disturb the peace to have war.

COSIMO: Truly, this reasoning of yours appears to me well considered: nonetheless, as it is almost contrary to what I have thought up to now, my mind is not yet purged of every doubt. For I see many Lords and Gentlemen who provide for themselves in times of peace through the training for war, as do your equals who obtain provisions from Princes and the Community. I also see almost all the men at arms remaining in the garrisons of the city and of the fortresses. So that it appears to me that there is a long time of peace for everyone.

FABRIZIO: I do not believe that you believe this, that everyone has a place in time of peace; for other reasons can be cited for their being stationed there, and the small number of people who remain in the places mentioned by you will answer your question. What is the proportion of infantry needed to be employed in time of war to that in peace? For while the fortresses and the city are garrisoned in times of peace, they are much more garrisoned in times of war; to this should be added the soldiers kept in the field who are a great number, but all of whom are released in time of peace. And concerning the garrisons of States, who are a small number, Pope Julius and you have shown how much they are to be feared who do not know any other profession than war, as you have taken them out of your garrisons because of their insolence, and placed the Swiss there, who are born and raised under the laws and are chosen by the community in an honest election; so do not say further that in peace there is a place for every man. As to the men at arms continued in their enlistment in peacetime, the answer appears more difficult. Nonetheless, whoever considers everything well, will easily find the answer, for this thing of keeping on the men at arms is a corrupt thing and not good. The reason is this; as there are men who do not have any art (trade or profession), a thousand evils will arise every day in those States where they exist, and especially so if they were to be joined by a great number of companions: but as they are few, and unable by themselves to constitute an army, they therefore, cannot do any serious damage. Nonetheless, they have done so many times, as I said of Francesco and of Sforza, his father, and of Braccio of Perugia. So I do not approve of this custom of keeping men at arms, both because it is corrupt and because it can cause great evils.

COSIMO: Would you do without them? Or if you keep them, how would you do so?

FABRIZIO: By means of an ordinance, not like those of the King of France, because they are as dangerous and insolent as ours, but like those of the ancients, who created horsemen (cavalry) from their subjects, and in times of peace sent them back to their homes to live from the practice of their own profession, as I shall discuss at length before I finish this discussion. So, if this part of the army can now live by such a practice even when there is peace, it stems from a corrupt order. As to the provisions that are reserved for me and the other leaders, I say to you that this likewise is a most corrupt order, for a wise Republic ought not to give them to anyone, rather it ought to employ its citizens as leaders in war, and in time of peace desire that they return to their professions. Thus also, a wise King ought not to give (provisions) to them, or if he does give them, the reasons ought to be either as a reward for some excellent act, or in order to avail himself of such a man in peace as well as in war. And because you have mentioned me, I want the example to include me, and I say I have never practiced war as a profession, for my profession is to govern my subjects, and defend them, and in order to defend them, I must love peace but know how to make war; and my King does not reward and esteem me so much for what I know of war, as because I know also how to counsel him in peace. Any King ought not, therefore, to want to have next to him anyone who is not thusly constituted, if he is wise and wants to govern prudently; for if he has around him either too many lovers of peace or too many lovers of war, they will cause him to err. I cannot, in this first discussion of mine and according to my suggestion, say otherwise, and if this is not enough for you, you must seek one which satisfies you better. You can begin to recognize how much difficulty there is in bringing the ancient methods into modem wars, and what preparations a wise man must make, and what opportunities he can hope for to put them into execution. But little by little you will know these things better if the discussion on bringing any part of the ancient institutions to the present order of things does not weary you.

COSIMO: If we first desired to hear your discussion of these matters, truly what you have said up to now redoubles that desire. We thank you, therefore, for what we have had and ask you for the rest.

FABRIZIO: Since this is your pleasure, I want to begin to treat of this matter from the beginning being able in that way to demonstrate it more fully, so that it may be better understood. The aim of those who want to make war is to be able to combat in the field with every (kind) of enemy, and to be able to win the engagement. To want to do this, they must raise an army. In raising an army, it is necessary to find men, arm them, organize them, train them in small and large (battle) orders, lodge them, and expose them to the enemy afterwards, either at a standstill or while marching. All the industry of war in the field is placed in these things, which are the more necessary and honored (in the waging of war). And if one does well in offering battle to the enemy, all the other errors he may make in the conduct of the war are supportable: but if he lacks this organization, even though he be valiant in other particulars, he will never carry on a war to victory (and honor). For, as one engagement that you win cancels out every other bad action of yours, so likewise, when you lose one, all the things you have done well before become useless. Since it is necessary, therefore, first to find men, you must come to the *Deletto* (Draft) of them, as thus the ancients called it, and which we call *Scelta* (Selection): but in order to call it by a more honored name, I want us to preserve the name of *Deletto*. Those who have drawn up regulations for war want men to be chosen from temperate countries as they have spirit and are prudent; for warm countries give rise to men who are prudent but not spirited, and cold (countries) to men who are spirited but not prudent. This regulation is drawn up well for one who is the Prince of all the world, and is therefore permitted to draw men from those places that appear best to him: but wanting to draw up a regulation that anyone can use, one must say that every Republic and every Kingdom ought to take soldiers from their own country, whether it is hot, cold, or temperate. For, from ancient examples, it is seen that in every country, good soldiers are made by training; because where nature is lacking, industry supplies it, which, in this case, is worth more than nature: And selecting them from another place cannot be called *Deletto*, because *Deletto* means to say to take the best of a province, and to have the power to select as well those who do not want to fight as those who do want to. This *Deletto* therefore, cannot be made unless the places are subject to you; for you cannot take whoever you want in the countries that are not yours, but you need to take those who want to come.

COSIMO: And of those who want to come, it can even be said, that they turn and leave you, and because of this, it can then be called a *Deletto*.

FABRIZIO: In a certain way, you say what is true: but consider the defects that such as *Deletto* has in itself, for often it happens that it is not a *Deletto*. The first thing (to consider), is that those who are not your subjects and do not willingly want to fight, are not of the best, rather they are of the worst of a province; for if nay are troublesome, idle, without restraint, without religion, subject to the rule of the father, blasphemous, gamblers, and in every way badly brought up, they are those who want to fight, (and) these habits cannot be more contrary to a true and good military life. When there are so many of such men offered to you that they exceed the number you had designated, you can select them; but if the material is bad, it is impossible for the *Deletto* to be good: but many times it happens that they are not so many as (are needed) to fill the number you require: so that being forced to take them all, it results that it can no longer be called the making of a *Deletto*, but in enlisting of infantry. The armies of Italy and other places are raised today with these evils, except in Germany, where no one is enlisted by command of the Prince, but according to the wishes of those who want to fight. Think, therefore, what methods of those ancients can now be introduced in an army of men put together by similar means.

COSIMO: What means should be taken therefore?

FABRIZIO: What I have just said: select them from your own subjects, and with the authority of the Prince.

COSIMO: Would you introduce any ancient form in those thus selected?

FABRIZIO: You know well it would be so; if it is a Principality, he who should command should be their Prince or an ordinary Lord; or if it is a Republic, a citizen who for the time should be Captain: otherwise it is difficult to do the thing well.

COSIMO: Why?

FABRIZIO: I will tell you in time: for now, I want this to suffice for you, that it cannot be done well in any other way.

COSIMO: If you have, therefore, to make *ibis Deletto* in your country, whence do you judge it better to draw them, from the City or the Countryside?

FABRIZIO: Those who have written of this all agree that it is better to select them from the Countryside, as they are men accustomed to discomfort, brought up on hard work, accustomed to be in the sun and avoid the shade, know how to handle the sword, dig a ditch, carry a load, and are without cunning or malice. But on this subject, my opinion would be, that as soldiers are of two kinds, afoot and on horseback, that those afoot be selected from the Countryside, and those on horseback from the City.

COSIMO: Of what age would you draw them?

FABRIZIO: If I had to raise a (entirely) new army, I would draw them from seventeen to forty years of age; if the army already exists and I had to replenish it, at seventeen years of age always.

COSIMO: I do not understand this distinction well.

FABRIZIO: I will tell you: if I should have to organize an army where there is none, it would be necessary to select all those men who were more capable, as long as they were of military age, in order to instruct them as I would tell them: but if I should have to make the *Deletto* in places where the army was (already) organized, in order to supplement it, I would take those of seventeen years of age, because the others having been taken for some time would have been selected and instructed.

COSIMO: Therefore you would want to make an ordinance similar to that which exists in our countries.
FABRIZIO: You say well: it is true that I would arm them, captain them, train them, and organize them, in a way which I do not know whether or not you have organized them similarly.
COSIMO: Therefore you praise the ordinance?
FABRIZIO: Why would you want me to condemn it?
COSIMO: Because many wise men have censured it.
FABRIZIO: You say something contrary, when you say a wise man censured the ordinance: for he can be held a wise man and to have censured them wrongly.
COSIMO: The wrong conclusion that he has made will always cause us to have such an opinion.
FABRIZIO: Watch out that the defect is not yours, but his: as that which you recognized before this discussion furnishes proof.
COSIMO: You do a most gracious thing. But I want to tell you that you should be able to justify yourself better in that of which those men are accused. These men say thusly: either that it is useless and our trusting in it will cause us to lose the State, or it is of virtue, and he who governs through it can easily deprive her of it. They cite the Romans, who by their own arms lost their liberty: They cite the Venetians and the King of France, of whom they say that the former, in order not to obey one of its Citizens employed the arms of others, and the King disarmed his People so as to be able to command them more easily. But they fear the uselessness of this much more; for which uselessness they cite two principal reasons: the one, because they are inexpert; the other, for having to fight by force: because they say that they never learn anything from great men, and nothing good is ever done by force.
FABRIZIO: All the reasons that you mention are from men who are not far sighted, as I shall clearly show. And first, as to the uselessness, I say to you that no army is of more use than your own, nor can an army of your own be organized except in this way. And as there is no debating over this, which all the examples of ancient history does for us, I do not want to lose time over it. And because they cite inexperience and force, I say (as it is true) that inept experience gives rise to little spirit (enthusiasm) and force makes for discontent: but experience and enthusiasm gains for themselves the means for arming, training, and organizing them, as you will see in the first part of this discussion. But as to force, you must understand that as men are brought to the army by commandment of the Prince, they have to come, whether it is entirely by force or entirely voluntarily: for if it were entirely from desire, there would not be a *Deletto* as only a few of them would go; so also, the (going) entirely by force would produce bad results; therefore, a middle way ought to be taken where neither the entirely forced or entirely voluntarily (means are used), but they should come, drawn by the regard they have for the Prince, where they are more afraid of his anger then the immediate punishment: and it will always happen that there will be a compulsion mixed with willingness, from which that discontent cannot arise which causes bad effects. Yet I do not claim that an army thus constituted cannot be defeated; for many times the Roman armies were overcome, and the army of Hannibal was defeated: so that it can be seen that no army can be so organized that a promise can be given that it cannot be routed. These wise men of yours, therefore, ought not measure this uselessness from having lost one time, but to believe that just as they can lose, so too they can win and remedy the cause of the defeat. And if they should look into this, they will find that it would not have happened because of a defect in the means, but of the organization which was not sufficiently perfect. And, as I have said, they ought to provide for you, not by censuring the organization, but by correcting it: as to how this ought to be done, you will come to know little by little.
As to being apprehensive that such organization will not deprive you of the State by one who makes himself a leader, I reply, that the arms carried by his citizens or subjects, given to them by laws and ordinances, never do him harm, but rather are always of some usefulness, and preserve the City uncorrupted for a longer time by means of these (arms), than without (them). Rome remained free four hundred years while armed: Sparta

eight hundred: Many other Cities have been disarmed, and have been free less than forty years; for Cities have need of arms, and if they do not have arms of their own, they hire them from foreigners, and the arms of foreigners more readily do harm to the public good than their own; for they are easier to corrupt, and a citizen who becomes powerful can more readily avail himself, and can also manage the people more readily as he has to oppress men who are disarmed. In addition to this, a City ought to fear two enemies more than one. One which avails itself of foreigners immediately has to fear not only its citizens but the foreigners that it enlists; and, remembering what I told you a short while ago of Francesco Sforza, (you will see that) that fear ought to exist. One which employs its own arms, has not other fear except of its own Citizens. But of all the reasons which can be given, I want this one to serve me, that no one ever established any Republic or Kingdom who did not think that it should be defended by those who lived there with arms: and if the Venetians had been as wise in this as in their other institutions, they would have created a new world Kingdom; but who so much more merit censure, because they had been the first who were armed by their founders. And not having dominion on land, they armed themselves on the sea, where they waged war with virtue, and with arms in hand enlarged their country. But when the time came when they had to wage war on land to defend Venice and where they ought to have sent their own citizens to fight (on land), they enlisted as their captain (a foreigner), the Marquis of Mantua. This was the sinister course which prevented them from rising to the skies and expanding. And they did this in the belief that, as they knew how to wage war at sea, they should not trust themselves in waging it on land; which was an unwise belief (distrust), because a Sea captain, who is accustomed to combat with winds, water, and men, could more easily become a Captain on land where the combat is with men only, than a land Captain become a sea one. And my Romans, knowing how to combat on land and not on the sea, when the war broke out with the Carthaginians who were powerful on the sea, did not enlist Greeks or Spaniards experienced at sea, but imposed that change on those citizens they sent (to fight) on land, and they won. If they did this in order that one of their citizens should not become Tyrant, it was a fear that was given little consideration; for, in addition to the other reasons mentioned a short while ago concerning such a proposal, if a citizen (skilled) in (the use of) arms at sea had never been made a Tyrant in a City situated in the sea, so much less would he be able to do this if he were (skilled) in (the use of arms) on land. And, because of this, they ought to have seen that arms in the hands of their own citizens could not create Tyrants, but the evil institutions of a Government are those which cause a City to be tyrannized; and, as they had a good Government, did not have to fear arms of their own citizens. They took an imprudent course, therefore, which was the cause of their being deprived of much glory and happiness. As to the error which the King of France makes in not having his people disciplined to war, from what has been cited from examples previously mentioned, there is no one (devoid of some particular passion of theirs) who does not judge this defect to be in the Republic, and that this negligence alone is what makes it weak. But I have made too great a digression and have gotten away from my subject: yet I have done this to answer you and to show you, that no reliance can be had on arms other than ones own, and ones own arms cannot be established otherwise than by way of an ordinance, nor can forms of armies be introduced in any place, nor military discipline instituted. If you have read the arrangements which the first Kings made in Rome, and most especially of Servius Tullus, you will find that the institution of classes is none other than an arrangement to be able quickly to put together an army for the defense of that City. But turning to our *Deletto*, I say again, that having to replenish an established (old) organization, I would take the seventeen year olds, but having to create a new one, I would take them of every age between seventeen and forty in order to avail myself of them quickly.

COSIMO: Would you make a difference of what profession (art) you would choose them from?

FABRIZIO: These writers do so, for they do not want that bird hunters, fishermen, cooks, procurers, and anyone who makes amusement his calling should be taken, but they want that, in addition to tillers of the soil, smiths and blacksmiths, carpenters, butchers, hunters, and such like, should be taken. But I would make little difference in conjecturing from his calling how good the man may be, but how much I can use him with the greatest usefulness. And for this reason, the peasants, who are accustomed to working the land, are more useful than anyone else, for of all the professions (arts), this one is used more than any other in the army: After this, are the forgers (smiths), carpenters, blacksmiths, shoemakers; of whom it is useful to have many, for their skills succeed in many things, as they are a very good thing for a soldier to have, from whom you draw double service.

COSIMO: How are those who are or are not suitable to fight chosen?

FABRIZIO: I want to talk of the manner of selecting a new organization in order to make it after wards into an army; which yet also apply in the discussion of the selection that should be made in re-manning an old (established) organization. I say, therefore, that how good the man is that you have to select as a soldier is recognized either from his experience, shown by some excellent deeds of his, or by conjecture. The proof of virtue cannot be found in men who are newly selected, and who never before have been selected; and of the former, few or none are found in an organization which is newly established. It is necessary, therefore, lacking experience to have recourse to conjecture, which is derived from their age, profession, and physical appearance. The first two have been discussed: it remains to talk of the third. And yet I say that some have wanted that the soldier be big, among whom was Pyrrhus: Some others have chosen them only from the strength of the body, as Caesar did: which strength of body is conjectured from the composition of the members and the gracefulness of aspect. And yet some of those who write say that he should have lively and merry eyes, a nervy neck, a large breast, muscular arms, long fingers, a small stomach, round hips, sleek legs and feet: which parts usually render a man strong and agile, which are the two things sought above everything else in a soldier. He ought, above all, to have regard for his habits and that there should be in him a (sense of) honesty and shame, otherwise there will be selected only an instrument of trouble and a beginning of corruption; for there is no one who believes that in a dishonest education and in a brutish mind, there can exist some virtue which in some part may be praiseworthy. Nor does it appear to me superfluous, rather I believe it necessary, in order for you to understand better the importance of this selection, to tell you the method that the Roman Consuls at the start of their Magistracy observed in selecting the Roman legions. In which *Deletto*, because those who had to be selected were to be a mixture of new and veteran men (because of the continuing wars), they proceeded from experience with regard to the old (veteran) men, and from conjecture with regard to the new. And this ought to be noted, that these *Deletti* are made, either for immediate training and use, or for future employment.

I have talked, and will talk, of those that are made for future employment, because my intention is to show you how an army can be organized in countries where there is no military (organization), in which countries I cannot have *Deletti* in order to make use of them. But in countries where it is the custom to call out armies, and by means of the Prince, these (*Deletti*) exist, as was observed at Rome and is today observed among the Swiss. For in these *Deletti*, if they are for the (selection of) new men, there are so many others accustomed to being under military orders, that the old (veteran) and new, being mixed together, make a good and united body. Notwithstanding this, the Emperors, when they began to hold fixed the (term of service of the) soldiers, placed new men in charge over the soldiers, whom they called Tironi, as teachers to train them, as is seen in the life of the Emperor Maximus: which thing, while Rome was free, was instituted, not in the army, but within the City: and as the military exercises where the young men were trained were in the City, there resulted that those then chosen to go to war, being accustomed in the method of mock warfare, could easily adapt themselves to real war. But afterwards, when these Emperors discontinued these exercises, it was necessary to employ the methods I have described to you. Arriving, therefore, at the methods of the Roman Selection, I say that, as soon as the Roman Consuls, on whom was imposed the carrying on of the war, had assumed the Magistracy, in wanting to organize their armies (as it was the custom that each of them had two legions of Roman men, who were the nerve (center) of their armies), created twenty four military Tribunes, proposing six for each legion, who filled that office which today is done by those whom we call Constables. After they had assembled all the Roman men adept at carrying arms, and placed the Tribunes of each legion apart from each of the others. Afterwards, by lot they drew the Tribes, from which the first Selection was to be made, and of that Tribe they selected four of their best men, from whom one was selected by the Tribunes of the first legion, and of the other three, one was selected by the Tribunes of the second legion; of the other two, one was selected by the Tribunes of the third, and that last belonged to the fourth legion. After these four, four others were selected, of whom the first man was selected by the Tribunes of the second legion, the second by those of the third, the third by those of the fourth, the fourth remained to the first. After, another four were chosen: the first man was selected by the (Tribunes of the) third (legion), the second by the fourth, the third by the first, the fourth remained to the second. And thus this method of selection changed successively, so that the selection came to be equal, and the legions equalized. And as we said above, this was done where the men were to be used immediately: and as it was formed of men of whom a good part were experienced in real warfare, and everyone in mock battles, this *Deletto* was able to be based on conjecture and experience. But when a new army was to be organized and the selection made for future employment, this *Deletto* cannot be based except on conjecture, which is done by age and physical appearance.

COSIMO: I believe what you have said is entirely true: but before you pass on to other discussion, I want to ask about one thing which you have made me remember, when you said that the *Deletto* which should be made where these men are not accustomed to fighting should be done by conjecture: for I have heard our organization censured in many of its parts, and especially as to number; for many say that a lesser number ought to be taken, of whom those that are drawn would be better and the selection better, as there would not be as much hardship imposed on the men, and some reward given them, by means of which they would be more content and could be better commanded. Whence I would like to know your opinion on this part, and if you preferred a greater rather than a smaller number, and what methods you would use in selecting both numbers.

FABRIZIO: Without doubt the greater number is more desirable and more necessary than the smaller: rather, to say better, where a great number are not available, a perfect organization cannot be made, and I will easily refute all the reasons cited in favor of this. I say, therefore, first, that where there are many people, as there are for example in Tuscany, does not cause you to have better ones, or that the *Deletto* is more selective; for desiring in the selection of men to judge them on the basis of experience, only a very few would probably be found in that country who would have had this experience, as much because few have been in a war, as because of those few who have been, very few have ever been put to the test, so that because of this they merit to be chosen before the others: so that whoever is in a similar situation should select them, must leave experience to one side and take them by conjecture: and if I were brought to such a necessity, I would want to see, if twenty young men of good physical appearance should come before me, with what rule I ought to take some or reject some: so that without doubt I believe that every man will confess that it is a much smaller error to take them all in arming and training them, being unable to know (beforehand) which of them are better, and to reserve to oneself afterwards to make a more certain *Deletto* where, during the exercises with the army, those of greater courage and vitality may be observed. So that, considering everything, the selection in this case of a few in order to have them better, is entirely false. As to causing less hardship to the country and to the men, I say that the ordinance, whether it is bad or insufficient, does not cause any hardship: for this order does not take men away from their business, and does not bind them so that they cannot go to carry out their business, because it only obliges them to come together for training on their free days, which proposition does not do any harm either to the country or the men; rather, to the young, it ought to be delightful, for where, on holidays they remain basely indolent in their hangouts, they would now attend these exercises with pleasure, for the drawing of arms, as it is a beautiful spectacle, is thus delightful to the young men. As to being able to pay (more to) the lesser number, and thereby keeping them more content and obedient, I reply, that no organization of so few can be made, who are paid so continually, that their pay satisfies them. For instance, if an army of five thousand infantry should be organized, in wanting to pay them so that it should be believed they would be contented, they must be given at least ten thousand ducats a month. To begin with, this number of infantry is not enough to make an army, and the payment is unendurable to a State; and on the other hand, it is not sufficient to keep the men content and obligated to respect your position. So that in doing this although much would be spent, it would provide little strength, and would not be sufficient to defend you, or enable you to undertake any enterprise. If you should give them more, or take on more, so much more impossible would it be for you to pay them: if you should give them less, or take on fewer, so much less would be content and so much less useful would they be to you. Therefore, those who consider things which are either useless or impossible. But it is indeed necessary to pay them when they are levied to send to war.

But even if such an arrangement should give some hardship to those enrolled in it in times of peace, which I do not see, they are still recompensed by all those benefits which an army established in a City bring; for without them, nothing is secure. I conclude that whoever desires a small number in order to be able to pay them, or for any other reason cited by you, does not know (what he is doing); for it will also happen, in my opinion, that any number will always diminish in your hands, because of the infinite impediments that men have; so that the small number will succeed at nothing. However, when you have a large organization, you can at your election avail yourself of few or of many. In addition to this, it serves you in fact and reputation, for the large number will always give you reputation. Moreover, in creating the organization, in order to keep men trained, if you enroll a small number of men in many countries, and the armies are very distant from each other, you cannot without the gravest injury to them assemble them for (joint) exercises, and without this training the organization is useless, as will be shown in its proper place.

COSIMO: What you have said is enough on my question: but I now desire that you resolve another doubt for me. There are those who say that such a multitude of armed men would cause confusion, trouble, and disorder in the country.

FABRIZIO: This is another vain opinion for the reason I will tell you. These organized under arms can cause disorders in two ways: either among themselves, or against others; both of these can be obviated where discipline by itself should not do so: for as to troubles among themselves, the organization removes them, not brings them up, because in the organization you give them arms and leaders. If the country where you organize them is so unwarlike that there are not arms among its men, and so united that there are no leaders, such an organization will make them more ferocious against the foreigner, but in no way will make it more disunited, because men well organized, whether armed or unarmed, fear the laws, and can never change, unless the leaders you give them cause a change; and I will later tell you the manner of doing this. But if the country where you have organized an army is warlike and disunited, this organization alone is reason enough to unite them, for these men have arms and leaders for themselves: but the arms are useless for war, and the leaders causes of troubles; but this organization gives them arms useful for war, and leaders who will extinguish troubles; for as soon as some one is injured in that country, he has recourse to his (leader) of the party, who, to maintain his reputation, advises him to avenge himself, (and) not to remain in peace. The public leader does the contrary. So that by this means, the causes for trouble are removed, and replaced by those for union; and provinces which are united but effeminate (unwarlike) lose their usefulness but maintain the union, while those that are disunited and troublesome remain united; and that disordinate ferocity which they usually employ is turned to public usefulness.

As to desiring that they do us injury against others, it should be kept in mind that they cannot do this except by the leaders who govern them. In desiring that the leaders do not cause disorders, it is necessary to have care that they do not acquire too much authority over them. And you have to keep in mind that this authority is acquired either naturally or by accident: And as to nature, it must be provided that whoever is born in one place is not put in charge of men enrolled in another place, but is made a leader in those places where he does not have any natural connections. As to accidents, the organization should be such that each year the leaders are exchanged from command to command; for continuous authority over the same men generates so much unity among them, which can easily be converted into prejudice against the Prince. As to these exchanges being useful to those who have employed them, and injurious to those who have not observed them, is known from the example of the Kingdom of Assyria and from the Empire of the Romans, in which it is seen that the former Kingdom endured a thousand years without tumult and without civil war; which did not result from anything else than the exchanges of those Captains, who were placed in charge of the care of the armies, from place to place every year. Nor, for other reasons, (did it result) in the Roman Empire; once the blood (race) of Caesar was extinguished, so many civil wars arose among the Captains of the armies, and so many conspiracies of the above mentioned Captains against the Emperors, resulting from the continuing of those Captains in their same Commands. And if any of those Emperors, and any who later held the Empire by reputation, such as Hadrian, Marcus, Severus, and others like them, would have observed such happenings, and would have introduced this custom of exchanging Captains in that Empire, without doubt they would have made it more tranquil and lasting; for the Captains would have had fewer opportunities for creating tumults, and the Emperors fewer causes to fear them, and the Senate, when there was a lack in the succession, would have had more authority in the election of Emperors, and consequently, better conditions would have resulted. But the bad customs of men, whether from ignorance or little diligence, or from examples of good or bad, are never put aside.

COSIMO: I do not know if, with my question, I have gone outside the limits you set; for from the *Deletto* we have entered into another discussion, and if I should not be excused a little, I shall believe I merit some reproach.

FABRIZIO: This did us no harm; for all this discussion was necessary in wanting to discuss the Organization (of an Army), which, being censured by many, it was necessary to explain it, if it is desired that this should take place before the *Deletto*. And before I discuss the other parts, I want to discuss the *Deletto* for men on horseback. This (selection) was done by the ancients from among the more wealthy, having regard both for the age and quality of the men, selecting three hundred for each legion: so that the Roman cavalry in every Consular army did not exceed six hundred.

COSIMO: Did you organize the cavalry in order to train them at home and avail yourself of them in the future?

FABRIZIO: Actually it is a necessity and cannot be done otherwise, if you want to have them take up arms for you, and not to want to take them away from those who make a profession of them.

COSIMO: How would you select them?

FABRIZIO: I would imitate the Romans: I would take the more wealthy, and give them leaders in the same manner as they are given to others today, and I would arm them, and train them.

COSIMO: Would it be well to give these men some provision?

FABRIZIO: Yes, indeed: but only as much as is necessary to take care of the horse; for, as it brings an expense to your subjects, they could complain of you. It would be necessary, therefore, to pay them for the horse and its upkeep.

COSIMO: How many would you make? How would you arm them?

FABRIZIO: You pass into another discussion. I will tell you in its place, which will be when I have said how the infantry ought to be armed, and how they should prepare for an engagement.

SECOND BOOK

I believe that it is necessary, once the men are found, to arm them; and in wanting to do this, I believe it is necessary to examine what arms the ancients used, and from them select the best. The Romans divided their infantry into the heavily and lightly armed. The light armed they gave the name Veliti. Under this name they included all those who operated with the sling, crossbow, and darts: and the greater part of them carried a helmet (head covering) and a shield on the arm for their defense. These men fought outside the regular ranks, and apart from the heavy armor, which was a Casque that came up to the shoulders, they also carried a Cuirass which, with the skirt, came down to the knees, and their arms and legs were covered by shin-guards and bracelets; they also carried a shield on the arm, two arms in length and one in width, which had an iron hoop on it to be able to sustain a blow, and another underneath, so that in rubbing on the ground, it should not be worn out. For attacking, they had cinched on their left side a sword of an arm and a half-length, and a dagger on the right side. They carried a spear, which they called Pilus, and which they hurled at the enemy at the start of a battle. These were the important Roman arms, with which they conquered the world. And although some of the ancient writers also gave them, in addition to the aforementioned arms, a shaft in the hand in the manner of a spit, I do not know how a staff can be used by one who holds a shield, for in managing it with two hands it is impeded by the shield, and he cannot do anything worthwhile with one hand because of its heaviness. In addition to this, to combat in the ranks with the staff (as arms) is useless, except in the front rank where there is ample space to deploy the entire staff, which cannot be done in the inner ranks, because the nature of the battalions (as I will tell you in their organization) is to press its ranks continually closer together, as this is feared less, even though inconvenient, than for the ranks to spread further apart, where the danger is most apparent. So that all the arms which exceed two arms in length are useless in tight places; for if you have a staff and want to use it with both hands, and handled so that the shield should not annoy you, you cannot attack an enemy with it who is next to you. If you take it in one hand in order to serve yourself of the shield, you cannot pick it up except in the middle, and there remains so much of the staff in the back part, that those who are behind impede you in using it. And that this is true, that the Romans did not have the staff, or, having it, they valued it little, you will read in all the engagements noted by Titus Livius in his history, where you will see that only very rarely is mention made of the shaft, rather he always says that, after hurling the spears, they put their hands on the sword. Therefore I want to leave this staff, and relate how much the Romans used the sword for offense, and for defense, the shield together with the other arms mentioned above.

The Greeks did not arm so heavily for defense as did the Romans, but in the offense relied more on this staff than on the sword, and especially the Phalanxes of Macedonia, who carried staffs which they called Sarisse, a good ten arms in length, with which they opened the ranks of the enemy and maintained order in the Phalanxes. And although other writers say they also had a shield, I do not know (for the reasons given above) how the Sarisse and the shield could exist together. In addition to this, in the engagement that Paulus Emilius had with Perseus, King of Macedonia, I do not remember mention being made of shields, but only of the Sarisse and the difficulty the Romans had in overcoming them. So that I conjecture that a Macedonian Phalanx was nothing else than a battalion of Swiss is today, who have all their strength and power in their pikes. The Romans (in addition to the arms) ornamented the infantry with plumes; which things make the sight of an army beautiful to friends, and terrible to the enemy. The arms for men on horseback in the original ancient Roman (army) was a round shield, and they had the head covered, but the rest (of the body) was without armor. They had a sword and a staff with an iron point, long and thin; whence they were unable to hold the shield firm, and only make weak movements with the staff, and because they had no armor, they were exposed to wounds. Afterwards, with time, they were armed like the infantry, but the shield was much smaller and square, and the staff more solid and with two iron tips, so that if the one side was encumbered, they could avail themselves of the other. With these arms, both for the infantry and the cavalry, my Romans occupied all the world, and it must be believed, from the fruits that are observed, that they were the best armed armies that ever existed.

And Titus Livius, in his histories, gives many proofs, where, in coming to the comparison with enemy armies, he says, "but the Romans were superior in virtue, kinds of arms, and discipline". And, therefore, I have discussed more in particular the arms of the victors than those of the losers. It appears proper to me to discuss only the present methods of arming. The infantry have for their defense a breast plate of iron, and for offense a lance nine arm-lengths long, which they call a pike, and a sword at their side, rather round in the point than sharp. This is the ordinary armament of the infantry today, for few have their arms and shins (protected by) armor, no one the head; and those few carry a halberd in place of a pike, the shaft of which (as you know) is three arm-lengths long, and has the iron attached as an axe. Among them they have three Scoppettieri (Exploders, i.e., Gunners), who, with a burst of fire fill that office which anciently was done by slingers and bowmen. This method of arming was established by the Germans, and especially by the Swiss, who, being poor and wanting to live in freedom, were, and are, obliged to combat with the ambitions of the Princes of Germany, who were rich and could raise horses, which that people could not do because of poverty: whence it happened that being on foot and wanting to defend themselves from enemies who were on horseback, it behooved them to search the ancient orders and find arms which should defend them from the fury of horses. This necessity has caused them to maintain or rediscover the ancient orders, without which, as every prudent man affirms, the infantry is entirely useless. They therefore take up pikes as arms, which are most useful not only in sustaining (the attacks of) horses, but to overcome them. And because of the virtue of these arms and ancient orders, the Germans have assumed so much audacity, that fifteen or twenty thousand of them would assault any great number of horse, and there have been many examples of this seen in the last twenty five years. And this example of their virtue founded on these arms and these orders have been so powerful, that after King Charles passed into Italy, every nation has imitated them: so that the Spanish armies have come into a very great reputation.

COSIMO: What method of arms do you praise more, this German one or the ancient Roman?

FABRIZIO: The Roman without any doubt, and I will tell you the good and the bad of one and the other. The German infantry can sustain and overcome the cavalry. They are more expeditious in marching and in organizing themselves, because they are not burdened with arms. On the other hand, they are exposed to blows from near and far because of being unarmed. They are useless in land battles and in every fight where there is stalwart resistance. But the Romans sustained and overcame the cavalry, as these (Germans) do. They were safe from blows near and far because they were covered with armor. They were better able to attack and sustain attacks having the shields. They could more actively in tight places avail themselves of the sword than these (Germans) with the pike; and even if the latter had the sword, being without a shield, they become, in such a case, (equally) useless. They (the Romans) could safely assault towns, having the body covered, and being able to cover it even better with the shield. So that they had no other inconvenience than the heaviness of the arms (armor) and the annoyance of having to carry them; which inconveniences they overcame by accustoming the body to hardships and inducing it to endure hard work. And you know we do not suffer from things to which we are accustomed. And you must understand this, that the infantry must be able to fight with infantry and cavalry, and those are always useless who cannot sustain the (attacks of the) cavalry, or if they are able to sustain them, nonetheless have fear of infantry who are better armed and organized than they. Now if you will consider the German and the Roman infantry, you will find in the German (as we have said) the aptitude of overcoming cavalry, but great disadvantages when fighting with an infantry organized as they are, and armed as the Roman. So that there will be this advantage of the one over the other, that the Romans could overcome both the infantry and the cavalry, and the Germans only the cavalry.

COSIMO: I would desire that you give some more particular example, so that we might understand it better.

FABRIZIO: I say thusly, that in many places in our histories you will find the Roman infantry to have defeated numberless cavalry, but you will never find them to have been defeated by men on foot because of some defect they may have had in their arms or because of some advantage the enemy had in his. For if their manner of arming had been defective, it was necessary for them to follow one of two courses: either when they found one who was better armed than they, not to go on further with the conquest, or that they take up the manner of the foreigner, and leave off theirs: and since neither ensued, there follows, what can be easily conjectured, that this method of arming was better than that of anyone else. This has not yet occurred with the German infantry; for it has been seen that anytime they have had to combat with men on foot organized and as obstinate as they, they have made a bad showing; which results from the disadvantage they have in trying themselves against the arms of the enemy. When Filippo Visconti, Duke of Milan, was assaulted by eighteen thousand Swiss, he sent against them Count Carmingnuola, who was his Captain at that time. This man with six thousand cavalry and a few infantry went to encounter them, and, coming hand to hand with them, was repulsed with very great damage. Whence Carmingnuola as a prudent man quickly recognized the power of the enemy arms, and how much they prevailed against cavalry, and the weakness of cavalry against those on foot so organized; and regrouping his forces, again went to meet the Swiss, and as they came near he made his men-at-arms descend from their horses, and in that manner fought with them, and killed all but three thousand, who, seeing themselves consumed without having any remedy, threw their arms on the ground and surrendered.

COSIMO: Whence arises such a disadvantage?

FABRIZIO: I have told you a little while ago, but since you have not understood it, I will repeat it to you. The German infantry (as was said a little while ago) has almost no armor in defending itself, and use pikes and swords for offense. They come with these arms and order of battle to meet the enemy, who (if he is well equipped with armor to defend himself, as were the men-at-arms of Carmingnuola who made them descend to their feet) comes with his sword and order of battle to meet him, and he has no other difficulty than to come near the Swiss until he makes contact with them with the sword; for as soon as he makes contact with them, he combats them safely, for the German cannot use the pike against the enemy who is next to him because of the length of the staff, so he must use the sword, which is useless to him, as he has no armor and has to meet an enemy that is (protected) fully by armor. Whence, whoever considers the advantages and disadvantages of one and the other, will see that the one without armor has no remedy, but the one well armored will have no difficulty in overcoming the first blow and the first passes of the pike: for in battles, as you will understand better when I have demonstrated how they are put together, the men go so that of necessity they accost each other in a way that they are attacked on the breast, and if one is killed or thrown to the ground by the pike, those on foot who remain are so numerous that they are sufficient for victory. From this there resulted that Carmingnuola won with such a massacre of the Swiss, and with little loss to himself.

COSIMO: I see that those with Carmingnuola were men-at-arms, who, although they were on foot, were all covered with iron (armor), and, therefore, could make the attempt that they made; so that I think it would be necessary to arm the infantry in the same way if they want to make a similar attempt.

FABRIZIO: If you had remembered how I said the Romans were armed, you would not think this way. For an infantryman who has his head covered with iron, his breast protected by a cuirass and a shield, his arms and legs with armor, is much more apt to defend himself from pikes, and enter among them, than is a man-at-arms (cavalryman) on foot. I want to give you a small modem example. The Spanish infantry had descended from Sicily into the Kingdom of Naples in order to go and meet Consalvo who was besieged in Barletta by the French. They came to an encounter against Monsignor D'Obigni with his men-at-arms, and with about four thousand German infantry. The Germans, coming hand to hand with their pikes low, penetrated the (ranks of the) Spanish infantry; but the latter, aided by their spurs and the agility of their bodies, intermingled themselves with the Germans, so that they (the Germans) could not get near them with their swords; whence resulted the death of almost all of them, and the victory of the Spaniards. Everyone knows how many German infantry were killed in the engagement at Ravenna, which resulted from the same causes, for the Spanish infantry got as close as the reach of their swords to the German infantry, and would have destroyed all of them, if the German infantry had not been succored by the French Cavalry: nonetheless, the Spaniards pressing together made themselves secure in that place. I conclude, therefore, that a good infantry not only is able to sustain the (attack of) cavalry but does not have fear of infantry, which (as I have said many times) proceeds from its arms (armor) and organization (discipline).

COSIMO: Tell us, therefore, how you would arm them.

FABRIZIO: I would take both the Roman arms and the German, and would want half to be armed as the Romans, and the other half as the Germans. For, if in six thousand infantry (as I shall explain a little later) I should have three thousand infantry with shields like the Romans, and two thousand pikes and a thousand gunners like the Germans, they would be enough for me; for I would place the pikes either in the front lines of the battle, or where I should fear the cavalry most; and of those with the shield and the sword, I would serve myself to back up the pikes and to win the engagement, as I will show you. So that I believe that an infantry so organized should surpass any other infantry today.

COSIMO: What you have said to us is enough as regards infantry, but as to cavalry, we desire to learn which seems the more strongly armed to you: ours or that of the ancients?

FABRIZIO: I believe in these times, with respect to saddles and stirrups not used by the ancients, one stays more securely on the horse than at that time. I believe we arm more securely: so that today one squadron of very heavily (armed) men-at-arms comes to be sustained with much more difficulty than was the ancient cavalry. With all of this, I judge, nonetheless, that no more account ought to be taken of the cavalry than was taken anciently; for (as has been said above) they have often in our times been subjected to disgrace by the infantry armed (armored) and organized as (described) above. Tigranus, King of Armenia, came against the Roman army of which Lucullus was Captain, with (an army) of one hundred fifty thousand cavalry, among whom were many armed as our men-at-arms, whom they called Catafratti, while on the other side the Romans did not total more than six thousand (cavalry) and fifteen thousand infantry; so that Tigranus, when he saw the army of the enemy, said: "These are just about enough horsemen for an embassy". Nonetheless, when they came to battle, he was routed; and he who writes of that battle blames those Catafratti, showing them to be useless, because, he says, that having their faces covered, their vision was impaired and they were little adept at seeing and attacking the enemy, and as they were heavily burdened by the armor, they could not regain their feet when they fell, nor in any way make use of their persons. I say, therefore, that those People or Kingdoms which esteem the cavalry more than the infantry, are always weaker and more exposed to complete ruin, as has been observed in Italy in our times, which has been plundered, ruined, and overrun by foreigners, not for any other fault than because they had paid little attention to the foot soldiers and had mounted all their soldiers on horses. Cavalry ought to be used, but as a second and not the first reliance of an army; for they are necessary and most useful in undertaking reconnaissance, in overrunning and despoiling the enemy country, and to keep harassing and troubling the enemy army so as to keep it continually under arms, and to impede its provisions; but as to engagements and battles in the field, which are the important things in war and the object for which armies are organized, they are more useful in pursuing than in routing the enemy, and are much more inferior to the foot soldier in accomplishing the things necessary in accomplishing such (defeats).

COSIMO: But two doubts occur to me: the one, that I know that the Parthians did not engage in war except with cavalry, yet they divided the world with the Romans: the other, that I would like you to tell me how the (attack of) the cavalry can be sustained by the infantry, and whence arises the virtue of the latter and the weakness of the former?

FABRIZIO: Either I have told you, or I meant to tell you, that my discussion on matters of war is not going beyond the limits of Europe. Since this is so, I am not obliged to give reasons for that which is the custom in Asia. Yet, I have this to say, that the army of Parthia was completely opposite to that of the Romans, as the Parthians fought entirely on horseback, and in the fighting was about confused and disrupted, and was a way of fighting unstable and full of uncertainties. The Romans, it may be recalled, were almost all on foot, and fought pressed closely together, and at various times one won over the other, according as the site (of the battle) was open or tight; for in the latter the Romans were superior, but in the former the Parthians, who were able to make a great trial with that army with respect to the region they had to defend, which was very open with a seacoast a thousand miles distant, rivers two or three days (journey) apart from each other, towns likewise, and inhabitants rare: so that a Roman army, heavy and slow because of its arms and organization, could not pursue him without suffering great harm, because those who defended the country were on horses and very speedy, so that he would be in one place today, and tomorrow fifty miles distant. Because of this, the Parthians were able to prevail with cavalry alone, and thus resulted the ruin of the army of Crassus, and the dangers to those of Marcantonio. But (as I have said) I did not intend in this discussion of mine to speak of armies outside of Europe; and, therefore, I want to continue on those which the Romans and Greeks had organized in their time, and that the Germans do today.

But let us come to the other question of yours, in which you desire to know what organization or what natural virtue causes the infantry to be superior to the cavalry. And I tell you, first, that the horses cannot go in all the places that the infantry do, because it is necessary for them either to turn back after they have come forward, or turning back to go forward, or to move from a stand-still, or to stand still after moving, so that, without doubt, the cavalry cannot do precisely thus as the infantry. Horses cannot, after being put into disorder from some attack, return to the order (of the ranks) except with difficulty, and even if the attack does not occur; the infantry rarely do this. In addition to this, it often occurs that a courageous man is mounted on a base horse, and a baseman on a courageous horse, whence it must happen that this difference in courage causes disorders. Nor should anyone wonder that a Knot (group) of infantry sustains every attack of the cavalry, for the horse is a sensible animal and knows the dangers, and goes in unwillingly. And if you would think about what forces make him (the horse) go forward and what keep him back, without doubt you will see that those which hold him back are greater than those which push him; for spurs make him go forward, and, on the other hand, the sword and the pike retain him. So that from both ancient and modem experiences, it has been seen that a small group of infantry can be very secure from, and even actually insuperable to, the cavalry. And if you should argue on this that the Elan with which he comes makes it more furious in hurling himself against whoever wants to sustain his attack, and he responds less to the pike than the spur, I say that, as soon as the horse so disposed begins to see himself at the point of being struck by the points of the pikes, either he will by himself check his gait, so that he will stop as soon as he sees himself about to be pricked by them, or, being pricked by them, he will turn to the right or left. If you want to make a test of this, try to run a horse against a wall, and rarely will you find one that will run into it, no matter with what Elan you attempt it. Caesar, when he had to combat the Swiss in Gaul, dismounted and made everyone dismount to their feet, and had the horses removed from the ranks, as they were more adept at fleeing than fighting.

But, notwithstanding these natural impediments that horses have, the Captain who leads the infantry ought to select roads that have as many obstacles for horses as possible, and rarely will it happen that the men will not be able to provide for their safety from the kind of country. If one marches among hills, the location of the march should be such that you may be free from those attacks of which you may be apprehensive; and if you go on the plains, rarely will you find one that does not have crops or woods which will provide some safety for you, for every bush and embankment, even though small, breaks up that dash, and every cultivated area where there are vines and other trees impedes the horses. And if you come to an engagement, the same will happen to you as when marching, because every little impediment which the horse meets cause him to lose his fury. None the less, I do not want to forget to tell you one thing, that although the Romans esteemed much their own discipline and trusted very much on their arms (and armor), that if they had to select a place, either so rough to protect themselves from horses and where they could not be able to deploy their forces, or one where they had more to fear from the horses but where they were able to spread out, they would always take the latter and leave the former.

But, as it is time to pass on to the training (of the men), having armed this infantry according to the ancient and modem usage, we shall see what training they gave to the Romans before the infantry were led to battle. Although they were well selected and better armed, they were trained with the greatest attention, because without this training a soldier was never any good. This training consisted of three parts: The first, to harden the body and accustom it to endure hardships, to act faster, and more dexterously. Next, to teach the use of arms: The third, to teach the trainees the observance of orders in marching as well as fighting and encamping. These are the three principal actions which make an army: for if any army marches, encamps, and fights, in a regular and practical manner, the Captain retains his honor even though the engagement should not have a good ending. All the ancient Republics, therefore, provided such training, and both by custom and law, no part was left out. They therefore trained their youth so as to make them speedy in running, dexterous in jumping, strong in driving stakes and wrestling. And these three qualities arc almost necessary in a soldier; for speed makes him adept at occupying places before the enemy, to come upon him unexpectedly, and to pursue him when he is routed. Dexterity makes him adept at avoiding blows, jumping a ditch and climbing over an embankment. Strength makes him better to carry arms, hurl himself against an enemy, and sustain an attack. And above all, to make the body more inured to hardships, they accustom it to carry great weights. This accustoming is necessary, for in difficult expeditions it often happens that the soldier, in addition to his arms, must carry provisions for many days, and if he had not been accustomed to this hard work, he would not be able to do it, and, hence, he could neither flee from a danger nor acquire a victory with fame.

As to the teaching of the use of arms, they were trained in this way. They had the young men put on arms (armor) which weighed more than twice that of the real (regular) ones, and, as a sword, they gave them a leaded club which in comparison was very heavy. They made each one of them drive a pole into the ground so that three arm-lengths remained (above ground), and so firmly fixed that blows would not drive it to one side or have it fall to the ground; against this pole, the young men were trained with the shield and the club as against an enemy, and sometime they went against it as if they wanted to wound the head or the face, another time as if they wanted to puncture the flank, sometimes the legs, sometime they drew back, another time they went forward. And in this training, they had in mind making themselves adept at covering (protecting) themselves and wounding the enemy; and since the feigned arms were very heavy, the real ones afterwards seemed light. The Romans wanted their soldiers to wound (the enemy) by the driving of a point against him, rather than by cutting (slashing), as much because such a blow was more fatal and had less defense against it, as also because it left less uncovered (unprotected) those who were wounding, making him more adept at repeating his attack, than by slashing. Do you not wonder that those ancients should think of these minute details, for they reasoned that where men had to come hand to hand (in battle), every little advantage is of the greatest importance; and I will remind you of that, because the writers say of this that I have taught it to you. Nor did the ancients esteem it a more fortunate thing in a Republic than to have many of its men trained in arms; for it is not the splendor of jewels and gold that makes the enemy submit themselves to you, but only the fear of arms. Moreover, errors made in other things can sometimes be corrected afterwards, but those that are made in war, as the punishment happens immediately, cannot be corrected. In addition to this, knowing how to fight makes men more audacious, as no one fears to do the things which appear to him he has been taught to do. The ancients, therefore, wanted their citizens to train in every warlike activity; and even had them throw darts against the pole heavier than the actual ones: which exercise, in addition to making men expert in throwing, also makes the arm more limber and stronger. They also taught them how to draw the bow and the sling, and placed teachers in charge of doing all these things: so that when (men) were selected to go to war, they were already soldiers in spirit and disposition. Nor did these remain to teach them anything else than to go by the orders and maintain themselves in them whether marching or combating: which they easily taught by mixing themselves with them, so that by knowing how to keep (obey) the orders, they could exist longer in the army.

COSIMO: Would you have them train this way now?

FABRIZIO: Many of those which have been mentioned, like running wrestling, making them jump, making them work hard under arms heavier than the ordinary, making them draw the crossbow and the sling; to which I would add the light gun, a new instrument (as you know), and a necessary one. And I would accustom all the youth of my State to this training: but that part of them whom I have enrolled to fight, I would (especially) train with greater industry and more solicitude, and I would train them always on their free days. I would also desire that they be taught to swim, which is a very useful thing, because there are not always bridges at rivers, nor ships ready: so that if your army does not know how to swim, it may be deprived of many advantages, and many opportunities, to act well are taken away. The Romans, therefore, arranged that the young men be trained on the field of Mars, so that having the river Tiber nearby, they would be able after working hard in exercises on land to refresh themselves in the water, and also exercise them in their swimming.

I would also do as the ancients and train those who fight on horseback: which is very necessary, for in addition to knowing how to ride, they would know how to avail themselves of the horse (in maneuvering him). And, therefore, they arranged horses of wood on which they straddled, and jumped over them armed and unarmed without any help and without using their hands: which made possible that in a moment, and at a sign from the Captain, the cavalry to become as foot soldiers, and also at another sign, for them to be remounted. And as such exercises, both on foot and horseback, were easy at that time, so now it should not be difficult for that Republic or that Prince to put them in practice on their youth, as is seen from the experience of Western Cities, where these methods similar to these institutions are yet kept alive.

They divide all their inhabitants into several parts, and assign one kind of arms of those they use in war to each part. And as they used pikes, halberds, bows, and light guns, they called them pikemen, halberdiers, archers, and gunners. It therefore behooved all the inhabitants to declare in what order they wanted to be enrolled. And as all, whether because of age or other impediment, are not fit for war (combat), they make a selection from each order and they call them the Giurati (Sworn Ones), who, on their free days, are obliged to exercise themselves in those arms in which they are enrolled: and each one is assigned his place by the public where such exercises are to be carried on, and those who are of that order but are not sworn, participate by (contributing) money for those expenses which are necessary for such exercises. That which they do, therefore, we can do; but our little prudence does not allow us to take up any good proceeding.

From these exercises, it resulted that the ancients had good infantry, and that now those of the West have better infantry than ours, for the ancients exercised either at home as did those Republics, or in the armies as did those Emperors, for the reasons mentioned above. But we do not want to exercise at home, and we cannot do so in the field because they are not our subjects and we cannot obligate them to other exercises than they themselves want. This reason has caused the armies to die out first, and then the institutions, so that the Kingdoms and the Republics, especially the Italian, exist in such a weak condition today.

But let us return to our subject, and pursuing this matter of training, I say, that it is not enough in undertaking good training to have hardened the men, made them strong, fast and dexterous, but it is also necessary to teach them to keep discipline, obey the signs, the sounds (of the bugle), and the voice of the Captain; to know when to stand, to retire, to go forward, and when to combat, to march, to maintain ranks; for without this discipline, despite every careful diligence observed and practiced, an army is never good. And without doubt, bold but undisciplined men are more weak than the timid but disciplined ones; for discipline drives away fear from men, lack of discipline makes the bold act foolishly. And so that you may better understand what will be mentioned below, you have to know that every nation has made its men train in the discipline of war, or rather its army as the principal part, which, if they have varied in name, they have varied little in the numbers of men involved, as all have comprised six to eight thousand men. This number was called a Legion by the Romans, a Phalanx by the Greeks, a Caterna by the Gauls. This same number, by the Swiss, who alone retain any of that ancient military umbrage, in our times is called in their language what in ours signifies a Battalion. It is true that each one is further subdivided into small Battaglia (Companies), and organized according to its purpose. It appears to me, therefore, more suitable to base our talk on this more notable name, and then according to the ancient and modern systems, arrange them as best as is possible. And as the Roman Legions were composed of five or six thousand men, in ten Cohorts, I want to divide our Battalion into ten Companies, and compose it of six thousand men on foot; and assign four hundred fifty men to each Company, of whom four hundred are heavily armed and fifty lightly armed: the heavily armed include three hundred with shields and swords, and will be called Scudati (shield bearers), and a hundred with pikes, and will be called pikemen: the lightly armed are fifty infantry armed with light guns, cross-bows, halberds, and bucklers, and these, from an ancient name, are called regular (ordinary) Veliti: the whole ten Companies, therefore, come to three thousand shield bearers; a thousand ordinary pikemen, and one hundred fifty ordinary Veliti, all of whom comprise (a number of) four thousand five hundred infantry. And we said we wanted to make a Battalion of six thousand men; therefore it is necessary to add another one thousand five hundred infantry, of whom I would make a thousand with pikes, whom I will call extraordinary pikemen, (and five hundred light armed, whom I will call extraordinary Veliti): and thus my infantry would come (according as was said a little while ago) to be composed half of shield bearers and half among pikemen and other arms (carriers). In every Company, I would put in charge a Constable, four Centurions, and forty Heads of Ten, and in addition, a Head of the ordinary Veliti with five Heads of Ten. To the thousand extraordinary pikemen, I would assign three Constables, ten Centurions, and a hundred Heads of Ten: to the extraordinary Veliti, two Constables, five Centurions, and fifty Heads of Ten. I would also assign a general Head for the whole Battalion. I would want each Constable to have a distinct flag and (bugle) sound.

Summarizing, therefore, a Battalion would be composed of ten Companies, of three thousand shield bearers, a thousand ordinary pikemen, a thousand extraordinary pikemen, five hundred ordinary Veliti, and five hundred extraordinary Veliti: thus they would come to be six thousand infantry, among whom there would be one thousand five hundred Heads of Ten, and in addition fifteen Constables, with fifteen Buglers and fifteen flags, fifty five Centurions, ten Captains of ordinary Veliti, and one Captain for the whole Battalion with its flag and Bugler. And I have knowingly repeated this arrangement many times, so that then, when I show you the methods for organizing the Companies and the armies, you will not be confounded.

I say, therefore, that any King or Republic which would want to organize its subjects in arms, would provide them with these parties and these arms, and create as many battalions in the country as it is capable of doing: and if it had organized it according to the division mentioned above, and wanting to train it according to the orders, they need only to be trained Company by Company. And although the number of men in each of them could not be themselves provide a reasonably (sized) army, nonetheless, each man can learn to do what applies to him in particular, for two orders are observed in the armies: the one, what men ought to do in each

Company: the other, what the Company ought to do afterwards when it is with others in an army: and those men who carry out the first, will easily observe the second: but without the first, one can never arrive at the discipline of the second. Each of these Companies, therefore, can by themselves learn to maintain (discipline in) their ranks in every kind and place of action, and then to know how to assemble, to know its (particular bugle) call, through which it is commanded in battle; to know how to recognize by it (as galleys do from the whistle) as to what they have to do, whether to stay put, or go forward, or turn back, or the time and place to use their arms. So that knowing how to maintain ranks well, so that neither the action nor the place disorganizes them, they understand well the commands of the leader by means of the (bugle) calls, and knowing how to reassemble quickly, these Companies then can easily (as I have said), when many have come together, learn to do what each body of them is obligated to do together with other Companies in operating as a reasonably (sized) army. And as such a general practice also is not to be esteemed little, all the Battalions can be brought together once or twice in the years of peace, and give them a form of a complete army, training it for several days as if it should engage in battle, placing the front lines, the flanks, and auxiliaries in their (proper) places.

And as a Captain arranges his army for the engagement either taking into account the enemy he sees, or for that which he does not see but is apprehensive of, the army ought to be trained for both contingencies, and instructed so that it can march and fight when the need arises, showing your soldiers how they should conduct themselves if they should be assaulted by this band or that. And when you instruct them to fight against an enemy they can see, show them how the battle is enkindled, where they have to retire without being repulsed, who has to take their places, what signs, what (bugle) calls, and what voice they should obey, and to practice them so with Companies and by mock attacks, that they have the desire for real battle. For a courageous army is not so because the men in it are courageous, but because the ranks are well disciplined; for if I am of the first line fighters, and being overcome, I know where I have to retire, and who is to take my place, I will always fight with courage seeing my succor nearby: If I am of the second line fighters, I would not be dismayed at the first line being pushed back and repulsed, for I would have presupposed it could happen, and I would have desired it in order to be he who, as it was not them, would give the victory to my patron. Such training is most necessary where a new army is created; and where the army is old (veteran), it is also necessary for, as the Romans show, although they knew the organization of their army from childhood, nonetheless, those Captains, before they came to an encounter with the enemy, continually exercised them in those disciplines. And Joseph in his history says, that the continual training of the Roman armies resulted in all the disturbance which usually goes on for gain in a camp, was of no effect in an engagement, because everyone knew how to obey orders and to fight by observing them. But in the armies of new men which you have to put together to combat at the time, or that you caused to be organized to combat in time, nothing is done without this training, as the Companies are different as in a complete army; for as much discipline is necessary, it must be taught with double the industry and effort to those who do not have it, and be maintained in those who have it, as is seen from the fact that many excellent Captains have tired themselves without any regard to themselves.

COSIMO: And it appears to me that this discussion has somewhat carried you away, for while you have not yet mentioned the means with which Companies are trained, you have discussed engagements and the complete army.

FABRIZIO: You say the truth, and truly the reason is the affection I have for these orders, and the sorrow that I feel seeing that they are not put into action: none the less, have no fear, but I shall return to the subject. As I have told you, of first importance in the training of the Company is to know how to maintain ranks. To do this, it is necessary to exercise them in those orders, which they called Chiocciole (Spiralling). And as I told you that one of these Companies ought to consist of four hundred heavily armed infantry, I will stand on this number. They should, therefore, be arranged into eighty ranks (files), with five per file. Then continuing on either strongly or slowly, grouping them and dispersing them; which, when it is done, can be demonstrated better by deeds than by words: afterwards, it becomes less necessary, for anyone who is practiced in these exercises knows how this order proceeds, which is good for nothing else but to accustom the soldiers to maintain ranks. But let us come and put together one of those Companies.

I say that these can be formed in three ways: the first and most useful is to make it completely massive and give it the form of two squares: the second is to make the square with a homed front: the third is to make it with a space in the center, which they call Piazza (plaza). The method of putting together the first form can be in two steps. The first is to have the files doubled, that is, that the second file enters the first, the fourth into the third, and sixth into the fifth, and so on in succession; so that where there were eighty files and five (men) per file, they become forty files and ten per file. Then make them double another time in the same manner, placing one file within the other, and thus they become twenty files of twenty men per file. This makes almost a square, for although there are so many men on one side (of the square) as the other, nonetheless, on the side of the front, they come together so that (the side of) one man touches the next; but on the other side (of the square) the men are distant at least two arm lengths from each other, so that the square is longer from the front to the back (shoulders), then from one side (flank) to the other. (So that the rectangle thus formed is called two squares).

And as we have to talk often today of the parts in front, in the rear, and on the side of this Company, and of the complete army, you will understand that when I will say either head or front, I mean to say the part in front; when I say shoulder, the part behind (rear); when I say flanks, the parts on the side.

The fifty ordinary Veliti of the company are not mixed in with the other files, but when the company is formed, they extend along its flanks.

The other method of putting together (forming) the company is this; and because it is better than the first, I want to place in front of your eyes in detail how it ought to be organized. I believe you remember the number of men and the heads which compose it, and with what arms it is armed. The form, therefore, that this company ought to have is (as I have said) of twenty files, twenty men per file, five files of pikemen in front, and fifteen files of shield bearers on the shoulders (behind); two centurions are in front and two behind in the shoulders who have the office of those whom the ancients called Tergiduttori (Rear-leaders): The Constable, with the flag and bugler, is in that space which is between the five files of pikemen and the fifteen of shield-bearers: there is one of the Captains of the Ten on every flank, so that each one is alongside his men, those who are on the left side of his right hand, those on the right side on his left hand. The fifty Veliti are on the flanks and shoulders (rear) of the company. If it is desired, now, that regular infantry be employed, this company is put together in this form, and it must organize itself thusly: Have the infantry be brought to eighty files, five per file, as we said a little while ago, leaving the Veliti at the head and on the tail (rear), even though they are outside this arrangement; and it ought to be so arranged that each Centurion has twenty files behind him on the shoulders, and those immediately behind every Centurion are five files of pikemen, and the remaining shield-bearers: the Constable, with his flag and bugler, is in that space that is between the pikemen and the shield-bearers of the second Centurion, and occupies the places of three shield-bearers: twenty of the Heads of Ten are on the Flanks of the first Centurion on the left hand, and twenty are on the flanks of the last Centurion on the right hand. And you have to understand, that the Head of Ten who has to guide (lead) the pikemen ought to have a pike, and those who guide the shield-bearers ought to have similar arms.

The files, therefore, being brought to this arrangement, and if it is desired, by marching, to bring them into the company to form the head (front), you have to cause the first Centurion to stop with the first file of twenty, and the second to continue to march; and turning to the right (hand) he goes along the flanks of the twenty stopped files so that he comes head-to-head with the other Centurion, where he too stops; and the third

Centurion continues to march, also turning to the right (hand), and marches along the flanks of the stopped file so that he comes head-to-head with the other two Centurions; and when he also stops, the other Centurion follows with his file, also going to the right along the flanks of the stopped file, so that he arrives at the head (front) with the others, and then he stops; and the two Centurions who are alone quickly depart from the front and go to the rear of the company, which becomes formed in that manner and with those orders to the point which we showed a little while ago. The Veliti extend themselves along its flanks, according as they were disposed in the first method; which method is called Doubling by the straight line, and this last (method) is called Doubling by the flanks.

The first method is easier, while this latter is better organized, and is more adaptable, and can be better controlled by you, for it must be carried out by the numbers, that from five you make ten, ten twenty, twenty forty: so that by doubling at your direction, you cannot make a front of fifteen, or twenty five or thirty or thirty five, but you must proceed to where the number is less. And yet, every day, it happens in particular situations, that you must make a front with six or eight hundred infantry, so that the doubling by the straight line will disarrange you: yet this (latter) method pleases me more, and what difficulty may exist, can be more easily overcome by the proper exercise and practice of it.

I say to you, therefore, that it is more important than anything to have soldiers who know how to form themselves quickly, and it is necessary in holding them in these Companies, to train them thoroughly, and have them proceed bravely forward or backward, to pass through difficult places without disturbing the order; for the soldiers who know how to do this well, are experienced soldiers, and although they may have never met the enemy face to face, they can be called seasoned soldiers; and, on the contrary, those who do not know how to maintain this order, even if they may have been in a thousand wars, ought always to be considered as new soldiers. This applies in forming them when they are marching in small files: but if they are formed, and then become broken because of some accident that results either from the location or from the enemy, to reorganize themselves immediately is the important and difficult thing, in which much training and practice is needed, and in which the ancients placed much emphasis. It is necessary, therefore, to do two things: first, to have many countersigns in the Company: the other, always to keep this arrangement, that the same infantry always remain in the same file. For instance, if one is commanded to be in the second (file), he will afterwards always stay there, and not only in this same file, but in the same position (in the file); it is to be observed (as I have said) how necessary are the great number of countersigns, so that, coming together with other companies, it may be recognized by its own men. Secondly, that the Constable and Centurion have tufts of feathers on their headdress different and recognizable, and what is more important, to arrange that the Heads of Ten be recognized. To which the ancients paid very much attention, that nothing else would do, but that they wrote numbers on their bucklers, calling then the first, second, third, fourth, etc. And they were not above content with this, but each soldier had to write on his shield the number of his file, and the number of his place assigned him in that file. The men, therefore, being thus countersigned (assigned), and accustomed to stay within these limits, if they should be disorganized, it is easy to reorganize them all quickly, for the flag staying fixed, the Centurions and Heads of Ten can judge their place by eye, and bring the left from the right, or the right from the left, with the usual distances between; the infantry guided by their rules and by the difference in countersigns, can quickly take their proper places, just as, if you were the staves of a barrel which you had first countersigned, I would wager you would put it (the barrel) back together with great ease, but if you had not so countersigned them (the staves), it is impossible to reassemble (the barrel). This system, with diligence and practice, can be taught quickly, and can be quickly learned, and once learned are forgotten with difficulty; for new men are guided by the old, and in time, a province which has such training, would become entirely expert in war. It is also necessary to teach them to turn in step, and do so when he should turn from the flanks and by the soldiers in the front, or from the front to the flanks or shoulders (rear). This is very easy, for it is sufficient only that each man turns his body toward the side he is commanded to, and the direction in which they turned becomes the front. It is true that when they turn by the flank, the ranks which turn go outside their usual area, because there is a small space between the breast to the shoulder, while from one flank to the other there is much space, which is all contrary to the regular formation of the company. Hence, care should be used in employing it. But this is more important and where more practice is needed, is when a company wants to turn entirely, as if it was a solid body. Here, great care and practice must be employed, for if it is desired to turn to the left, for instance, it is necessary that the left wing be halted, and those who are closer to the halted one, march much slower then those who are in the right wing and have to run; otherwise everything would be in confusion.

But as it always happens when an army marches from place to place, that the companies not situated in front, not having to combat at the front, or at the flanks or shoulders (rear), have to move from the flank or shoulder quickly to the front, and when such companies in such cases have the space necessary as we indicated above, it is necessary that the pikemen they have on that flank become the front, and the Heads of the Ten, Centurions, and Constables belonging to it relocate to their proper places. Therefore, in wanting to do this, when forming them it is necessary to arrange the eighty files of five per file, placing all the pikemen in the first twenty files, and placing five of the Heads of Ten (of it) in the front of them and five in the rear: the other sixty files situated behind are all shield-bearers, who total to three hundred. It should therefore be so arranged, that the first and last file of every hundred of Heads of Ten; the Constable with his flag and bugler be in the middle of the first hundred (century) of shield-bearers; and the Centurions at the head of every century. Thus arranged, when you want the pikemen to be on the left flank, you have to double them, century by century, from the right flank: if you want them to be on the right flank, you have to double them from the left. And thus this company turns with the pikemen on the flank, with the Heads of Ten on the front and rear, with the Centurions at the front of them, and the Constable in the middle. Which formation holds when going forward; but when the enemy comes and the time for the (companies) to move from the flanks to the front, it cannot be done unless all the soldiers face toward the flank where the pikemen are, and then the company is turned with its files and heads in that manner that was described above; for the Centurions being on the outside, and all the men in their places, the Centurions quickly enter them (the ranks) without difficulty. But when they are marching frontwards, and have to combat in the rear, they must arrange the files so that, in forming the company, the pikes are situated in the rear; and to do this, no other order has to be maintained except that where, in the formation of the company ordinarily every Century has five files of pikemen in front, it now has them behind, but in all the other parts, observe the order that I have mentioned.

COSIMO: You have said (if I remember well) that this method of training is to enable them to form these companies into an army, and that this training serves to enable them to be arranged within it. But if it should occur that these four hundred fifty infantry have to operate as a separate party, how would you arrange them?

FABRIZIO: I will now guide you in judging where he wants to place the pikes, and who should carry them, which is not in any way contrary to the arrangement mentioned above, for although it may be the method that is observed when, together with other companies, it comes to an engagement, nonetheless, it is a rule that serves for all those methods, in which it should happen that you have to manage it. But in showing you the other two methods for arranging the companies, proposed by me, I will also better satisfy your question; for either they are never used, or they are used when the company is above, and not in the company of others.

And to come to the method of forming it with two horns (wings), I say, that you ought to arrange the eighty files at five per file in this way: place a Centurion in the middle, and behind him twenty-five files that have two pikemen (each) on the left side, and three shield-bearers on the right: and after the first five, in the next twenty, twenty Heads of Ten be placed, all between the pikemen and shield-bearers, except that those (Heads) who carry pikes stay with the pikemen. Behind these twenty-five files thusly arranged, another

Centurion is placed who has fifteen files of shield-bearers behind him. After these, the Constable between the flag and the bugler, who also has behind him another fifteen files of shield-bearers. The third Centurion is placed behind these, and he has twenty-five files behind him, in each of which are three shield-bearers on the left side and two pikemen on the right: and after the first five files are twenty Heads of Ten placed between the pikemen and the shield-bearers. After these files, there is the fourth Centurion. If it is desired, therefore, to arrange these files to form a company with two horns (wings), the first Centurion has to be halted with the twenty-five files which are behind him. The second Centurion then has to be moved with the fifteen shield-bearers who are on his rear, and turning to the right, and on the right flank of the twenty-five files to proceed so far that he comes to the fifteen files, and here he halts. After, the Constable has to be moved with the fifteen files of shield bearers who are behind, and turning around toward the right, over by the right flank of the fifteen files which were moved first, marches so that he comes to their front, and here he halts. After, move the third Centurion with the twenty-five files and with the fourth Centurion who is behind them, and turning to the right, march by the left flank of the last fifteen files of shield-bearers, and he does not halt until he is at the head of them, but continues marching up until the last files of twenty-five are in line with the files behind. And, having done this, the Centurion who was Head of the first fifteen files of shield-bearers leaves the place where he was, and goes to the rear of the left angle. And thus he will turn a company of twenty-five solid files, of twenty infantry per file, with two wings, on each side of his front, and there will remain a space between then, as much as would (be occupied by) by ten men side by side. The Captain will be between the two wings, and a Centurion in each corner of the wing. There will be two files of pikemen and twenty Heads of Ten on each flank. These two wings (serve to) hold between them that artillery, whenever the company has any with it, and the carriages. The Veliti have to stay along the flanks beneath the pikemen. But, in wanting to bring this winged (formed) company into the form of the piazza (plaza), nothing else need be done than to take eight of the fifteen files of twenty per file and place them between the points of the two horns (wings), which then from wings become the rear (shoulder) of the piazza (plaza). The carriages are kept in this plaza, and the Captain and the flag there, but not the artillery, which is put either in the front or along the flanks. These are the methods which can be used by a company when it has to pass by suspicious places by itself. Nonetheless, the solid company, without wings and without the plaza, is best. But in wanting to make safe the disarmed ones, that winged one is necessary.

The Swiss also have many forms of companies, among which they form one in the manner of a cross, as in the spaces between the arms, they keep their gunners safe from the attacks of the enemy. But since such companies are good in fighting by themselves, and my intention is to show how several companies united together combat with the enemy, I do not belabor myself further in describing it.

COSIMO: And it appears to me I have very well comprehended the method that ought to be employed in training the men in these companies, but (if I remember well) you said that in addition to the ten companies in a Battalion, you add a thousand extraordinary pikemen and four hundred extraordinary Veliti. Would you not describe how to train these?

FABRIZIO: I would, and with the greatest diligence: and I would train the pikemen, group by group, at least in the formations of the companies, as the others; for I would serve myself of these more than of the ordinary companies, in all the particular actions, how to escort, to raid, and such things. But the Veliti I would train at home without bringing them together with the others, for as it is their office to combat brokenly (in the open, separately), it is not as necessary that they come together with the others or to train in common exercises, than to train them well in particular exercises. They ought, therefore, (as was said in the beginning, and now it appears to me laborious to repeat it) to train their own men in these companies so that they know how to maintain their ranks, know their places, return there quickly when either the evening or the location disrupts them; for when this is caused to be done, they can easily be taught the place the company has to hold and what its office should be in the armies. And if a Prince or a Republic works hard and puts diligence in these formations and in this training, it will always happen that there will be good soldiers in that country, and they will be superior to their neighbors, and will be those who give, and not receive, laws from other men. But (as I have told you) the disorder in which one exists, causes them to disregard and not to esteem these things, and, therefore, our training is not good: and even if there should be some heads or members naturally of virtue, they are unable to demonstrate it.

COSIMO: What carriages would you want each of these companies to have?

FABRIZIO: The first thing I would want is that the Centurions or the Heads of Ten should not go on horseback: and if the Constables want to ride mounted, I would want them to have a mule and not a horse. I would permit them two carriages, and one to each Centurion, and two to every three Heads of Ten, for they would quarter so many in each encampment, as we will narrate in its proper place. So that each company would have thirty six carriages, which I would have (them) to carry the necessary tents, cooking utensils, hatchets, digging bars, sufficient to make the encampment, and after that anything else of convenience.

COSIMO: I believe that Heads assigned by you in each of the companies are necessary: nonetheless, I would be apprehensive that so many commanders would be confusing.

FABRIZIO: They would be so if I would refer to one, but as I refer to many, they make for order; actually, without those (orders), it would be impossible to control them, for a wall which inclines on every side would need many and frequent supports, even if they are not so strong, but if few, they must be strong, for the virtue of only one, despite its spacing, can remedy any ruin. And so it must be that in the armies and among every ten men there is one of more life, of more heart, or at least of more authority, who with his courage, with words and by example keeps the others firm and disposed to fight. And these things mentioned by me, as the heads, the flags, the buglers, are necessary in an army, and it is seen that we have all these in our (present day) armies, but no one does his duty. First, the Heads of Ten, in desiring that those things be done because they are ordered, it is necessary (as I have said) for each of them to have his men separate, lodge with them, go into action with them, stay in the ranks with them, for when they are in their places, they are all of mind and temperament to maintain their ranks straight and firm, and it is impossible for them to become disrupted, or if they become disrupted, do not quickly reform their ranks. But today, they do not serve us for anything other than to give them more pay than the others, and to have them do some particular thing. The same happens with the flags, for they are kept rather to make a beautiful show, than for any military use. But the ancients served themselves of it as a guide and to reorganize themselves, for everyone, when the flag was standing firm, knew the place that he had to be near his flag, and always returned there. He also knew that if it were moving or standing still, he had to move or halt. It is necessary in an army, therefore, that there be many bodies, and that each body have its own flag and its own guide; for if they have this, it needs must be they have much courage and consequently, are livelier. The infantry, therefore, ought to march according to the flag, and the flag move according to the bugle (call), which call, if given well, commands the army, which proceeding in step with those, comes to serve the orders easily. Whence the ancients having whistles (pipes), fifes, and bugles, controlled (modulated) them perfectly; for, as he who dances proceeds in time with the music, and keeping with it does not make a miss-step, so an army obedient in its movement to that call (sound), will not become disorganized. And, therefore, they varied the calls according as they wanted to enkindle or quiet, or firm the spirits of men. And as the sounds were various, so they named them variously. The Doric call (sound) brought on constancy, Frigio, fury (boldness): whence they tell, that Alexander being at table, and someone sounding the Frigio call, it so excited his spirit that he took up arms. It would be necessary to rediscover all these methods, and if this is difficult, it ought not at least to be (totally) put aside by those who teach the soldier to obey; which each one can vary and arrange in his own way, so long as with practice he accustoms the ears of his soldiers to recognize them. But today, no benefit is gotten from these sounds in great part, other than to make noise.

COSIMO: I would desire to learn from you, if you have ever pondered this with yourself, whence such baseness and disorganization arises, and such negligence of this training in our times?

FABRIZIO: I will tell you willingly what I think. You know of the men excellent in war, there have been many famed in Europe, few in Africa, and less in Asia. This results from (the fact that) these last two parts of the world have had a Principality or two, and few Republics; but Europe alone has had some Kingdoms and an infinite number of Republics. And men become excellent, and show their virtue, according as they are employed and recognized by their Prince, Republic, or King, whichever it may be. It happens, therefore, that where there is much power, many valiant men spring up, where there is little, few. In Asia, there are found Ninus, Cyrus, Artafersus, Mithradates, and very few others to accompany these. In Africa, there are noted (omitting those of ancient Egypt) Maximinius, Jugurtha, and those Captains who were raised by the Carthaginian Republic, and these are very few compared to those of Europe; for in Europe there are excellent men without number, and there would be many more, if there should be named together with them those others who have been forgotten by the malignity of the time, since the world has been more virtuous when there have been many States which have favored virtue, either from necessity or from other human passion. Few men, therefore, spring up in Asia, because, as that province was entirely subject to one Kingdom, in which because of its greatness there was indolence for the most part, it could not give rise to excellent men in business (activity). The same happened in Africa: yet several, with respect to the Carthaginian Republic, did arise. More excellent men come out of Republics than from Kingdoms, because in the former virtue is honored much of the time, in the Kingdom it is feared; whence it results that in the former, men of virtu are raised, in the latter they are extinguished. Whoever, therefore, considers the part of Europe, will find it to have been full of Republics and Principalities, which from the fear one had of the other, were constrained to keep alive their military organizations, and honor those who greatly prevailed in them. For in Greece, in addition to the Kingdom of the Macedonians, there were many Republics, and many most excellent men arose in each of them. In Italy, there were the Romans, the Samnites, the Tuscans, the Cisalpine Gauls. France and Germany were full of Republics and Princes. Spain, the very same. And although in comparison with the Romans, very few others were noted, it resulted from the malignity of the writers, who pursued fortune and to whom it was often enough to honor the victors. For it is not reasonable that among the Samnites and Tuscans, who fought fifty years with the Roman People before they were defeated, many excellent men should not have sprung up. And so likewise in France and Spain. But that virtue which the writers do not commemorate in particular men, they commemorate generally in the peoples, in which they exalt to the stars (skies) the obstinacy which existed in them in defending their liberty. It is true, therefore, that where there are many Empires, more valiant men spring up, and it follows, of necessity, that those being extinguished, little by little, virtu is extinguished, as there is less reason which causes men to become virtuous. And as the Roman Empire afterwards kept growing, and having extinguished all the Republics and Principalities of Europe and Africa, and in greater part those of Asis, no other path to virtue was left, except Rome. Whence it resulted that men of virtue began to be few in Europe as in Asia, which virtue ultimately came to decline; for all the virtue being brought to Rome, and as it was corrupted, so almost the whole world came to be corrupted, and the Scythian people were able to come to plunder that Empire, which had extinguished the virtue of others, but did not know how to maintain its own. And although afterwards that Empire, because of the inundation of those barbarians, became divided into several parts, this virtue was not renewed: first, because a price is paid to recover institutions when they are spoiled; another, because the mode of living today, with regard to the Christian religion, does not impose that necessity to defend it that anciently existed, in which at the time men, defeated in war, were either put to death or remained slaves in perpetuity, where they led lives of misery: the conquered lands were either desolated or the inhabitants driven out, their goods taken away, and they were sent dispersed throughout the world, so that those overcome in war suffered every last misery. Men were terrified from the fear of this, and they kept their military exercises alive, and honored those who were excellent in them. But today, this fear in large part is lost, and few of the defeated are put to death, and no one is kept prisoner long, for they are easily liberated. The Citizens, although they should rebel a thousand times, are not destroyed, goods are left to their people, so that the greatest evil that is feared is a ransom; so that men do not want to subject themselves to dangers which they little fear. Afterwards, these provinces of Europe exist under very few Heads as compared to the past, for all of France obeys a King, all of Spain another, and Italy exists in a few parts; so that weak Cities defend themselves by allying themselves with the victors, and strong States, for the reasons mentioned, do not fear an ultimate ruin.

COSIMO: And in the last twenty-five years, many towns have been seen to be pillaged and lost their Kingdoms; which examples ought to teach others to live and reassume some of the ancient orders.

FABRIZIO: That is what you say, but if you would note which towns are pillaged, you would not find them to be the Heads (Chief ones) of the States, but only members: as is seen in the sacking of Tortona and not Milan, Capua and not Naples, Brescia and not Venice, Ravenna and not Rome. Which examples do not cause the present thinking which governs to change, rather it causes them to remain in that opinion of being able to recover themselves by ransom: and because of this, they do not want to subject themselves to the bother of military training, as it appears to them partly unnecessary, partly a tangle they do not understand. Those others who are slave, to whom such examples ought to cause fear, do not have the power of remedying (their situation), and those Princes who have lost the State, are no longer in time, and those who have (the State) do not have (military training) and those Princes who have lost the State, are no longer in time, and those who have (the State) do not have (military training) or want it; for they want without any hardship to remain (in power) through fortune, not through their own virtue, and who see that, because there is so little virtue, fortune governs everything, and they want it to master them, not they master it. And that that which I have discussed is true, consider Germany, in which, because there are many Principalities and Republics, there is much virtue, and all that is good in our present army, depends on the example of those people, who, being completely jealous of their State (as they fear servitude, which elsewhere is not feared) maintain and honor themselves all us Lords. I want this to suffice to have said in showing the reasons for the present business according to my opinion. I do not know if it appears the same to you, or if some other apprehension should have risen from this discussion.

COSIMO: None, rather I am most satisfied with everything. I desire above, returning to our principal subject, to learn from you how you would arrange the cavalry with these companies, and how many, how captained, and how armed.

FABRIZIO: And it, perhaps, appears to you that I have omitted these, at which do not be surprised, for I speak little of them for two reasons: one, because this part of the army is less corrupt than that of the infantry, for it is not stronger than the ancient, it is on a par with it. However, a short while before, the method of training them has been mentioned. And as to arming them, I would arm them as is presently done, both as to the light cavalry as to the men-at-arms. But I would want the light cavalry to be all archers, with some light gunners among them, who, although of little use in other actions of war, are most useful in terrifying the peasants, and place them above a pass that is to be guarded by them, for one gunner causes more fear to them (the enemy) than twenty other armed men. And as to numbers, I say that departing from imitating the Roman army, I would have not less than three hundred effective cavalry for each battalion, of which I would want one hundred fifty to be men-at-arms, and a hundred fifty light cavalry; and I would give a leader to each of these parts, creating among them fifteen Heads of Ten per hand, and give each one a flag and a bugler. I would want that every ten men-at-arms have five carriages and every ten light cavalrymen two, which, like those of the infantry, should carry the tents, (cooking) utensils, hitches, poles, and in addition over the others, their tools. And do not think this is out of place seeing that men-at-arms have four horses at their service, and that such a practice is a corrupting one; for in Germany, it is seen that those men-at-arms are alone with their horses, and only every twenty have a cart which carries the necessary things behind them. The horsemen of the Romans were likewise alone: it is true that the Triari encamped near the cavalry and were obliged to render aid to it in the handling of the horses: this can easily be imitated by us, as will be shown in the distribution of quarters. That, therefore, which the Romans did, and that which the Germans do, we also can do; and in not doing it, we make a mistake. These cavalrymen, enrolled and organized together with a battalion, can often be assembled when the companies are assembled, and caused to make some semblance of attack among them, which should be done more so that they may be recognized among them than for any necessity. But I have said enough on this subject for now, and let us descend to forming an army which is able to offer battle to the enemy, and hope to win it; which is the end for which an army is organized, and so much study put into it.

THIRD BOOK

COSIMO: Since we are changing the discussion, I would like the questioner to be changed, so that I may not be held to be presumptuous, which I have always censured in others. I, therefore, resign the speakership, and I surrender it to any of these friends of mine who want it.

ZANOBI: It would be most gracious of you to continue: but since you do not want to, you ought at least to tell us which of us should succeed in your place.

COSIMO: I would like to pass this burden on the Lord Fabrizio.

FABRIZIO: I am content to accept it, and would like to follow the Venetian custom, that the youngest talks first; for this being an exercise for young men, I am persuaded that young men are more adept at reasoning, than they are quick to follow.

COSIMO: It therefore falls to you Luigi: and I am pleased with such a successor, as long as you are satisfied with such a questioner.

FABRIZIO: I am certain that, in wanting to show how an army is well organized for undertaking an engagement, it would be necessary to narrate how the Greeks and the Romans arranged the ranks in their armies. Nonetheless, as you yourselves are able to read and consider these things, through the medium of ancient writers, I shall omit many particulars, and will cite only those things that appear necessary for me to imitate, in the desire in our times to give some (part of) perfection to our army. This will be done, and, in time, I will show how an army is arranged for an engagement, how it faces a real battle, and how it can be trained in mock ones. The greatest mistake that those men make who arrange an army for an engagement is to give it only one front, and commit it to only one onrush and one attempt (fortune). This results from having lost the method the ancients employed of receiving one rank into the other; for without this method, one cannot help the rank in front, or defend them, or change them by rotation in battle, which was practiced best by the Romans. In explaining this method, therefore, I want to tell how the Romans divided each Legion into three parts, namely, the Astati, the Princeps, and the Triari; of whom the Astati were placed in the first line of the army in solid and deep ranks, (and) behind them were the Princeps, but placed with their ranks more open: and behind these they placed the Triari, and with ranks so sparse, as to be able, if necessary, to receive the Princeps and the Astati between them. In addition to these, they had slingers, bowmen (archers), and other lightly armed, who were not in these ranks, but were situated at the head of the army between the cavalry and the infantry. These light armed men, therefore, enkindled the battle, and if they won (which rarely happened), they pursued the victory: if they were repulsed, they retired by way of the flanks of the army, or into the intervals (gaps) provided for such a result, and were led back among those who were not armed: after this proceeding, the Astati came hand to hand with the enemy, and who, if they saw themselves being overcome, retired little by little through the open spaces in the ranks of the Princeps, and, together with them, renewed the fight. If these also were forced back, they all retired into the thin lines of the Triari, and all together, en masse, recommenced the battle; and if these were defeated, there was no other remedy, as there was no way left to reform themselves. The cavalry were on the flanks of the army, placed like two wings on a body, and they some times fought on horseback, and sometimes helped the infantry, according as the need required. This method of reforming themselves three times is almost impossible to surpass, as it is necessary that fortune abandon you three times, and that the enemy has so much virtue that he overcomes you three times. The Greeks, with their Phalanxes, did not have this method of reforming themselves, and although these had many ranks and Leaders within them, nonetheless, they constituted one body, or rather, one front. So that in order to help one another, they did not retire from one rank into the other, as the Romans, but one man took the place of another, which they did in this way. Their Phalanxes were (made up) of ranks, and supposing they had placed fifty men per rank, when their front came against the enemy, only the first six ranks of all of them were able to fight, because their lances, which they called Sarisse, were so long, that the points of the lances of those in the sixth rank reached past the front rank. When they fought, therefore, if any of the first rank fell, either killed or wounded, whoever was behind him in the second rank immediately entered into his place, and whoever was behind him in the third rank immediately entered into the place in the second rank which had become vacant, and thus successively all at once the ranks behind restored the deficiencies of those in front, so that the ranks were always remained complete, and no position of the combatants was vacant except in the last rank, which became depleted because there was no one in its rear to restore it. So that the injuries which the first rank suffered, depleted the last, and the first rank always remained complete; and thus the Phalanxes, because of their arrangement, were able rather to become depleted than broken, since the large (size of its) body made it more immobile. The Romans, in the beginning, also employed Phalanxes, and instructed their Legions in a way similar to theirs. Afterwards, they were not satisfied with this arrangement, and divided the Legion into several bodies; that is, into Cohorts and Maniples; for they judged (as was said a little while ago) that that body should have more life in it (be more active) which should have more spirit, and that it should be composed of several parts, and each regulate itself. The Battalions of the Swiss, in these times, employed all the methods of the Phalanxes, as much in the size and entirety of their organization, as in the method of helping one another, and when coming to an engagement they place the Battalions one on the flank of the other, or they place them one behind the other. They have no way in which the first rank, if it should retire, to be received by the second, but with this arrangement, in order to help one another, they place one Battalion in front and another behind it to the right, so that if the first has need of aid, the latter can go forward and succor it. They put a third Battalion behind these, but distant a gun shot. This they do, because if the other two are repulsed, this (third) one can make its way forward, and the others have room in which to retire, and avoid the onrush of the one which is going forward; for a large multitude cannot be received (in the same way) as a small body, and, therefore, the small and separate bodies that existed in a Roman Legion could be so placed together as to be able to receive one another among themselves, and help each other easily. And that this arrangement of the Swiss is not as good as that of the ancient Romans is demonstrated by the many examples of the Roman Legions when they engaged in battle with the Greek Phalanxes, and the latter were always destroyed by the former, because the kinds of arms (as I mentioned before) and this method of reforming themselves, was not able to maintain the solidity of the Phalanx. With these examples, therefore, if I had to organize an army, I would prefer to retain the arms and the methods, partly of the Greek Phalanxes, partly of the Roman Legions; and therefore I have mentioned wanting in a Battalion two thousand pikes, which are the arms of the Macedonian Phalanxes, and three thousand swords and shield, which are the arms of the Romans. I have divided the Battalion into ten Companies, as the Romans (divided) the Legion into ten Cohorts. I have organized the Veliti, that is the light armed, to enkindle the battle, as they (the Romans did). And thus, as the arms are mixed, being shared by both nations and as also the organizations are shared, I have arranged that each company have five ranks of pikes (pikemen) in front, and the remainder shields (swordsmen with shields), in order to be able with this front to resist the cavalry, and easily penetrate the enemy companies on foot, and the enemy at the first encounter would meet the pikes, which I would hope would suffice to resist him, and then the shields (swordsmen) would defeat him. And if you would note the virtue of this arrangement, you will see all these arms will execute their office completely. First, because pikes are useful against cavalry, and when they come against infantry, they do their duty well before the battle closes in, for when they are pressed, they become useless. Whence the Swiss, to avoid this disadvantage, after every three ranks of pikemen place one of halberds, which, while it is not enough, gives the pikemen room (to maneuver). Placing, therefore, our pikes in the front and the shields (swordsmen) behind, they manage to resist the cavalry, and in enkindling the battle, lay open and attack the infantry: but when the battle closes in, and they become useless, the shields and swords take their place, who are able to take care of themselves in every strait.

LUIGI: We now await with desire to learn how you would arrange the army for battle with these arms and with these organizations.

FABRIZIO: I do not now want to show you anything else other than this. You have to understand that in a regular Roman army, which they called a Consular Army, there were not more than two Legions of Roman Citizens, which consist of six hundred cavalry and about eleven thousand infantry. They also had as many more infantry and cavalry which were sent to them by their friends and confederates, which they divided into two parts, and they called one the right wing, and the other the left wing, and they never permitted this (latter) infantry to exceed the number of the infantry of the Legion. They were well content that the cavalry should be greater in number. With this army which consisted of twenty two thousand infantry and about two thousand cavalry effectives, a Consul undertook every action and went on every enterprise. And when it was necessary to face a large force, they brought together two Consuls with two armies. You ought also to note that ordinarily in all three of the principal activities in which armies engage, that is, marching, camping, and fighting, they place the Legion in the middle, because they wanted that virtue in which they should trust most should be greater unity, as the discussion of all these three activities will show you. Those auxiliary infantry, because of the training they had with the infantry of the Legion, were as effective as the latter, as they were disciplined as they were, and therefore they arranged them in a similar way when organizing (for) and engagement. Whoever, therefore, knows how they deployed the entire (army). Therefore, having told you how they divided a Legion into three lines, and how one line would receive the other, I have come to tell you how the entire army was organized for an engagement.

If I would want, therefore, to arrange (an army for) an engagement in imitation of the Romans, just as they had two Legions, I would take two Battalions, and these having been deployed, the disposition of an entire Army would be known: for by adding more people, nothing else is accomplished than to enlarge the organization. I do not believe it is necessary that I remind you how many infantry there are in a Battalion, and that it has ten companies, and what Leaders there are per company, and what arms they have, and who are the ordinary (regular) pikemen and Veliti, and who the extraordinary, because a little while I distinctly told you, and I reminded you to commit it to memory as something necessary if you should want to understand all the other arrangements: and, therefore, I will come to the demonstration of the arrangement, without repeating these again. And it appears to me that ten Companies of a Battalion should be placed on the left flank, and the ten others of the other on the right. Those on the left should be arranged in this way. The five companies should be placed one alongside the other on the front, so that between one and the next there would be a space of four arm lengths which come to occupy an area of one hundred forty one arm lengths long, and forty wide. Behind these five Companies I would place three others, distant in a straight line from the first ones by forty arm lengths, two of which should come behind in a straight line at the ends of the five, and the other should occupy the space in the middle. Thus these three would come to occupy in length and width the same space as the five: but where the five would have a distance of four arm lengths between one another, this one would have thirty three. Behind these I would place the last two companies, also in a straight line behind the three, and distant from those three forty arm lengths, and I would place each of them behind the ends of the three, so that the space between them would be ninety one arm lengths. All of these companies arranged thusly would therefore cover (an area of) one hundred forty one arm lengths long and two hundred wide. The extraordinary pikemen I would extend along the flanks of these companies on the left side, distant twenty arm lengths from it, creating a hundred forty three files of seven per file, so that they should cover the entire length of the ten companies arranged as I have previously described; and there would remain forty files for protecting the wagons and the unarmed people in the tail of the army, (and) assigning the Heads of Ten and the Centurions in their (proper) places: and, of the three Constables, I would put one at the head, another in the middle, and the third in the last file, who should fill the office of Tergiduttore, as the ancients called the one placed in charge of the rear of the Army. But returning to the head (van) of the Army I say, that I would place the extraordinary Veliti alongside the extraordinary pikemen, which, as you know, are five hundred, and would place them at a distance of forty arm lengths. On the side of these, also on the left hand, I would place the men-at-arms, and would assign them a distance of a hundred fifty arm lengths away. Behind these, the light cavalry, to whom I would assign the same space as the men-at-arms. The ordinary Veliti I would leave around their companies, who would occupy those spaces which I placed between one company and another, who would act to minister to those (companies) unless I had already placed them under the extraordinary pikemen; which I would do or not do according as it should benefit my plans. The general Head of all the Battalions I would place in that space that exists between the first and second order of companies, or rather at the head, and in that space with exists between the last of the first five companies and the extraordinary pikemen, according as it should benefit my plans, surrounded by thirty or sixty picked men, (and) who should know how to execute a commission prudently, and stalwartly resist an attack, and should also be in the middle of the buglers and flag carriers. This is the order in which I would deploy a Battalion on the left side, which would be the deployment of half the Army, and would cover an area five hundred and eleven arm lengths long and as much as mentioned above in width, not including the space which that part of the extraordinary pikemen should occupy who act as a shield for the unarmed men, which would be about one hundred arm lengths. The other Battalions I would deploy on the right side exactly in the same way as I deployed those on the left, having a space of thirty arm lengths between our battalions and the other, in the head of which space I would place some artillery pieces, behind which would be the Captain general of the entire Army, who should have around him in addition to the buglers and flag carriers at least two hundred picked men, the greater portion on foot, among whom should be ten or more adept at executing every command, and should be so provided with arms and a horse as to be able to go on horseback or afoot as the needs requires. Ten cannon of the artillery of the Army suffice for the reduction of towns, which should not exceed fifty pounds per charge, of which in the field I would employ more in the defense of the encampment than in waging a battle, and the other artillery should all be rather often than fifteen pounds per charge. This I would place in front of the entire army, unless the country should be such that I could situate it on the flank in a safe place, where it should not be able to be attacked by the enemy.

This formation of the Army thusly arranged, in combat, can maintain the order both of the Phalanxes and of the Roman Legions, because the pikemen are in front and all the infantry so arranged in ranks, that coming to battle with the enemy, and resisting him, they should be able to reform the first ranks from those behind according to the usage of the Phalanxes. On the other hand, if they are attacked so that they are compelled to break ranks and retire, they can enter into the spaces of the second company behind them, and uniting with them, (and) en masse be able to resist and combat the enemy again: and if this should not be enough, they can in the same way retire a second time, and combat a third time, so that in this arrangement, as to combating, they can reform according to both the Greek method, and the Roman. As to the strength of the Army, it cannot be arranged any stronger, for both wings are amply provided with both leaders and arms, and no part is left weak except that part behind which is unarmed, and even that part has its flanks protected by the extraordinary pikemen. Nor can the enemy assault it in any part where he will not find them organized, and the part in the back cannot be assaulted, because there cannot be an enemy who has so much power that he can assail every side equally, for it there is one, you don't have to take the field with him. But if he should be a third greater than you, and as well organized as you, if he weakens himself by assaulting you in several places, as soon as you defeat one part, all will go badly for him. If his cavalry should be greater than yours, be most assured, for the ranks of pikemen that gird you will defend you from every onrush of theirs, even if your cavalry should be repulsed. In addition to this, the Heads are placed on the side so that they are able easily to command and obey. And the spaces that exist between one company and the next one, and between one rank and the next, not only serve to enable one to receive the other, but also to provide a place for the messengers who go and come by order of the Captain. And as I told you before, as the Romans had about twenty thousand men in an Army, so too ought this one have: and as other soldiers borrowed their mode of fighting and the formation of their Army from the Legions, so too those soldiers that you assembled into your two Battalions would have to borrow their formation and organization. Having given an example of these things, it is an easy matter to initiate it: for if the army is increased either by two Battalions, or by as many men as are contained in them, nothing else has to be done than to double the arrangements, and where ten companies are placed on the left side, twenty are now placed, either by increasing or extending the ranks, according as the place or the enemy should command you.

LUIGI: Truly, (my) Lord, I have so imagined this army, that I see it now, and have a desire to see it facing us, and not for anything in the world would I desire you to become Fabius Maximus, having thoughts of holding the enemy at bay and delaying the engagement, for I would say worse of you, than the Roman people said of him.

FABRIZIO: Do not be apprehensive. Do you not hear the artillery? Ours has already fired, but harmed the enemy little; and the extraordinary Veliti come forth from their places together with the light cavalry, and spread out, and with as much fury and the loudest shouts of which they are capable, assault the enemy, whose artillery has fired one time, and has passed over the heads of our infantry without doing them an injury. And as it is not able to fire a second time, our Veliti and cavalry have already seized it, and to defend it, the enemy has moved forward, so that neither that of friend or enemy can perform its office. You see with what virtu our men fight, and with what discipline they have become accustomed because of the training they have had, and from the confidence they have in the Army, which you see with their stride, and with the men-at-arms alongside, in marching order, going to rekindle the battle with the adversary. Your see our artillery, which to make place for them, and to leave the space free, has retired to the place from which the Veliti went forth. You see the Captain who encourages them and points out to them certain victory. You see the Veliti and light cavalry have spread out and returned to the flanks of the Army, in order to see if they can cause any injury to the enemy from the flanks. Look, the armies are facing each other: watch with what virtue they have withstood the onrush of the enemy, and with what silence, and how the Captain commands the men-at-arms that they should resist and not attack, and do not detach themselves from the ranks of the infantry. You see how our light cavalry are gone to attack a band of enemy gunners who wanted to attach by the flank, and how the enemy cavalry have succored them, so that, caught between the cavalry of the one and the other, they cannot fire, and retire behind their companies. You see with what fury our pikemen attack them, and how the infantry is already so near each other that they can no longer manage their pikes: so that, according to the discipline taught by us, our pikemen retire little by little among the shields (swordsmen). Watch how in this (encounter), so great an enemy band of men-at-arms has pushed back our men-at-arms on the left side and how ours, according to discipline, have retired under the extraordinary pikemen, and having reformed the front with their aid, have repulsed the adversary, and killed a good part of them. In fact all the ordinary pikemen of the first company have hidden themselves among the ranks of the shields (swordsmen), and having left the battle to the swordsmen, who, look with what virtu, security, and leisure, kill the enemy. Do you not see that, when fighting, the ranks are so straitened, that they can handle the swords only with much effort? Look with what hurry the enemy moves; for, armed with the pike and their swords useless (the one because it is too long, the other because of finding the enemy too greatly armed) in part they fall dead or wounded, in part they flee. See them flee on the right side. They also flee on the left. Look, the victory is ours. Have we not won an engagement very happily? But it would have been won with greater felicity if I should have been allowed to put them in action and see that it was not necessary to avail ourselves of either the second or third ranks, that our first line was sufficient to overcome them. In this part, I have nothing else to tell you, except to dissolve any doubts that should arise in you.

LUIGI: You have won this engagement with so much fury, that I am astonished, and in fact so stupefied, that I do not believe I can well explain if there is any doubt left in my mind. Yet, trusting in your prudence, I will take courage to say that I intend. Tell me first, why did you not let your artillery fire more than one time? And why did you have them quickly retire within the army, nor afterward make any other mention of them? It seems to me also that you pointed the enemy artillery high, and arranged it so that it should be of much benefit to you. Yet, if it should occur (and I believe it happens often) that the lines are pierced, what remedy do you provide? And since I have commenced on artillery, I want to bring up all these questions so as not to have to discuss it any more. I have heard many disparage the arms and the organization of the ancient Armies, arguing that today they could do little, or rather how useless they would be against the fury of artillery, for these are superior to their arms and break the ranks, so that it appears to them to be madness to create an arrangement that cannot be held, and to endure hardship in carrying a weapon that cannot defend you.

FABRIZIO: This question of yours has need (because it has so many items) of a long answer. It is true that I did not have the artillery fire more than one time, and because of it one remains in doubt. The reason is, that it is more important to one to guard against being shot than shooting the enemy. You must understand that, if you do not want the artillery to injure you, it is necessary to stay where it cannot reach you, or to put yourself behind a wall or embankment. Nothing else will stop it; but it is necessary for them to be very strong. Those Captains who must make an engagement cannot remain behind walls or embankments, nor can they remain where it may reach them. They must, therefore, since they do not have a way of protecting themselves, find one by which they are injured less; nor can they do anything other than to undertake it quickly. The way of doing this is to go find it quickly and directly, not slowly or en masse; for, speed does not allow them to shoot again, and because the men are scattered, they can injure only a few of them. A band of organized men cannot do this, because if they march in a straight line, they become disorganized, and if they scatter, they do not give the enemy the hard work to rout them, for they have routed themselves. And therefore I would organize the Army so that it should be able to do both; for having placed a thousand Veliti in its wings, I would arrange, that after our artillery had fired, they should issue forth together with the light cavalry to seize the enemy artillery. And therefore I did not have my artillery fire again so as not to give the enemy time, for you cannot give me time and take it from others. And for that, the reason I did not have it fired a second time, was not to allow it to be fired first; because, to render the enemy artillery useless, there is no other remedy than to assault it; which, if the enemy abandons it, you seize it; if they want to defend it, it is necessary that they leave it behind, so that in the hands of the enemy or of friends, it cannot be fired. I believe that, even without examples, this discussion should be enough for you; yet, being able to give you some from the ancients, I will do so. Ventidius, coming to battle with the Parthians, the virtu of whom (the latter) in great part consisted in their bows and darts, he allowed them to come almost under his encampments before he led the Army out, which he only did in order to be able to seize them quickly and not give them time to fire. Caesar in Gaul tells, that in coming to battle with the enemy, he was assaulted by them with such fury, that his men did not have time to draw their darts according to the Roman custom. It is seen, therefore, that, being in the field, if you do not want something fired from a distance to injure you, there is no other remedy than to be able to seize it as quickly as possible. Another reason also caused me to do without firing the artillery, at which you may perhaps laugh, yet I do not judge it is to be disparaged. And there is nothing that causes greater confusion in an Army than to obstruct its vision, whence most stalwart Armies have been routed for having their vision obstructed either by dust or by the sun. There is also nothing that impedes the vision than the smoke which the artillery makes when fired: I would think, therefore, that it would be more prudent to let the enemy blind himself, than for you to go blindly to find him. I would, therefore, not fire, or (as this would not be approved because of the reputation the artillery has) I would put it in the wings of the Army, so that firing it, its smoke should not blind the front of what is most important of our forces. And that obstructing the vision of the enemy is something useful, can be adduced from the example of Epaminondas, who, to blind the enemy Army which was coming to engage him, had his light cavalry run in front of the enemy so that they raised the dust high, and which obstructed their vision, and gave him the victory in the engagement. As to it appearing to you that I aimed the shots of artillery in my own manner, making it pass over the heads of the infantry, I reply that there are more times, and without comparison, that the heavy artillery does not penetrate the infantry than it does, because the infantry lies so low, and they (the artillery) are so difficult to fire, that any little that you raise them, (causes) them to pass over the heads of the infantry, and if you lower them, they damage the ground, and the shot does not reach them (the infantry). Also, the unevenness of the ground saves them, for every little mound or height which exists between the infantry and it (the artillery) impedes it. And as to cavalry, and especially men-at-arms, because they are taller and can more easily be hit, they can be kept in the rear (tail) of the Army until the time the artillery has fired. It is true that often they injure the smaller artillery and the gunners more that the latter (cavalry), to which the best remedy is to come quickly to grips (hand to hand): and if in the first assault some are killed (as some always do die) a good Captain and a good Army do not have to fear an injury that is confined, but a general one; and to imitate the Swiss, who never shun an engagement even if terrified by artillery, but rather they punish with the capital penalty those who because of fear of it either break ranks or by their person give the sign of fear. I made them (once it had been fired) to retire into the Army because it left the passage free to the companies. No other mention of it was made, as something useless, once the battle was started.

You have also said in regard to the fury of this instrument that many judge the arms and the systems of the ancients to be useless, and it appears from your talk that the modems have found arms and systems which are useful against the artillery. If you know this, I would be pleased for you to show it to me, for up to now I do not know of any that have been observed, nor do I believe any can be found. So that I would like to learn from those men for what reasons the soldiers on foot of our times wear the breastplate or the corselet of iron, and those on horseback go completely covered with armor, since, condemning the ancient armor as useless with respect to artillery, they ought also to shun these. I would also like to learn for what reason the Swiss, in imitation of the ancient systems, for a close (pressed) company of six or eight thousand infantry, and for what reason all the others have imitated them, bringing the same dangers to this system because of the artillery as the others brought which had been imitated from antiquity. I believe that they would not know what to answer; but if you asked the soldiers who should have some experience, they would answer, first that they go armed because, even if that armor does not protect them from the artillery, it does every other injury inflicted by an enemy, and they would also answer that they go closely together as the Swiss in order to be better able to attack the infantry, resist the cavalry, and give the enemy more difficulty in routing them. So that it is observed that soldiers have to fear many other things besides the artillery, from which they defend themselves with armor and organization. From which it follows that as much as an Army is better armed, and as much as its ranks are more serrated and more powerful, so much more is it secure. So that whoever is of the opinion you mentioned must be either of little prudence, or has thought very little on this matter; for if we see the least part of the ancient way of arming in use today, which is the pike, and the least part of those systems, which are the battalions of the Swiss, which do us so much good, and lend so much power to our Armies, why shouldn't we believe that the other arms and other systems that they left us are also useful? Moreover, if we do not have any regard for the artillery when we place ourselves close together, like the Swiss, what other system than that can make us afraid? Inasmuch as there is no other arrangement that can make us afraid than that of being pressed together. In addition to this, if the enemy artillery does not frighten me when I lay siege to a town, where he may injure me with great safety to himself, and where I am unable to capture it as it is defended from the walls, but can stop him only with time with my artillery, so that he is able to redouble his shots as he wishes, why do I have to be afraid of him in the field where I am able to seize him quickly? So that I conclude this, that the artillery, according to my opinion, does not impede anyone who is able to use the methods of the ancients, and demonstrate the ancient virtue. And if I had not talked another time with you concerning this instrument, I would extend myself further, but I want to return to what I have now said.

LUIGI: We are able to have a very good understanding since you have so much discoursed about artillery, and in sum, it seems to me you have shown that the best remedy that one has against it when he is in the field and having an Army in an encounter, is to capture it quickly. Upon which, a doubt rises in me, for it seems to me the enemy can so locate it on a side of his army from which he can injure you, and would be so protected by the other sides, that it cannot be captured. You have (if you will remember) in your army's order for battle, created intervals of four arm lengths between one company and the next, and placed twenty of the extraordinary pikemen of the company there. If the enemy should organize his army similarly to yours, and place his artillery well within those intervals, I believe that from here he would be able to injure you with the greatest safety to himself, for it would not be possible to enter among the enemy forces to capture it.

FABRIZIO: You doubt very prudently, and I will endeavor either to resolve the doubt, or to give you a remedy. I have told you that these companies either when going out or when fighting are continually in motion, and by nature always end up close together, so that if you make the intervals small, in which you would place the artillery, in a short time, they would be so closed up that the artillery can no longer perform its function: if you make them large to avoid this danger, you incur a greater, so that, because of those intervals, you not only give the enemy the opportunity to capture your artillery, but to rout you. But you have to know that it is impossible to keep the artillery between the ranks, especially those that are mounted on carriages, for the artillery travel in one direction, and are fired in the other, so that if they are desired to be fired while traveling, it is necessary before they are fired that they be turned, and when they are being turned they need so much space, that fifty carriages of artillery would disrupt every Army. It is necessary, therefore, to keep them outside the ranks where they can be operated in the manner which we showed you a short time ago. But let us suppose they can be kept there, and that a middle way can be found, and of a kind which, when closed together, should not impede the artillery, yet not be so open as to provide a path for the enemy, I say that this is easily remedied at the time of the encounter by creating intervals in your army which give a free path for its shots, and thus its fury will be useless. Which can be easily done, because the enemy, if it wants its artillery to be safe, must place it in the end portions of the intervals, so that its shots, if they should not harm its own men, must pass in a straight line, and always in the same line, and, therefore, by giving them room, can be easily avoided. Because this is a general rule, that you must give way to those things which cannot be resisted, as the ancients did to the elephants and chariots with sickles. I believe, rather I am more than certain, that it must appear to you that I prepared and won an engagement in my own manner; none the less, I will repeat this, if what I have said up to now is now enough, that it would be impossible for an Army thus organized and armed not to overcome, at the first encounter, every other Army organized as modem Armies are organized, which often, unless they have shields (swordsmen), do not form a front, and are of an unarmed kind, which cannot defend themselves from a near-by enemy; and so organized that, that if they place their companies on the flanks next to each other, not having a way of receiving one another, they cause it to be confused, and apt to be easily disturbed. And although they give their Armies three names, and divide them into three ranks, the Vanguard, the Company (main body) and the Rearguard, none the less, they do not serve for anything else than to distinguish them in marching and in their quarters: but in an engagement, they are all pledged to the first attack and fortune.

LUIGI: I have also noted that in making your engagement, your cavalry was repulsed by the enemy cavalry, and that it retired among the extraordinary pikemen, whence it happened that with their aid, they withstood and repulsed the enemy in the rear. I believe the pikemen can withstand the cavalry, as you said, but not a large and strong Battalion, as the Swiss do, which, in your Army, have five ranks of pikemen at the head, and seven on the flank, so that I do not know how they are able to withstand them.

FABRIZIO: Although I have told you that six ranks were employed in the Phalanxes of Macedonia at one time, none the less, you have to know that a Swiss Battalion, if it were composed of ten thousand tanks could not employ but four, or at most five, because the pikes are nine arm lengths long and an arm length and a half is occupied by the hands; whence only seven and a half arm lengths of the pike remain to the first rank. The second rank, in addition to what the hand occupies, uses up an arm's length of the space that exists between one rank and the next; so that not even six arm lengths of pike remain of use. For the same reasons, these remain four and one half arm lengths to the third rank, three to the fourth, and one and a half to the fifth. The other ranks are useless to inflict injury; but they serve to replace the first ranks, as we have said, and serve as reinforcements for those (first) five ranks. If, therefore, five of their ranks can control cavalry, why cannot five of ours control them, to whom five ranks behind them are also not lacking to sustain them, and give the same support, even though they do not have pikes as the others do? And if the ranks of extraordinary pikemen which are placed along the flanks seem thin to you, they can be formed into a square and placed by the flank of the two companies which I place in the last ranks of the army, from which place they would all together be able easily to help the van and the rear of the army, and lend aid to the cavalry according as their need may require.

LUIGI: Would you always use this form of organization, when you would want to engage in battle?

FABRIZIO: Not in every case, for you have to vary the formation of the army according to the fitness of the site, the kind and numbers of the enemy, which will be shown before this discussion is furnished with an example. But this formation that is given here, not so much because it is stronger than others, which is in truth very strong, as much because from it is obtained a rule and a system, to know how to recognize the manner of organization of the others; for every science has its generations, upon which, in good part, it is based. One thing only, I would remind you, that you never organize an army so that whoever fights in the van cannot be helped by those situated behind, because whoever makes this error renders useless the great part of the army, and if any virtue is eliminated, he cannot win.

LUIGI: And on this part, some doubt has arisen in me. I have seen that in the disposition of the companies you form the front with five on each side the center with three, and the rear with two; and I would believe that it should be better to arrange them oppositely, because I think that an army can be routed with more difficulty, for whoever should attack it, the more he should penetrate into it, so much harder would he find it: but the arrangement made by you appears to me results, that the more one enters into it, the more he finds it weak.

FABRIZIO: If you would remember that the Triari, who were the third rank of the Roman Legions, were not assigned more than six hundred men, you would have less doubt, when you leave that they were placed in the last ranks, because you will see that I (motivated by this example) have placed two companies in the last ranks, which comprise nine-hundred infantry; so that I come to err rather with the Roman people in having taken away too many, than few. And although this example should suffice, I want to tell you the reasons, which is this. The first front (line) of the army is made solid and dense because it has to withstand the attack of the enemy, and does not have to receive any friends into it, and because of this, it must abound in men, for few men would make it weak both from their sparseness and their numbers. But the second line, because it has to relieve the friends from the first who have withstood the enemy, must have large intervals, and therefore must have a smaller number than the first; for if it should be of a greater or equal number, it would result in not leaving any intervals, which would cause disorder, or if some should be left, it would extend beyond the ends of those in front, which would make the formation of the army incomplete (imperfect). And what you say is not true, that the more the enemy enters into the Battalions, the weaker he will find them; for the enemy can never fight with the second line, if the first one is not joined up with it: so that he will come to find the center of the Battalion stronger and not weaker, having to fight with the first and second (lines) together. The same thing happens if the enemy should reach the third line, because here, he will not only have to fight with two fresh companies, but with the entire Battalion. And as this last part has to receive more men, its spaces must be larger, and those who receive them lesser in number.

LUIGI: And I like what you have said; but also answer me this. If the five companies retire among the second three, and afterwards, the eight among the third two, does it not seem possible that the eight come together then the ten together, are able to crowd together, whether they are eight or ten, into the same space which the five occupied.

FABRIZIO: The first thing that I answer is, that it is not the same space; for the five have four spaces between them, which they occupy when retiring between one Battalion and the next, and that which exists between the three or the two: there also remains that space which exists between the companies and the extraordinary pikemen, which spaces are all made large. There is added to this whatever other space the companies have when they are in the lines without being changed, for, when they are changed, the ranks are either compressed or enlarged. They become enlarged when they are so very much afraid, that they put themselves in flight: they become compressed when they become so afraid, that they seek to save themselves, not by flight, but by defense; so that in this case, they would compress themselves, and not spread out. There is added to this, that the five ranks of pikemen who are in front, once they have started the battle, have to retire among their companies in the rear (tail) of the army to make place for the shield-bearers (swordsmen) who are able to fight: and when they go into the tail of the army they can serve whoever the captain should judge should employ them well, whereas in the front, once the fight becomes mixed, they would be completely useless. And therefore, the arranged spaces come to be very capacious for the remaining forces. But even if these spaces should not suffice, the flanks on the side consist of men and not walls, who, when they give way and spread out, are able to create a space of such capacity, which should be sufficient to receive them.

LUIGI: The ranks of the extraordinary pikemen, which you place on the flank of the army when the first company retires into the second, do you want them to remain firm, and become as two wings of the army or do you also want them to retire with the company. Which, if they have to do this, I do not see how they can, as they do not have companies behind them with wide intervals which would receive them.

FABRIZIO: If the enemy does not fight them when he faces the companies to retire, they are able to remain firm in their ranks, and inflict injury on the enemy on the flank since the first companies had retired: but if they should also fight them, as seems reasonable, being so powerful as to be able to force the others to retire, they should cause them also to retire. Which they are very well able to do, even though they have no one behind who should receive them, for from the middle forward they are able to double on the right, one file entering into the other in the manner we discussed when we talked of the arrangement for doubling themselves. It is true, that when doubling, they should want to retire behind, other means must be found than that which I have shown you, since I told you that the second rank had to enter among the first, the fourth among the third, and so on little by little, and in this case, it would not be begun from the front, but from the rear, so that doubling the ranks, they should come to retire to the rear, and not to turn in front. But to reply to all of that, which (you have asked) concerning this engagement as shown by me, it should be repeated, (and) I again say that I have so organized this army, and will (again) explain this engagement to you for two reasons: one, to show you how it (the army) is organized: the other, to show you how it is trained. As to the systems, I believe you all most knowledgeable. As to the army, I tell you that it may often be put together in this form, for the Heads are taught to keep their companies in this order: and because it is the duty of each individual soldier to keep (well) the arrangement of each company, and it is the duty of each Head to keep (well) those in each part of the Army, and to know well how to obey the commands of the general Captain. They must know, therefore, how to join one company with another, and how to take their places instantly: and therefore, the banner of each company must have its number displayed openly, so that they may be commanded, and the Captain and the soldiers will more readily recognize that number. The Battalions ought also to be numbered, and have their number on their principal banner. One must know, therefore, what the number is of the Battalion placed on the left or right wing, the number of those placed in the front and the center, and so on for the others. I would want also that these numbers reflect the grades of positions in the Army. For instance, the first grade is the Head of Ten, the second is the head of fifty ordinary Veliti, the third the Centurion, the fourth the head of the first company, the fifth that of the second (company), the sixth of the third, and so on up to the tenth Company, which should be in the second place next to the general Captain of the Battalion; nor should anyone arrive to that Leadership, unless he had (first) risen through all these grades. And, as in addition to these Heads, there are the three Constables (in command) of the extraordinary pikemen, and the two of the extraordinary Veliti, I would want them to be of the grade of Constable of the first company, nor would I care if they were men of equal grade, as long as each of them should vie to be promoted to the second company. Each one of these Captains, therefore, knowing where his Company should be located, of necessity it will follow that, at the sound of the trumpet, once the Captain's flag was raised, all of the Army would be in its proper places. And this is the first exercise to which an Army ought to become accustomed, that is, to assemble itself quickly: and to do this, you must frequently each day arrange them and disarrange them.

LUIGI: What signs would you want the flags of the Army to have, in addition to the number?

FABRIZIO: I would want the one of the general Captain to have the emblem of the Army: all the others should also have the same emblem, but varying with the fields, or with the sign, as it should seem best to the Lord of the Army, but this matters little, so long as their effect results in their recognizing one another.

But let us pass on to another exercise in which an army ought to be trained, which is, to set it in motion, to march with a convenient step, and to see that, while in motion, it maintains order. The third exercise is, that they be taught to conduct themselves as they would afterwards in an engagement; to fire the artillery, and retire it; to have the extraordinary Veliti issue forth, and after a mock assault, have them retire; have the first company, as if they were being pressed, retire within the intervals of the second (company), and then both into the third, and from here each one return to its place; and so to accustom them in this exercise, that it become understood and familiar to everyone, which with practice and familiarity, will readily be learned. The fourth exercise is that they be taught to recognize commands of the Captain by virtue of his (bugle) calls and flags, as they will understand, without other command, the pronouncements made by voice. And as the importance of the commands depends on the (bugle) calls, I will tell you what sounds (calls) the ancients used. According as Thucydides affirms, whistles were used in the army of the Lacedemonians, for they judged that its pitch was more apt to make their Army proceed with seriousness and not with fury. Motivated by the same reason, the Carthaginians, in their first assault, used the zither. Alliatus, King of the Lydians, used the zither and whistles in war; but Alexander the Great and the Romans used horns and trumpets, like those who thought the courage of the soldiers could be increased by virtue of such instruments, and cause them to combat more bravely. But just as we have borrowed from the Greek and Roman methods in equipping our Army, so also in choosing sounds should we serve ourselves of the customs of both those nations. I would, therefore, place the trumpets next to the general Captain, as their sound is apt not only to inflame the Army but to be heard over every noise more than any other sound. I would want that the other sounds existing around the Constables and Heads of companies to be (made by) small drums and whistles, sounded not as they are presently, but as they are customarily sounded at banquets. I would want, therefore, for the Captain to use the trumpets in indicating when they should stop or go forward or turn back, when they should fire the artillery, when to move the extraordinary Veliti, and by changes in these sounds (calls) point out to the Army all those moves that generally are pointed out; and those trumpets afterwards followed by drums. And, as training in these matters is of great importance, I would follow them very much in training your Army. As to the cavalry, I would want to use the same trumpets, but of lower volume and different pitch of sounds from those of the Captain. This is all that occurs to me concerning the organization and training of the Army.

LUIGI: I beg you not to be so serious in clearing up another matter for me: why did you have the light cavalry and the extraordinary Veliti move with shouts and noise and fury when they attacked, but they in rejoining the Army you indicated the matter was accomplished with great silence: and as I do not understand the reason for this fact, I would desire you to clarify it for me.

FABRIZIO: When coming to battle, there have been various opinions held by the ancient Captains, whether they ought either to accelerate the step (of the soldiers) by sounds, or have them go slowly in silence. This last manner serves to keep the ranks firmer and have them understand the commands of the Captain better: the first serves to encourage the men more. And, as I believe consideration ought to be given to both these methods, I made the former move with sound, and the latter in silence. And it does not seem to me that in any case the sounds are planned to be continuous, for they would impede the commands, which is a pernicious thing. Nor is it reasonable that the Romans, after the first assault, should follow with such sounds, for it is frequently seen in their histories that soldiers who were fleeing were stopped by the words and advice of the Captains, and changed the orders in various ways by his command: which would not have occurred if the sounds had overcome his voice.

FOURTH BOOK

LUIGI: Since an engagement has been won so honorably under my Rule, I think it is well if I do not tempt fortune further, knowing how changeable and unstable it is. And, therefore, I desire to resign my speakership, and that, wanting to follow the order that belongs to the youngest, Zanobi now assume this office of questioning. And I know he will not refuse this honor, or we would rather say, this hard work, as much in order to (give) pleasure, as also because he is naturally more courageous than I: nor should he be afraid to enter into these labors, where he can thus be overcome, as he can overcome.

ZANOBI: I intend to stay where you put me, even though I would more willingly stay to listen, because up to now I am more satisfied with your questions than those which occurred to me in listening to your discussions pleased me. But I believe it is well, Lords, that since you have time left, and have patience, we do not annoy you with these ceremonies of ours.

FABRIZIO: Rather you give me pleasure, because this change of questioners makes me know the various geniuses, and your various desires. Is there anything remaining of the matter discussed which you think should be added?

ZANOBI: There are two things I desire before we pass on to another part: the one is, that you would show me if there is another form of organizing the Army which may occur to you: the other, what considerations ought a Captain have before going to battle, and if some accident should arise concerning it, what remedies can be made.

FABRIZIO: I will make an effort to satisfy you, I will not reply to your questions in detail; for, when I answer one, often it will also answer another. I have told you that I proposed a form for the Army which should fill all the requirements according to the (nature of) the enemy and the site, because in this case, one proceeds according to the site and the enemy. But note this, that there is no greater peril than to over extend the front of your army, unless you have a very large and very brave Army: otherwise you have to make it rather wide and of short length, than of long length and very narrow. For when you have a small force compared to the enemy, you ought to seek other remedies; for example, arrange your army so that you are girded on a side by rivers or swamps, so that you cannot be surrounded or gird yourself on the flanks with ditches, as Caesar did in Gaul. In this case, you have to take the flexibility of being able to enlarge or compress your front, according to the numbers of the enemy: and if the enemy is of a lesser number, you ought to seek wide places, especially if you have your forces so disciplined, that you are able not only to surround the enemy, but extend your ranks, because in rough and difficult places, you do not have the advantage of being able to avail yourself of (all) your ranks. Hence it happened that the Romans almost always sought open fields, and avoided the difficult ones. On the other hand (as I have said) you ought to, if you have either a small force or a poorly disciplined one, for you have to seek places where a small number can defend you, or where inexperience may not cause you injury. Also, higher places ought to be sought so as to be able more easily to attack (the enemy). Nonetheless, one ought to be aware not to arrange your Army on a beach and in a place near the adjoining hills, where the enemy Army can come; because in this case, with respect to the artillery, the higher place would be disadvantageous to you, because you could continuously and conveniently be harmed by the enemy artillery, without being able to undertake any remedy, and similarly, impeded by your own men, you cannot conveniently injure him. Whoever organizes an Army for battle, ought also to have regard for both the sun and the wind, that the one and the other do not strike the front, because both impede your vision, the one with its rays, the other with dust. And in addition, the wind does not aid the arms that are thrown at the enemy, and makes their blows more feeble. And as to the sun, it is not enough that you take care that it is not in your face at the time, but you must think about it not harming you when it comes up. And because of this, in arranging the army, I would have it (the sun) behind them, so that much time should pass before it should come in front of you. This method was observed by Hannibal at Cannae and by Marius against the Cimbrians. If you should be greatly inferior in cavalry, arrange your army between vines and trees, and such impediments, as the Spaniards did in our times when they routed the French in the Kingdom (of Naples) on the Cirignuola. And it has been frequently seen that the same soldiers, when they changed only their arrangement and the location, from being overcome became victorious, as happened to the Carthaginians, who, after having been often defeated by Marius Regulus, were afterwards victorious, through the counsel of Xantippe, the Lacedemonian, who had them descend to the plain, where, by the virtu of their cavalry and Elephants, they were able to overcome the Romans. And it appears to me, according to the examples of the ancients, that almost all the excellent Captains, when they learned that the enemy had strengthened one side of the company, did not attack the stronger side, but the weaker, and the other stronger side they oppose to the weaker: then, when starting a battle, they cornered the stronger part that it only resist the enemy, and not push it back, and the weaker part that it allow itself to be overcome, and retire into the rear ranks of the Army. This causes two great disorders to the enemy: the first, that he finds his strongest part surrounded: the second is, that as it appears to them they will obtain the victory quickly, it rarely happens that he will not become disorganized, whence his defeat quickly results. Cornelius Scipio, when he was in Spain, (fighting) against Hasdrubal, the Carthaginian, and knowing that Hasdrubal was noted, that in arranging the Army, placed his legions in the center, which constituted the strongest part of his Army, and therefore, when Hasdrubal was to proceed in this manner, afterwards, when he came to the engagement, changed the arrangement, and put his Legions in the wings of the Army, and placed his weakest forces in the center. Then when they came hand to hand, he quickly had those forces in the center to walk slowly, and the wings to move forward swiftly: so that only the wings of both armies fought, and the ranks in the center, being distant from each other, did not join (in battle), and thus the strongest part of (the army of) Scipio came to fight the weakest part of (that of) Hasdrubal, and defeated it. This method at that time was useful, but today, because of the artillery, could not be employed, because that space that existed between one and the other army, gives them time to fire, which is most pernicious, as we said above. This method, therefore, must be set aside, and be used, as was said a short time ago, when all the Army is engaged, and the weaker part made to yield. When a Captain finds himself to have an army larger than that of the enemy, and not wanting to be prevented from surrounding him, arranges his Army with fronts equal to those of the enemy: then when the battle is started, has his front retire and the flanks extend little by little, and it will always happen that the enemy will find himself surrounded without being aware of it. When a Captain wants to fight almost secure in not being routed, he arranges his army in a place where he has a safe refuge nearby, either amid swamps or mountains or in a powerful city; for, in this manner, he cannot be pursued by the enemy, but the enemy cannot be pursued by him. This means was employed by Hannibal when fortune began to become adverse for him, and he was apprehensive of the valor of Marcus Marcellus. Several, in order to disorganize the ranks of the enemy, have commanded those who are lightly armed, that they begin the fight, and having begun it, retire among the ranks; and when the Armies afterwards have joined fronts together, and each front is occupied in fighting, they have allowed them to issue forth from the flanks of the companies, and disorganized and routed them. If anyone finds himself inferior in cavalry, he can, in addition to the methods mentioned, place a company of pikemen behind his cavalry, and in the fighting, arrange for them to give way for the pikemen, and he will always remain superior. Many have accustomed some of the lightly armed infantry to get used to combat amidst the cavalry, and this has been a very great help to the cavalry. Of all those who have organized Armies for battle, the most praiseworthy have been Hannibal and Scipio when they were fighting in Africa: and as Hannibal had his Army composed of Carthaginians and auxiliaries of various kinds, he placed eighty Elephants in the first van, then placed the auxiliaries, after these he placed his Carthaginians, and in the rear, he placed the Italians, whom he trusted little. He arranged matters thusly, because the auxiliaries, having the enemy in front and their rear closed by his men, they could not flee: so that being compelled to fight, they should overcome or tire out the Romans, thinking afterwards with his forces of virtue, fresh, he could easily overcome the already tired Romans. In the encounter with this arrangement, Scipio placed the Astati, the Principi, and the Triari, in the accustomed fashion for one to be able to receive the other, and one to help the other. He made the vans of the army full of intervals; and so that they should not be seen through, but rather appear united, he filled them with Veliti, whom he commanded that, as soon as the Elephants arrived, they should give way, and enter through the regular spaces among the legions, and leave the way open to the Elephants: and thus come to render their attack vain, so that coming hand to hand with them, he was superior.

ZANOBI: You have made me remember in telling me of this engagement, that Scipio, during the fight, did not have the Astati retire into the ranks of the Principi, but divided them and had them retire into the wings of the army, so as to make room for the Principi, if he wanted to push them forward. I would desire, therefore, that you tell me what reason motivated him not to observe the accustomed arrangement.

FABRIZIO: I will tell you. Hannibal had placed all the virtue of his army in the second line; whence Scipio, in order to oppose a similar virtu to it, assembled the Principi and the Triari; so that the intervals of the Principi being occupied by the Triari, there was no place to receive the Astati, and therefore, he caused the Astati to be divided and enter the wings of the army, and did not bring them among the Principi. But take note that this method of opening up the first lines to make a place for the second, cannot be employed except when the other are superior, because then the convenience exists to be able to do it, as Scipio was able to. But being inferior and repulsed, it cannot be done except with your manifest ruin: and, therefore, you must have ranks in the rear which will receive you. But let us return to our discussion. The ancient Asiatics (among other things thought up by them to injure the enemy) used chariots which had scythes on their sides, so that they not only served to open up the lines with their attack, but also kill the adversary with the scythes. Provisions against these attacks were made in three ways. It was resisted by the density of the ranks, or they were received within the lines as were the Elephants, or a stalwart resistance was made with some stratagems, as did Sulla, the Roman, against Archelaus, who had many of those chariots which they called Falcati; he (Sulla), in order to resist them, fixed many poles in the ground behind the first ranks, by which the chariots, being resisted, lost their impetus. And note is to be taken of the new method which Sulla used against this man in arranging the army, since he put the Veliti and the cavalry in the rear, and all the heavily armed in front, leaving many intervals in order to be able to send those in the rear forward if necessity should require it; whence when the battle was started, with the aid of the cavalry, to whom he gave the way, he obtained the victory. To want to worry the enemy during the battle, something must be made to happen which dismays him, either by announcing new help which is arriving, or by showing things which look like it, so that the enemy, being deceived by that sight, becomes frightened; and when he is frightened, can be easily overcome. These methods were used by the Roman Consuls Minucius Rufus and Accilius Glabrius, Caius Sulpicius also placed many soldier-packs on mules and other animals useless in war, but in a manner that they looked like men-at-arms, and commanded that they appear on a hill while they were (in) hand to hand (combat) with the Gauls: whence his victory resulted. Marius did the same when he was fighting against the Germans. Feigned assaults, therefore, being of great value while the battle lasts, it happens that many are benefited by the real (assaults), especially if, improvised in the middle of the battle, it is able to attack the enemy from behind or on the sides. Which can be done only with difficulty, unless the (nature of the) country helps you; for if it is open, part of your forces cannot be speeded, as must be done in such enterprises: but in wooded or mountainous places, and hence capable of ambush, part of your forces can be well hidden, so that the enemy may be assaulted, suddenly and without his expecting it, which will always be the cause of giving you the victory. And sometimes it has been very important, while the battle goes on, to plant voices which announce the killed of the enemy Captain, or to have defeated some other part of the army; and this often has given the victory to whoever used it. The enemy cavalry may be easily disturbed by unusual forms (sights) or noises; as did Croesus, who opposed camels to the cavalry of his adversaries, and Pyrrhus who opposed elephants to the Roman cavalry, the sight of which disturbed and disorganized it. In our times, the Turk routed the Shah in Persia and the Soldan in Syria with nothing else than the noise of guns, which so affected their cavalry by their unaccustomed noises, that the Turk was able easily to defeat it. The Spaniards, to overcome the army of Hamilcar, placed in their first lines chariots full of tow drawn by oxen, and when they had come to battle, set fire to them, whence the oxen, wanting to flee the fire, hurled themselves on the army of Hamilcar and dispersed it. As we mentioned, where the country is suitable, it is usual to deceive the enemy when in combat by drawing him into ambushes: but when it is open and spacious, many have employed the making (digging) of ditches, and then covering them lightly with earth and branches, but leaving several places (spaces) solid in order to be able to retire between them; then when the battle is started, retire through them, and the enemy pursuing, comes to ruin in them. If, during the battle, some accident befalls you which dismays your soldiers, it is a most prudent thing to know how to dissimulate and divert them to (something) good, as did Lucius Sulla, who, while the fighting was going on, seeing that a great part of his forces had gone over to the side of the enemy, and that this had dismayed his men, quickly caused it to be understood throughout the entire army that everything was happening by his order, and this not only did not disturb the army, but so increased its courage that it was victorious. It also happened to Sulla, that having sent certain soldiers to undertake certain business, and they having been killed, in order that his army would not be dismayed, said that because he had found them unfaithful, he had cunningly sent them into the hands of the enemy. Sertorious, when undertaking an engagement in Spain, killed one who had pointed out to him the slaying of one of his Heads, for fear that by telling the same to the others, he should dismay them. It is a difficult matter to stop an army already in flight, and return it to battle. And you have to make this distinction: either they are entirely in flight (motion) -- and here it is impossible to return them, or only a part are in flight, and here there is some remedy. Many Roman Captains, by getting in front of those fleeing, have stopped them, by making them ashamed of their flight, as did Lucius Sulla, who, when a part of his Legions had already turned, driven by the forces of Mithradates, with his sword in hand he got in front of them and shouted, "If anyone asks you where you have left your Captain, tell them, we have left him in Boetia fighting." The Consul Attilius opposed those who fled with those who did not flee, and made them understand that if they did not turn about, they would be killed by both friends and enemies. Phillip of Macedonia, when he learned that his men were afraid of the Scythian soldiers, put some of his most trusted cavalry behind his army, and commissioned them to kill anyone who fled; whence his men, preferring to die fighting rather than in flight, won. Many Romans, not so much in order to stop a flight, as to give his men an occasion to exhibit greater prowess, while they were fighting, have taken a banner out of their hands, and tossing it amid the enemy, offered rewards to whoever would recover it.

I do not believe it is out of order to add to this discussion those things that happen after a battle, especially as they are brief, and not to be omitted, and conform greatly to this discussion. I will tell you, therefore, how engagements are lost, or are won. When one wins, he ought to follow up the victory with all speed, and imitate Caesar in this case, and not Hannibal, who, because he had stopped after he had defeated the Romans at Cannae, lost the Empire of Rome. The other (Caesar) never rested after a victory, but pursued the routed enemy with great impetus and fury, until he had completely assaulted it. But when one loses, a Captain ought to see if something useful to him can result from this loss, especially if some residue of the army remains to him. An opportunity can arise from the unawareness of the enemy, which frequently becomes obscured after a victory, and gives you the occasion to attack him; as Martius, the Roman, attacked the Carthaginian army, which, having killed the two Scipios and defeated their armies, thought little of that remnant of the forces who, with Martius, remained alive; and was (in turn) attacked and routed by him. It is seen, therefore, that there is nothing so capable of success as that which the enemy believes you cannot attempt, because men are often injured more when they are less apprehensive. A Captain ought, therefore, when he cannot do this, at least endeavor with industry to restrict the injury caused by the defeat. And to do this, it is necessary for you to take steps that the enemy is not able to follow you easily, or give him cause for delay. In the first case some, after they realize they are losing, order their Leaders to flee in several parts by different paths, having (first) given an order where they should afterward reassemble, so that the enemy, fearing to divide his forces, would leave all or a greater part of them safe. In the second case, many have thrown down their most precious possessions in front of the enemy, so that being retarded by plundering, he gave them more time for flight. Titus Dimius used not a little astuteness in hiding the injury received in battle; for, after he had fought until nightfall with a loss of many of his men, caused a good many of them to be buried during the night; whence in the morning, the enemy seeing so many of their dead and so few Romans, believing they had had the disadvantage, fled. I believe I have thus confused you, as I said, (but) satisfied your question in good part: it is true, that concerning the shape of the army, there remains for me to tell you how sometimes it is customary for some Captains to make the front in the form of a wedge, judging in that way to be able more readily to open (penetrate) the Army of the enemy. In opposition to this shape they customarily would use a form of a scissor, so as to be able to receive that wedge into that space, and surround and fight it from every side. On this, I would like you to have this general rule, that the greatest remedy used against the design of the enemy, is to do that willingly which he designs for you to do by force, because doing it willingly you do it with order and to your advantage, but to his disadvantage: if you should do it by force, it would be to your ruin. As to the fortifying of this, I would not care to repeat anything already said. Does the adversary make a wedge in order to open your ranks? If you proceed with yours open, you disorganize him, and he does not disorganize you. Hannibal placed Elephants in front of his Army to open that of the Army of Scipio; Scipio went with his open and was the cause of his own victory and the ruin of the former (Hannibal). Hasdrubal placed his most stalwart forces in the center of the van of his Army to push back the forces of Scipio: Scipio commanded in like fashion that they should retire, and defeated him. So that such plans, when they are put forward, are the cause for the victory of him against whom they were organized. It remains for me yet, if I remember well, to tell you what considerations a Captain ought to take into account before going into battle: upon which I have to tell you first that a Captain never has to make an engagement, if he does not have the advantage, or if he is not compelled to. Advantages arise from the location, from the organization, and from having either greater or better forces. Necessity, (compulsion) arises when you see that, by not fighting, you must lose in an event; for example, when you see you are about to lack money, and therefore your Army has to be dissolved in any case; when hunger is about to assail you, or when you expect the enemy to be reinforced again by new forces. In these cases, one ought always to fight, even at your disadvantage; for it is much better to try your fortune when it can favor you, than by not trying, see your ruin sure: and in such a case, it is as serious an error for a Captain not to fight, as it is to pass up an opportunity to win, either from ignorance, or from cowardice. The enemy sometimes gives you the advantage, and sometimes (it derives from) your prudence. Many have been routed while crossing a river by an alert enemy of theirs, who waited until they were in the middle of the stream, and then assaulted them on every side; as Caesar did to the Swiss, where he destroyed a fourth part of them, after they had been split by the river. Some time you may find your enemy tired from having pursued you too inconsiderately, so that, finding yourself fresh, and rested, you ought not to lose such an opportunity. In addition to this, if an enemy offers you battle at a good hour of the morning, you can delay going out of your encampment for many hours: and if he has been under arms for a long time, and has lost that first ardor with which he started, you can then fight with him. Scipio and Metellus employed this method in Spain, the first against Hasdrubal, and the other against Sertorius. If the enemy has diminished in strength, either from having divided the Armies, as the Scipios (did) in Spain, or from some other cause, you ought to try (your) fortune. The greater part of prudent Captains would rather receive the onrush of the enemy, who impetuously go to assault them, for their fury is easily withstood by firm and resolute men, and that fury which was withstood, easily converts itself into cowardice. Fabius acted thusly against the Samnites and against the Gauls, and was victorious, but his colleague, Decius was killed. Some who feared the virtu of their enemy have begun the battle at an hour near nightfall, so that if their men were defeated, they might be able to be protected by its darkness and save themselves. Some, having known that the enemy Army, because of certain superstitions, does not want to undertake fighting at such a time, selected that time for battle, and won: which Caesar did in Gaul against Ariovistus, and Vespatianus in Syria against the Jews. The greater and more important awareness that a Captain ought to have, is (to see) that he has about him, men loyal and most expert in war, and prudent, with whom he counsels continually, and discusses his forces and those of the enemy with them: which are the greater in number, which are better armed or better trained, which are more apt to suffer deprivation, which to confide in more, the infantry or the cavalry. Also, they consider the location in which they are, and if it is more suitable for the enemy than for themselves; which of them has the better convenience of supply; whether it is better to delay the engagement or undertake it, and what benefit the weather might give you or take away from them; for often when the soldiers see the war becoming long, they become irritable, and weary from hard work and tedium, will abandon you. Above all, it is important for the Captain to know the enemy, and who he has around him: if he is foolhardy or cautious: if timid or audacious. See whether you can trust the auxiliary soldiers. And above all, you ought to guard against leading an army into battle which is afraid, or distrustful in any way of victory, for the best indication of defeat is when one believes he cannot win. And, therefore, in this case, you ought to avoid an engagement, either by doing as Fabius Maximus did, who, by encamping in strong places, did not give Hannibal courage to go and meet him, or by believing that the enemy, also in strong places, should come to meet you, you should depart from the field, and divide your forces among your towns, so that the tedium of capturing them will tire him.

ZANOBI: Can he not avoid the engagement in other ways than by dividing it (the army) into several parts, and putting them in towns?

FABRIZIO: I believe at another time I have discussed with some of you that whoever is in the field, cannot avoid an engagement if he has an enemy who wants to fight in any case; and he has but one remedy, and that is to place himself with his Army at least fifty miles distant from his adversary, so as to be in time to get out of his way if he should come to meet him. And Fabius Maximus never avoided an engagement with Hannibal, but wanted it at his advantage; and Hannibal did not presume to be able to overcome him by going to meet him in the places where he was encamped. But if he supposed he could defeat him, it was necessary for Fabius to undertake an engagement with him in any case, or to flee. Phillip, King of Macedonia, he who was the father of Perseus, coming to war with the Romans, placed his encampment on a very high mountain so as not to have an engagement with them; but the Romans went to meet him on that mountain, and routed him. Vercingetorix, a Captain of the Gauls, in order to avoid an engagement with Caesar, who unexpectedly had crossed the river, placed himself miles distant with his forces. The Venetians in our times, if they did not want to come to an engagement with the King of France, ought not to have waited until the French Army had crossed the Adda, but should have placed themselves distant from him, as did Vercingetorix: whence, having waited for him, they did not know how to take the opportunity of undertaking an engagement during the crossing, nor how to avoid it; for the French being near to them, as the Venetians decamped, assaulted and routed them. And so it is, that an engagement cannot be avoided if the enemy at all events wants to undertake it. Nor does anyone cite Fabius, for he avoided an engagement in cases like that, just as much as did Hannibal. It often happens that your soldiers are not willing to fight, and you know that because of their number or the location, or from some other cause, you have a disadvantage, and would like them to change their minds. It also happens that necessity or opportunity constrains you to (come to) an engagement, and that your soldiers are discontent and little disposed to fight, whence it is necessary for you in one case to frighten them, and in the other to excite them. In the first instance, if persuasion is not enough, there is no better way to have both those who fight and those who would not believe you, than to give some of them over to the enemy as plunder. It may also be well to do with cunning that which happened to Fabius Maximus at home. The Army of Fabius desired (as you know) to fight with the Army of Hannibal: his Master of cavalry had the same desire. It did not seem proper to Fabius to attempt the battle, so that in order to dispel such (desires), he had to divide the Army. Fabius kept his men in the encampments: and the other (the Master of cavalry) going forth, and coming into great danger, would have been routed, if Fabius had not succored him. By this example, the Master of the cavalry, together with the entire army, realized it was a wise course to obey Fabius. As to exciting them to fight, it is well to make them angry at the enemy, by pointing out that (the enemy) say slanderous things of them, and showing them to have with their intelligence (in the enemy camp) and having corrupted some part, to encamp on the side where they see they enemy, and undertake some light skirmishes with them; because things that are seen daily are more easily disparaged. By showing yourself indignant, and by making an oration in which you reproach them for their laziness, you make them so ashamed by saying you want to fight only if they do not accompany you. And above every thing, to have this awareness, if you want to make the soldiers obstinate in battle, not to permit them to send home any of their possessions, or settle in any place, until the war ends, so that they understand that if flight saves them their lives, it will not save them their possessions, the love of the latter, not less than the former, renders men obstinate in defense.

ZANOBI: You have told how soldiers can be made to turn and fight, by talking to them. Do you mean by this that he has to talk to the entire Army, or to its Heads?

FABRIZIO: To persuade or dissuade a few from something, is very easy; for if words are not enough, you can use authority and force: but the difficulty is to take away a sinister idea from a multitude, whether it may be in agreement or contrary to your own opinion, where only words can be used, which, if you want to persuade everyone, must be heard by everyone. Captains, therefore, must be excellent Orators, for without knowing how to talk to the entire Army, good things can only be done with difficulty. Which, in these times of ours, is completely done away with. Read the life (biography) of Alexander the Great, and see how many times it was necessary to harangue and speak publicly to the Army; otherwise he could never have them led them (having become rich and full of plunder) through the deserts of Arabia and into India with so much hardship and trouble; for infinite numbers of things arose by which an Army is ruined if a Captain does not know how or is not accustomed to talking to it; for this speaking takes away fear, incites courage, increases obstinacy, and sweeps away deceptions, promises rewards, points out dangers and the ways to avoid them, reprimands, begs, threatens, fills with hope, praises, slanders, and does all those things by which human passion are extinguished or enkindled. Whence that Prince or Republic planning to raise a new army, and to give this army reputation, ought to accustom the soldiers to listen to the talk of the Captain, and the Captain to know how to talk to them. Religion was (also) of much value in keeping the ancient soldiers well disposed and an oath was given to (taken by) them when they came into the army; for whenever they made a mistake, they were threatened not only by those evils that can be feared by men, but also by those that can be expected from the Deity. This practice, mixed with other religious means, often made an entire enterprise easy for the ancient Captains, and would always be so whenever religion was feared and observed. Sertorius availed himself of this when he told of talking with a Hind (female stag), which promised him victory on the part of the Deity. Sulla was said to talk with a Statue which he had taken from the Temple of Apollo. Many have told of God appearing to them in their sleep, and admonishing them to fight. In the times of our fathers, Charles the seventh, King of France, in the war he waged against the English, was said to counsel with a young girl sent by God, who is called the Maid of France, and who was the cause for victory. You can also take means to make your (soldiers) value the enemy little, as Agesilaus the Spartan did, who showed his soldiers some Persians in the nude, so that seeing their delicate members, they should have no cause for being afraid of them. Some have constrained them to fight from necessity, by removing from their paths all hope of saving themselves, except through victory. This is the strongest and the best provision that can be made when you want to make your soldiers obstinate, which obstinacy is increased by the confidence and the love either of the Captain or of the Country. Confidence is instilled by arms organization, fresh victories, and the knowledge of the Captain. Love of Country springs from nature: that of the Captain from (his) virtue more than any other good event. Necessities can be many, but that is the strongest, which constrains you either to win or to die.

FIFTH BOOK

FABRIZIO: I have shown you how to organize an army to battle another army which is seen posted against you, and I have told you how it is overcome, and also of the many circumstances which can occur because of the various incidents surrounding it, so that it appears to me now to be the time to show you how to organize an army against an enemy which is unseen, but which you are continually afraid will assault you. This happens when marching through country which is hostile, or suspected (of being so). And first you have to understand that a Roman Army ordinarily always sent ahead some groups of cavalry as observers for the march. Afterwards the right wing followed. After this came all the wagons which pertained to it. After those, another Legion, and next its wagons. After these come the left wing with its wagon in the rear, and the remainder of the cavalry followed in the last part. This was in effect the manner in which one ordinarily marched. And if it happened that the Army should be assaulted on the march in front or from the rear, they quickly caused all the wagons to be withdrawn either on the right, or on the left, according as it happened, or rather as best they could depending on the location, and all the forces together, free from their baggage, set up a front on that side from which the enemy was coming. If they were assaulted on the flank, they would withdraw the wagons to the side which was secure, and set up a front on the other. This method being good, and prudently conducted, appears to me ought to be imitated, sending cavalry ahead to observe the country, then having four battalions, having them march in line, and each with its wagons in the rear. And as the wagons are of two kinds, that is, those pertaining to individual soldiers, and the public ones for use by the whole camp, I would divide the public wagons into four parts, and assign a part to each Battalion, also dividing the artillery and all the unarmed men, so that each one of those armed should have its equal share of impedimenta. But as it sometimes happens that one marches in a country not only suspect, but hostile in fact, that you are afraid of being attacked hourly, in order to go on more securely, you are compelled to change the formation of the march, and go on in the regular way, so that in some unforeseen place, neither the inhabitants nor the Army can injure you. In such a case, the ancient Captains usually went on with the Army in squares, for such they called these formations, not because it was entirely square, but because it was capable of fighting on four sides, and they said that they were going prepared either for marching or for battle. I do not want to stray far from this method, and want to arrange my two Battalions, which I have taken as a rule for an Army, in this manner. If you want, therefore, to walk securely through the enemy country, and be able to respond from every side, if you had been assaulted by surprise, and wanting, in accordance with the ancients, to bring it into a square, I would plan to make a square whose hollow was two hundred arm lengths on every side in this manner. I would first place the flanks, each distant from the other by two hundred twelve arm lengths, and would place five companies in each flank in a file along its length, and distant from each other three arm lengths; these would occupy their own space, each company occupying (a space) forty arm lengths by two hundred twelve arm lengths. Between the front and rear of these two flanks, I would place another ten companies, five on each side, arranging them in such a way that four should be next to the front of the right flank, and five at the rear of the left flank, leaving between each one an interval (gap) of four arm lengths: one of which should be next to the front of the left flank, and one at the rear of the right flank. And as the space existing between the one flank and the other is two hundred twelve arm lengths, and these companies placed alongside each other by their width and not length, they would come to occupy, with the intervals, one hundred thirty four arm lengths, (and) there would be between the four companies placed on the front of the right flank, and one placed on the left, a remaining space of seventy eight arm lengths, and a similar space be left among the companies placed in the rear parts; and there would be no other difference, except that one space would be on the rear side toward the right wing, the other would be on the front side toward the left wing. In the space of seventy-eight arm lengths in front, I would place all the ordinary Veliti, and in that in the rear the extraordinary Veliti, who would come to be a thousand per space. And if you want that the space taken up by the Army should be two hundred twelve arm lengths on every side, I would see that five companies are placed in front, and those that are placed in the rear, should not occupy any space already occupied by the flanks, and therefore I would see that the five companies in the rear should have their front touch the rear of their flanks, and those in front should have their rear touch the front (of their flanks), so that on every side of that army, space would remain to receive another company. And as there are four spaces, I would take four banners away from the extraordinary pikemen and would put one on every corner: and the two banners of the aforementioned pikemen left to me, I would place in the middle of the hollow of their army (formed) in a square of companies, at the heads of which the general Captain would remain with his men around him. And as these companies so arranged all march in one direction, but not all fight in one, in putting them together, one has to arrange which sides are not guarded by other companies during the battle. And, therefore, it ought to be considered that the five companies in front protect all the other sides, except the front; and therefore these have to be assembled in an orderly manner (and) with the pikemen in front. The five companies behind protect all the sides, except the side in the back; and therefore ought to be assembled so that the pikemen are in the rear, as we will demonstrate in its place. The five companies on the right flank protect all the sides, from the right flank outward. The five on the left, engird all the sides, from the left flank outward: and therefore in arranging the companies, the pikemen ought to be placed so that they turn by that flank which in uncovered. And as the Heads of Ten are placed in the front and rear, so that when they have to fight, all the army and its members are in their proper places, the manner of accomplishing this was told when we discussed the methods of arranging the companies. I would divide the artillery, and one part I would place outside the right flank, and the other at the left. I would send the light cavalry ahead to reconnoiter the country. Of the men-at-arms, I would place part in the rear on the right wing, and part on the left, distant forty arms lengths from the companies. And no matter how you arrange your Army, you have to take up (as the cavalry) this general (rule), that you have to place them always either in the rear or on the flanks. Whoever places them ahead in front of the Army must do one of two things: either he places them so far ahead, that if they are repulsed they have so much room to give them time to be able to obtain shelter for themselves from your infantry and not collide with them; or to arrange them (the infantry) with so many intervals, that by means of them the cavalry can enter among them without disorganizing them. Let not anyone think little of this instruction, because many, not being aware of this, have been ruined, and have been disorganized and routed by themselves. The wagons and the unarmed men are placed in the plaza that exists within the Army, and so compartmented, that they easily make way for whoever wants to go from one side to the other, or from one front of the Army to the other. These companies, without artillery and cavalry, occupy two hundred eighty two arm lengths of space on the outside in every direction. And as this square is composed of two Battalions, it must be devised as to which part one Battalion makes up, and which part the other. And since the Battalions are called by number, and each of them has (as you know) ten companies and a general Head, I would have the first Battalion place its first five companies in the front, the other five on the left flank, and the Head should be in the left angle of the front. The first five companies of the second Battalion then should be placed on the right flank, and the other five in the rear, and the Head should be in the right angle, who would undertake the office of the Tergiduttore.

The Army organized in this manner is ready to move, and in its movement should completely observe this arrangement: and without doubt it is secure from all the tumults of the inhabitants. Nor ought the Captain make other provisions against these tumultuous assaults, than sometime to give a commission to some cavalry or band of Veliti to put them in their place. Nor will it ever happen that these tumultuous people will come to meet you within the drawing of a sword or pike, because disorderly people are afraid of order; and it will always be seen that they make a great assault with shouts and noises without otherwise approaching you in the way of yelping dogs around a mastiff. Hannibal, when he came to harm from the Romans in Italy, passed through all of France, and always took little account of the tumults of the French. When you want to march, you must have levelers and men with pick axes ahead who clear the road for you, and who are well protected by that cavalry sent ahead to reconnoiter. An Army will march in this order ten miles a day, and enough sunlight will remain for them to dine and camp, since ordinarily an Army marches twenty miles. If it happens that it is assaulted by an organized Army, this assault cannot arise suddenly, because an organized Army travels at its own rate (step), so that you are always in time to reorganize for the engagement, and quickly bring yourself to that formation, or similar to that formation of the Army, which I showed you above. For if you are assaulted on the front side, you do nothing except (to) have the artillery in the flanks and the cavalry behind come forward and take those places and with those distances mentioned above. The thousand Veliti who are forward, come forth from their positions, and dividing into groups of a hundred, enter into their places between the cavalry and the wings of the Army. Then, into the voids left by them, enter the two bands of extraordinary pikemen which I had placed in the plaza of the Army. The thousand Veliti that I had placed in the rear depart from there, and distribute themselves among the flanks of the companies to strengthen them: and from the open space they leave all the wagons and unarmed men issue forth and place themselves at the rear of the companies. The plaza, therefore, remains vacant as everyone has gone to their places, and the five companies that I placed in the rear of the Army come forward through the open void that exists between the one and the other flank, and march toward the company in the front, and the three approach them at forty arm lengths with equal intervals between one another, and two remain behind distant another forty arm lengths. This formation can be organized quickly, and comes to be almost the same as the first disposition of the Army which we described before: and if it becomes more straitened in the front, it becomes larger in the flanks, which does not weaken it. But as the five companies in the back have their pikemen in the rear for the reasons mentioned above, it is necessary to have them come from the forward part, if you want them to get behind the front of the Army; and, therefore, one must either make them turn company by company, as a solid body, or make them enter quickly between the ranks of the shield-bearers (swordsmen), and bring them forward; which method is more swift and less disorderly than to make them turn. And thus you ought to do with all those who are in the rear in every kind of assault, as I will show you. If it should happen that the enemy comes from the rear, the first thing that ought to be done is to have everyone turn to face the enemy, so that at once the front of the army becomes the rear, and the rear the front. Then all those methods of organizing the front should be followed, which I mentioned above. If the enemy attacks on the right flank, the entire army ought to be made to face in that direction, and then those things ought to be done to strengthen that (new) front which were mentioned above, so that the cavalry, the Veliti, and the artillery are in the position assigned in this front. There is only this difference, that in the changing of fronts, of those who move about, some have to go further, and some less. It is indeed true that when a front is made of the right flank, the Veliti would have to enter the intervals (gaps) that exist between the wings of the Army, and the cavalry would be those nearer to the left flank, in the position of those who would have to enter into the two bands of extraordinary pikemen placed in the center. But before they enter, the wagons and unarmed men stationed at the openings should clear the plaza and retire behind the left flank, which then becomes the rear of the army. And the other Veliti who should be placed in the rear according to the original arrangement, in this case should not be changed, as that place should not remain open, which, from being the rear, would become a flank. All the other things ought to be done as was said concerning the first front.

What has been said concerning making a front from the right flank, is intended also in making one from the left flank, since the same arrangements ought to be observed. If the enemy should happen to be large and organized to assault you on two sides, the two sides on which he assaults you ought to be strengthened from the two that are not assaulted, doubling the ranks in each one, and distributing the artillery, Veliti, and cavalry among each side. If he comes from three or four sides, it needs must be either you or he lacks prudence, for if you were wise, you would never put yourself on the side where the enemy could assault you from three or four sides with large and organized forces, and if he wanted to attach you in safety he must be so large and assault you on each side with a force almost as large as you have in your entire Army. And if you are so little prudent that you put yourself in the midst of the territory and forces of an enemy, who has three times the organized forces that you have, you cannot complain if evil happens to you, except of yourself. If it happens, not by your fault, but by some misadventure, the injury will be without shame, and it will happen to you as it did to the Scipios in Spain, and the Hasdrubal in Italy. But if the enemy has a much larger force than you, and in order to disorganize you wants to assault you on several sides, it will be his foolishness and his gamble; for to do this, he must go (spread) himself thin, that you can always attack on one side and resist on another, and in a brief time ruin him. This method of organizing an Army which is not seen, but who is feared, is necessary, and it is a most useful thing to accustom your soldiers to assemble, and march in such order, and in marching arrange themselves to fight according to the first front (planned), and then return to marching formation, from that make a front from the rear, and then from the flank, and from that return to the original formation. These exercises and accustomization are necessary matters if you want a disciplined and trained Army. Captains and Princes have to work hard at these things: nor is military discipline anything else, than to know how to command and how to execute these things, nor is a disciplined Army anything else, than an army which is well trained in these arrangements; nor would it be possible for anyone in these times who should well employ such discipline ever to be routed. And if this square formation which I have described is somewhat difficult, such difficulty is necessary, if you take it up as exercise; since knowing how to organize and maintain oneself well in this, one would afterwards know how to manage more easily those which not be as difficult.

ZANOBI: I believe as you say, that these arrangements are very necessary, and by myself, I would not know what to add or leave out. It is true that I desire to know two things from you: the one, when you want to make a front from the rear or from a flank, and you want them to turn, whether the command is given by voice or by sound (bugle call): the other, whether those you sent ahead to clear the roads in order to make a path for the Army, ought to be soldiers of your companies, or other lowly people assigned to such practices.

FABRIZIO: Your first question is very important, for often the commands of the Captain are not very well understood or poorly interpreted, have disorganized their Army; hence the voices with which they command in (times of) danger, ought to be loud and clear. And if you command with sounds (bugle calls), it ought to be done so that they are so different from each other that one cannot be mistaken for another; and if you command by voice, you ought to be alert to avoid general words, and use particular ones, and of the particular ones avoid those which might be able to be interpreted in an incorrect manner. Many times saying "go back, go back", has caused an Army to be ruined: therefore this expression ought to be avoided, and in its place use "Retreat". If you want them to turn so as to change the front, either from the rear or from the flank, never use "Turn around", but say, "To the left", "To the right", "To the rear", "To the front". So too, all the other words have to be simple and clear, as "Hurry", "Hold still", "Forward", "Return". And all those things which can be done by words are done; the others are done by sounds (calls). As to the (road) clearers, which is your second question, I would have this job done by my own soldiers, as much because the ancient military did so, as also because there would be fewer unarmed men and less impediments in the army: and I would draw the number needed from every company, and I would have them take up the tools suitable for clearing, and leave their arms in those ranks that are closest to them, which would carry them so that if the enemy should come, they would have nothing to do but take them up again and return to their ranks.

ZANOBI: Who would carry the clearing equipment?

FABRIZIO: The wagons assigned to carry such equipment.

ZANOBI: I'm afraid you have never led these soldiers of ours to dig.

FABRIZIO: Everything will be discussed in its place. For now I want to leave these parts alone, and discuss the manner of living of the Army, for it appears to me that having worked them so hard, it is time to refresh and restore it with food. You have to understand that a Prince ought to organize his army as expeditiously as possible, and take away from it all those things that add burdens to it and make the enterprise difficult. Among those that cause more difficulty, are to have to keep the army provided with wine and baked bread. The ancients did not think of wine, for lacking it, they drank water tinted with a little vinegar, and not wine. They did not cook bread in ovens, as is customary throughout the cities; but they provided flour, and every soldier satisfied himself of that in his own way, having lard and grease for condiment, which gave flavor to the bread they made, and which kept them strong. So that the provisions of living (eating) for the army were Flour, Vinegar, Lard (Bacon) and Grease (Lard), and Barley for the horses. Ordinarily, they had herds of large and small beasts that followed the Army, which (as they did not need to be carried) did not impede them much. This arrangement permitted an ancient Army to march, sometimes for many days, through solitary and difficult places without suffering hardship of (lack of) provisions, for it lived from things which could be drawn behind. The contrary happens in modern Armies, which, as they do not want to lack wine and eat baked bread in the manner that those at home do, and of which they cannot make provision for long, often are hungry; or even if they are provided, it is done with hardship and at very great expense. I would therefore return my Army to this form of living, and I would not have them eat other bread than that which they should cook for themselves. As to wine, I would not prohibit its drinking, or that it should come into the army, but I would not use either industry or any hard work to obtain it, and as to other provisions, I would govern myself entirely as the ancients. If you would consider this matter well, you will see how much difficulty is removed, and how many troubles and hardships an army and a Captain avoid, and what great advantage it will give any enterprise which you may want to undertake.

ZANOBI: We have overcome the enemy in the field, and then marched on his country: reason wants that there be no booty, ransoming of towns, prisoners taken. Yet I would like to know how the ancients governed themselves in these matters.

FABRIZIO: Here, I will satisfy you. I believe you have considered (since I have at another time discussed this with some of you) that modem wars impoverish as much those Lords who win, as those who lose; for if one loses the State, the other loses his money and (movable) possessions. Which anciently did not happen, as the winner of a war (then) was enriched. This arises from not keeping track in these times of the booty (acquired), as was done anciently, but everything is left to the direction of the soldiers. This method makes for two very great disorders: the one, that of which I have spoken: the other, that a soldier becomes more desirous of booty and less an observer of orders: and it has often been said that the cupidity for booty has made him lose who had been victorious. The Romans, however, who were Princes in this matter, provided for both these inconveniences, ordering that all the booty belong to the public, and that hence the public should dispense it as it pleased. And so they had Quaestors in the Army, who were, as we would say, chamberlains, to whom all the ransoms and booty was given to hold: from which the Consul served himself to give the soldiers their regular pay, to help the wounded and infirm, and to provide for the other needs of the army. The Consul could indeed, and often did concede a booty to the soldiers, but this concession did not cause disorders; for when the (enemy) army was routed, all the booty was placed in the middle and was distributed to each person, according to the merits of each. This method made for the soldiers attending to winning and not robbing, and the Roman legions defeating the enemy but not pursuing him: for they never departed from their orders: only the cavalry and lightly armed men pursued him, unless there were other soldiers than legionnaires, which, if the booty would have been kept by whoever acquired it, it was neither possible nor reasonable to (expect to) hold the Legion firm, and would bring on many dangers. From this it resulted, therefore that the public was enriched, and every Consul brought, with his triumphs, much treasure into the Treasury, which (consisted) entirely of ransoms and booty. Another thing well considered by the ancients, was the pay they gave to each soldier: they wanted a third part to be placed next to him who carried the flag of the company, who never was given any except that furnished by the war. They did this for two reasons: The first so that the soldier would make capital (save) of his pay: for the greater part of them being young and irresponsible, the more they had, the more they spent without need to. The other part because, knowing that their movable possessions were next to the flag, they would be forced to have greater care, and defend it with greater obstinacy: and thus this method made them savers, and strong. All of these things are necessary to observe if you want to bring the military up to your standards.

ZANOBI: I believe it is not possible for an army while marching from place to place not to encounter dangerous incidents, (and) where the industry of the Captain and the virtue of the soldier is needed if they are to be avoided; therefore, if you should have something that occurs to you, I would take care to listen.

FABRIZIO: I will willingly content you, especially as it is necessary, if I want to give you complete knowledge of the practice. The Captains, while they march with the Army, ought, above everything else, to guard against ambushes, which may happen in two ways: either you enter into them while marching, or the enemy cunningly draws you into them without your being aware of it. In the first case, if you want to avoid them, it is necessary to send ahead double the guard, who reconnoiter the country. And the more the country is suitable for ambush, as are wooded and mountainous countries, the more diligence ought to be used, for the enemy always place themselves either in woods or behind a hill. And, just as by not foreseeing an ambush you will be ruined, so by foreseeing it you will not be harmed. Birds or dust have often discovered the enemy, for where the enemy comes to meet you, he will always raise a great dust which will point out his coming to you. Thus often a Captain when he sees in a place whence he ought to pass, pigeons taking off and other birds flying about freely, circling and not setting, has recognized this to be the place of any enemy ambush, and knowing this has sent his forces forward, saving himself and injuring the enemy. As to the second case, being drawn into it (which our men call being drawn into a trap) you ought to look out not to believe readily those things that appear to be less reasonable than they should be: as would be (the case) if an enemy places some booty before you, you would believe that it to be (an act of) love, but would conceal deceit inside it. If many enemies are driven out by few of your man: if only a few of the enemy assault you: if the enemy takes to sudden and unreasonable flight: in such cases, you ought always to be afraid of deceit; and you should never believe that the enemy does not know his business, rather, if you want to deceive yourself less and bring on less danger, the more he appears weak, the more enemy appears more cautious, so much the more ought you to esteem (be wary) of him. And in this you have to use two different means, since you have to fear him with your thoughts and arrangements, but by words and other external demonstrations show him how much you disparage him; for this latter method causes your soldiers to have more hope in obtaining the victory, the former makes you more cautious and less apt to be deceived. And you have to understand that when you march through enemy country, you face more and greater dangers than in undertaking an engagement. And therefore, when marching, a Captain ought to double his diligence, and the first thing he ought to do, is to have all the country through which he marches described and depicted, so that he will know the places, the numbers, the distances, the roads, the mountains, the rivers, the marshes, and all their characteristics. And in getting to know this, in diverse ways one must have around him different people who know the places, and question them with diligence, and contrast their information, and make notes according as it checks out. He ought to send cavalry ahead, and with them prudent Heads, not so much to discover the enemy as to reconnoiter the country, to see whether it checks with the places and with the information received from them. He ought also to send out guides, guarded (kept loyal) by hopes of reward and fear of punishment. And above all, he ought to see to it that the Army does not know to which sides he guides them, since there is nothing more useful in war, than to keep silent (about) the things that have to be done. And so that a sudden assault does not disturb your soldiers, you ought to advise them to be prepared with their arms, since things that are foreseen cause less harm. Many have (in order to avoid the confusion of the march) placed the wagons and the unarmed men under the banners, and commanded them to follow them, so that having to stop or retire during the march, they are able to do so more easily: which I approve very much as something useful. He ought also to have an awareness during the march, that one part of the Army does not detach itself from another, or that one (part) going faster and the other more slowly, the Army does not become compacted (jumbled), which things cause disorganization. It is necessary, therefore, to place the Heads along the sides, who should maintain the steps uniform, restraining those which are too fast, and hastening the slow; which step cannot be better regulated than by sound (music). The roads ought to be widened, so that at least one company can always move in order. The customs and characteristics of the enemy ought to be considered, and if he wants to assault you in the morning, noon, or night, and if he is more powerful in infantry or cavalry, from what you have learned, you may organize and prepare yourself. But let us come to some incident in particular. It sometimes happens that as you are taking yourself away from in front of the enemy because you judge yourself to be inferior (to him), and therefore do not want to come to an engagement with him, he comes upon your rear as you arrive at the banks of a river, which causes you to lose times in its crossing, so that the enemy is about to join up and combat with you. There have been some who have found themselves in such a peril, their army girded on the rear side by a ditch, and filling it with tow, have set it afire, then have passed on with the army without being able to be impeded by the enemy, he being stopped by that fire which was in between.

ZANOBI: And it is hard for me to believe that this fire can check him, especially as I remember to have heard that Hanno, the Carthaginian, when he was besieged by the enemy, girded himself on that side from which he wanted to make an eruption with wood, and set fire to it. Whence the enemy not being intent to guard that side, had his army pass over the flames, having each (soldier) protect his face from the fire and smoke with his shield.

FABRIZIO: You say well; but consider what I have said and what Hanno did: for I said that he dug a ditch and filled it with tow, so that whoever wanted to pass had to contend with the ditch and the fire. Hanno made the fire without a ditch, and as he wanted to pass through it did not make it very large (strong), since it would have impeded him even without the ditch. Do you not know that Nabidus, the Spartan, when he was besieged in Sparta by the Romans, set fire to part of his own town in order to stop the passage of the Romans, who had already entered inside? And by those flames not only stopped their passage, but pushed them out. But let us return to our subject. Quintus Luttatius, the Roman, having the Cimbri at his rear, and arriving at a river, so that the enemy should give him time to cross, made as if to give him time to combat him, and therefore feigned to make camp there, and had ditches dug, and some pavilions raised, and sent some horses to the camps to be shod: so that the Cimbri believing he was encamping, they also encamped, and divided themselves into several parts to provide themselves with food: of which Luttatius becoming aware, he crossed the river without being able to be impeded by them. Some, in order to cross a river, not having a bridge, have diverted it, and having drawn a part of it in their rear, the other then became so low that they crossed it easily. If the rivers are rapid, (and) desiring that the infantry should cross more safely, the more capable horses are placed on the side above which holds back the water, and another part below which succor the infantry if any, in crossing, should be overcome by the river; rivers that are not forded are crossed by bridges, boats, and rafts: and it is therefore well to have skills in your Armies capable of doing all these things. It sometimes happens that in crossing a river, the enemy on the opposite bank impedes you. If you want to overcome this difficulty there is no better example known than that of Caesar, who, having his army on the bank of a river in Gaul, and his crossing being impeded by Vercingetorix, the Gaul, who had his forces on the other side of the river, marched for several days along the river, and the enemy did the same. And Caesar having made an encampment in a woody place (and) suitable to conceal his forces, withdrew three cohorts from every Legion, and had them stop in that place, commanding then that as soon as he should depart, they should throw a bridge across and fortify it, and he with the rest of his forces continued the march: Whence Vercingetorix seeing the number of Legions, and believing that no part had remained behind, also continued the march: but Caesar, as soon as he thought the bridge had been completed, turned back, and finding everything in order, crossed the river without difficulty.

ZANOBI: Do you have any rule for recognizing the fords?

FABRIZIO: Yes, we have. The river, in that part between the stagnant water and the current, always looks like a line to whoever looks at it, is shallower, and is a place more suitable for fording than elsewhere, for the river always places more material, and in a pack, which it draws (with it) from the bottom. Which thing, as it has been experienced many times, is very true.

ZANOBI: If it happens that the river has washed away the bottom of the ford, so that horses sink, what remedy do you have?

FABRIZIO: Make grids of wood, and place them on the bottom of the river, and cross over those. But let us pursue our discussion. If it happens that a Captain with his army is led (caught) between two mountains, and has but two ways of saving himself, either that in front, or the one in the rear, and both being occupied by the enemy, has, as a remedy, to do what some have done in the past, which is to dig a large ditch, difficult to cross, and show the enemy that by it you want to be able to hold him with all his forces, without having to fear those forces in the rear for which the road in front remains open. The enemy believing this, fortifies himself on the side open, and abandons the (side) closed, and he then throws a wooden bridge, planned for such a result, over the ditch, and without any impediment, passes on that side and freed himself from the hands of the enemy. Lucius Minutius, the Roman Consul, was in Liguria with the Armies, and had been enclosed between certain mountains by the enemy, from which he could not go out. He therefore sent some soldiers of Numidia, whom he had in his army, who were badly armed, and mounted on small and scrawny horses, toward those places which were guarded by the enemy, and the first sight of whom caused the enemy to assemble to defend the pass: but then when they saw those forces poorly organized, and also poorly mounted, they esteemed them little and loosened their guard. As soon as the Numidians saw this, giving spurs to their horses and attacking them, they passed by without the enemy being able to take any remedy; and having passed, they wasted and plundered the country, constraining the enemy to leave the pass free to the army of Lucius. Some Captain, who has found himself assaulted by a great multitude of the enemy, has tightened his ranks, and given the enemy the faculty of completely surrounding him, and then has applied force to that part which he has recognized as being weaker, and has made a path in that way, and saved himself. Marcantonio, while retiring before the army of the Parthians, became aware that every day at daybreak as he moved, the enemy assaulted him, and infested him throughout the march: so that he took the course of not departing before midday. So that the Parthians, believing he should not want to decamp that day returned to their quarters, and Marcantonio was able then for the remainder of the day to march without being molested. This same man, to escape the darts of the Parthians, commanded that, when the Parthians came toward them, they should kneel, and the second rank of the company should place their shields on the heads of (those in the) first, the third on (those of the) second, the fourth on the third, and so on successively: so that the entire Army came to be as under a roof, and protected from the darts of the enemy. This is as much as occurs to me to tell you of what can happen to an army when marching: therefore, if nothing else occurs to you, I will pass on to another part.

SIXTH BOOK

ZANOBI: I believe it is well, since the discussion ought to be changed, that Battista take up his office, and I resign mine; and in this case we would come to imitate the good Captains, according as I have already learned here from the Lord, who place the best soldiers in the front and in the rear of the Army, as it appears necessary to them to have those who bravely enkindle the battle, and those in the rear who bravely sustain it. Cosimo, therefore, begun this discussion prudently, and Battista will prudently finish it. Luigi and I have come in between these. And as each one of us has taken up his part willingly, so too I believe Battista is about to close it.

BATTISTA: I have allowed myself to be governed up to now, so too I will allow myself (to be governed) in the future. Be content, therefore, (my) Lords, to continue your discussions, and if we interrupt you with these questions (practices), you have to excuse us.

FABRIZIO: You do me, as I have already told you, a very great favor, since these interruptions of yours do not take away my imagination, rather they refresh it. But if we want to pursue our subject I say, that it is now time that we quarter this Army of ours, since you know that everything desires repose, and safety; since to repose oneself, and not to repose safely, is not complete (perfect) repose. I am afraid, indeed, that you should not desire that I should first quarter them, then had them march, and lastly to fight, and we have done the contrary. Necessity has led us to this, for in wanting to show when marching, how an army turns from a marching formation to that of battle, it was necessary first to show how they were organized for battle. But returning to our subject I say, that if you want the encampment to be safe, it must be Strong and Organized. The industry of the Captain makes it organized: Arts or the site make it Strong. The Greeks sought strong locations, and never took positions where there was neither grottoes (caves), or banks of rivers, or a multitude of trees or other natural cover which should protect them. But the Romans did not encamp safely so much from the location as by arts, nor ever made an encampment in places where they should not have been able to spread out all their forces, according to their discipline. From this resulted that the Romans were always able to have one form of encampment, for they wanted the site to obey them, and not they the site. The Greeks were not able to observe this, for as they obeyed the site, and the sites changing the formation, it behooved them that they too should change the mode of encamping and the form of their encampment. The Romans, therefore, where the site lacked strength, supplied it with (their) art and industry. And since in this narration of mine, I have wanted that the Romans be imitated, I will not depart from their mode of encamping, not, however, observing all their arrangements: but taking (only) that part which at the present time seems appropriate to me. I have often told you that the Romans had two Legions of Roman men in their consular armies, which comprised some eleven thousand infantry of forces sent by friends (allies) to aid them; but they never had more foreign soldiers in their armies than Romans, except for cavalry, which they did not care if they exceeded the number in their Legions; and that in every action of theirs, they place the Legions in the center, and the Auxiliaries on the sides. Which method they observed even when they encamped, as you yourselves have been able to read in those who write of their affairs; and therefore I am not about to narrate in detail how they encamped, but will tell you only how I would at present arrange to encamp my army, and then you will know what part of the Roman methods I have treated. You know that at the encounter of two Roman Legions I have taken two Battalions of six thousand infantry and three hundred cavalry effective for each Battalion, and I have divided them by companies, by arms, and names. You know that in organizing the army for marching and fighting, I have not made mention of other forces, but have only shown that in doubling the forces, nothing else had to be done but to double the orders (arrangements).

Since at present I want to show you the manner of encamping, it appears proper to me not to stay only with two Battalions, but to assemble a fair army, and composed like the Roman of two Battalions and as many auxiliary forces. I know that the form of an encampment is more perfect, when a complete army is quartered: which matter did not appear necessary to me in the previous demonstration. If I want, therefore, to quarter a fair (sized) army of twenty four thousand infantry and two thousand cavalry effectives, being divided into four companies, two of your own forces and two of foreigners, I would employ this method. When I had found the site where I should want to encamp, I would raise the Captain's flag, and around it I would draw a square which would have each face distant from it fifty arm lengths, of which each should look out on one of the four regions of the sky, that is, east, west, south and north, in which space I would put the quarters of the Captain. And as I believe it prudent, and because thus the Romans did in good part, I would divide the armed men from the unarmed, and separate the men who carry burdens from the unburdened ones. I would quarter all or a greater part of the armed men on the east side, and the unarmed and burdened ones on the west side, making the east the front and the west the rear of the encampment, and the south and north would be the flanks. And to distinguish the quarters of the armed men, I would employ this method. I would run a line from the Captain's flag, and would lead it easterly for a distance of six hundred eighty (680) arm lengths. I would also run two other lines which I would place in the middle of it, and be of the same length as the former, but distant from each of them by fifteen arm lengths, at the extremity of which, I would want the east gate to be (placed): and the space which exists between the two extreme (end) lines, I would make a road that would go from the gate to the quarters of the Captain, which would be thirty arm lengths in width and six hundred thirty (630) long (since the Captain's quarters would occupy fifty arm lengths) and call this the Captain's Way. I would then make another road from the south gate up to the north gate, and cross by the head of the Captain's Way, and along the east side of the Captain's quarters which would be one thousand two hundred fifty (1250) arm lengths long (since it would occupy the entire width of the encampment) and also be thirty arm lengths wide and be called the Cross Way. The quarters of the Captain and these two roads having been designed, therefore the quarters of the two battalions of your own men should begin to be designed; and I would quarter one on the right hand (side) of the Captain's Way, and one on the left. And hence beyond the space which is occupied by the width of the Cross Way, I would place thirty two quarters on the left side of the Captain's Way, and thirty two on the right side, leaving a space of thirty arm lengths between the sixteenth and seventeenth quarters which should serve as a transverse road which should cross through all of the quarters of the battalions, as will be seen in their partitioning. Of these two arrangements of quarters, in the first tents that would be adjacent to the Cross Way, I would quarter the heads of men-at-arms, and since each company has one hundred and fifty men-at-arms, there would be assigned ten men-at-arms to each of the quarters. The area (space) of the quarters of the Heads should be forty arm lengths wide and ten arm lengths long. And it is to be noted that whenever I say width, I mean from south to north, and when I say length, that from west to east. Those of the men-at-arms should be fifteen arm lengths long and thirty wide. In the next fifteen quarters which in all cases are next (which should have their beginning across the transverse road, and which would have the same space as those of the men-at-arms) I would quarter the light cavalry, which, since they are one hundred fifty, ten cavalrymen would be assigned to each quarter, and in the sixteenth which would be left, I would quarter their Head, giving him the same space which is given to the Head of men-at-arms. And thus the quarters of the cavalry of the two battalions would come to place the Captain's Way in the center and give a rule for the quarters of the infantry, as I will narrate. You have noted that I have quartered the three hundred cavalry of each battalion with their heads in thirty two quarters situated on the Captain's Way, and beginning with the Cross Way, and that from the sixteenth to the seventeenth there is a space of thirty arm lengths to make a transverse road. If I want, therefore, to quarter the twenty companies which constitute the two regular Battalions, I would place the quarters of every two companies behind the quarters of the cavalry, each of which should be fifteen arm lengths long and thirty wide, as those of the cavalry, and should be joined on the rear where they touch one another. And in every first quarter of each band that fronts on the Cross Way, I would quarter the Constable of one company, which would come to correspond with the quartering of the Head of the men-at-arms: and their quarters alone would have a space twenty arm lengths in width and ten in length. And in the other fifteen quarters in each group which follow after this up the Transverse Way, I would quarter a company of infantry on each side, which, as they are four hundred fifty, thirty would be assigned to each quarter. I would place the other fifteen quarters contiguous in each group to those of the cavalry with the same space, in which I would quarter a company of infantry from each group. In the last quarter of each group I would place the Constable of the company, who would come to be adjacent to the Head of the light cavalry, with a space of ten arm lengths long and twenty wide. And thus these first two rows of quarters would be half of cavalry and half of infantry.

And as I want (as I told you in its place) these cavalry to be all effective, and hence without retainers who help taking care of the horses or other necessary things, I would want these infantry quartered behind the cavalry should be obligated to help the owners (of the horses) in providing and taking care of them, and because of this should be exempt from other activities of the camp, which was the manner observed by the Romans. I would also leave behind these quarters on all sides a space of thirty arm lengths to make a road, and I would call one of the First Road on the right hand (side) and the other the First Road on the left, and in each area I would place another row of thirty two double quarters which should face one another on the rear, with the same spaces as those which I have mentioned, and also divided at the sixteenth in the same manner to create a Transverse Road, in which I would quarter in each area four companies of infantry with the Constables in the front at the head and foot (of each row). I would also leave on each side another space of thirty arm lengths to create a road which should be called the Second Road on the right hand (side) and on the other side the Second Road to the left; I would place another row in each area of thirty two double quarters, with the same distances and divisions, in which I would quarter on every side four companies (of infantry) with their Constables. And thus there would come to be quartered in three rows of quarters per area the cavalry and the companies (of infantry) of the two regular battalions, in the center of which I would place the Captain's Way. The two battalions of auxiliaries (since I had them composed of the same men) I would quarter on each side of these two regular battalions with the same arrangement of double quarters, placing first a row of quarters in which I should quarter half with cavalry and half infantry, distant thirty arm lengths from each other, to create two roads which I should call, one the Third Road on the right hand (side), the other the Third on the left hand. And then I would place on each side two other rows of quarters, separate but arranged in the same way, which are those of the regular battalions, which would create two other roads, and all of these would be called by the number and the band (side) where they should be situated. So that all this part of the Army would come to be quartered in twelve rows of double quarters, and on thirteen roads, counting the Captain's Way and the Cross Way.

I would want a space of one hundred arm lengths all around left between the quarters and the ditch (moat). And if you count all those spaces, you will see, that from the middle of the quarters of the Captain to the east gate, there are seven hundred arm lengths. There remains to us now two spaces, of which one is from the quarters of the Captain to the south gate, the other from there to the north gate, each of which comes to be, measuring from the center point, six hundred thirty five (635) arm lengths. I then subtract from each of these spaces fifty arm lengths which the quarters of the Captain occupies, and forty five arm lengths of plaza which I want to give to each side, and thirty arm lengths of road, which divides each of the mentioned spaces in the middle, and a hundred arm lengths which are left on each side between the quarters and the ditch, and there remains in each area a space left for quarters four hundred arm lengths wide and a hundred long, measuring the length to include the space occupied by the Captain's quarters. Dividing the said length in the middle, therefore, there would be on each side of the Captain forty quarters fifty arm lengths long and twenty wide, which would total eighty quarters, in which would be quartered the general Heads of the battalions, the

Chamberlains, the Masters of the camps, and all those who should have an office (duty) in the army, leaving some vacant for some foreigners who might arrive, and for those who should fight through the courtesy of the Captain. On the rear side of the Captain's quarters, I would create a road thirty arm lengths wide from north to south, and call it the Front Road, which would come to be located along the eighty quarters mentioned, since this road and the Cross Way would have between them the Captain's quarters and the eighty quarters on their flanks. From this Front road and opposite to the Captain's quarters, I would create another road which should go from there to the west gate, also thirty arm lengths wide, and corresponding in location and length to the Captain's Way, and I should call it the Way of the Plaza. These two roads being located, I would arrange the plaza where the market should be made, which I would place at the head of the Way of the Plaza, opposite to the Captain's quarters, and next to the Front Road, and would want it to be square, and would allow it a hundred twenty one arm lengths per side. And from the right hand and left hand of the said plaza, I would make two rows of quarters, and each row have eight double quarters, which would take up twelve arm lengths in length and thirty in width so that they should be on each side of the plaza, in which there would be sixteen quarters, and total thirty two all together, in which I would quarter that cavalry left over from the auxiliary battalions, and if this should not be enough, I would assign them some of the quarters about the Captain, and especially those which face the ditch.

It remains for us now to quarter the extraordinary pikemen and Veliti, which every battalion has; which you know, according to our arrangement, in addition to the ten companies (of infantry), each has a thousand extraordinary pikemen, and five hundred Veliti; so that each of the two regular battalions have two thousand extraordinary pikemen, and a thousand extraordinary pikemen, and five hundred Veliti; so that each of the two regular battalions have two thousand extraordinary pikemen, and a thousand extraordinary Veliti, and the auxiliary as many as they; so that one also comes to have to quarter six thousand infantry, all of whom I would quarter on the west side along the ditches. From the point, therefore, of the Front Road, and northward, leaving the space of a hundred arm lengths from those (quarters) to the ditch, I would place a row of five double quarters which would be seventy five arm lengths long and sixty in width: so that with the width divided, each quarters would be allowed fifteen arm lengths for length and thirty for width. And as there would be ten quarters, I would quarter three hundred infantry, assigning thirty infantry to each quarter. Leaving then a space of thirty one arm lengths, I would place another row of five double quarters in a similar manner and with similar spaces, and then another, so that there would be five rows of five double quarters, which would come to be fifty quarters placed in a straight line on the north side, each distant one hundred arm lengths from the ditches, which would quarter one thousand five hundred infantry. Turning then on the left hand side toward the west gate, I would want in all that tract between them and the said gate, five other rows of double quarters, in a similar manner and with the same spaces, (it is true that from one row to the other there would not be more than fifteen arm lengths of space) in which there would also be quartered a thousand five hundred infantry: and thus from the north gate to that on the west, following the ditches, in a hundred quarters, divided into ten rows of five double quarters per row, the extraordinary pikemen and Veliti of the regular battalions would be quartered. And so, too, from the west gate to that on the south, following the ditches, in exactly the same manner, in another ten rows of ten quarters per row, the extraordinary pikemen and Veliti of the auxiliary battalions would be quartered. Their Heads, or rather their Constables, could take those quarters on the side toward the ditches which appeared most convenient for themselves.

I would dispose the artillery all along the embankments of the ditches: and in all the other space remaining toward the west, I would quarter all the unarmed men and all the baggage (impedimenta) of the Camp. And it has to be understood that under this name of impedimenta (as you know) the ancients intended all those carriages (wagons) and all those things which are necessary to an Army, except the soldiers; as are carpenters (wood workers), smiths, blacksmiths, shoe makers, engineers, and bombardiers, and others which should be placed among the number of the armed: herdsmen with their herds of castrated sheep and oxen, which are used for feeding the Army: and in addition, masters of every art (trade), together with public wagons for the public provisions of food and arms. And I would not particularly distinguish their quarters: I would only designate the roads that should not be occupied by them. Then the other spaces remaining between the roads, which would be four, I would assign in general to all the impedimenta mentioned, that is, one to the herdsmen, another to Artificers and workmen, another to the public wagons for provisions, and the fourth to the armorers. The roads which I would want left unoccupied would be the Way of the Plaza, the Front Road, and in addition, a road that should be called the Center Road, which should take off at the north and proceed toward the south, and pass through the center of the Way of the Plaza, which, on the west side, should have the same effect as has the Transverse Road on the east side. And in addition to this, a road that should go around the rear along the quarters of the extraordinary pikemen and Veliti. And all these roads should be thirty arm lengths wide. And I would dispose the artillery along the ditches on the rear of the camp.

BATTISTA: I confess I do not understand, and I also do not believe that to say so makes me ashamed, as this is not my profession. Nonetheless, I like this organization very much: I would want only that you should resolve these doubts for me. The one: why you make the roads and the spaces around the quarters so wide. The other, which annoys me more, is this, how are these spaces that you designate for quarters to be used.

FABRIZIO: You know that I made all the roads thirty arm lengths wide, so that a company of infantry is able to go through them in order (formation): which, if you remember well, I told you that each of these (formations) were twenty-five to thirty arm lengths wide. The space between the ditch and the quarters, which is a hundred arm lengths wide, is necessary, since the companies and the artillery can be handled here, through which booty is taken, (and) when space is needed into which to retire, new ditches and embankments are made. The quarters very distant from the ditches are better, for they are more distant from the fires and other things that might be able to draw the enemy to attack them. As to the second question, my intention is not that every space designated by me is covered by only one pavilion, but is to be used as an all-round convenience for those who are quartered, with several or few tents, so long as they do not go outside its limits. And in designing these quarters, the men must be most experienced and excellent architects, who, as soon as the Captain has selected the site, know how to give it form, and divide it, and distinguishing the roads, dividing the quarters with cords and hatchets in such a practical manner, that they might be divided and arranged quickly. And if confusion is not to arise, the camp must always face the same way, so that everyone will know on which Road and in which space he has to find his quarters. And this ought to be observed at all times, in every place, and in a manner that it appears to be a movable City, which, wherever it goes, brings with it the same roads, the same houses, and the same appearance: which cannot be observed by those men who, seeking strong locations, have to change the form according to the variations in the sites. But the Romans made the places strong with ditches, ramparts, and embankments, for they placed a space around the camp, and in front of it they dug a ditch and ordinarily six arm lengths wide and three deep, which spaces they increased according to the (length of) time they resided in the one place, and according as they feared the enemy. For myself, I would not at present erect a stockade (rampart), unless I should want to winter in a place. I would, however, dig the ditch and embankment, not less than that mentioned, but greater according to the necessity. With respect to the artillery, on every side of the encampment, I would have a half circle ditch, from which the artillery should be able to batter on the flanks whoever should come to attack the moats (ditches). The soldiers ought also to be trained in this practice of knowing how to arrange an encampment, and work with them so they may aid him in designing it, and the soldiers quick in knowing their places. And none of these is difficult, as will be told in its proper place. For now I want to pass on to the protection of the camp, which, without the distribution (assignment) of guards, all the other efforts would be useless.

BATTISTA: Before you pass on to the guards, I would want you to tell me, what methods are employed when others want to place the camp near the enemy, for I do not know whether there is time to be able to organize it without danger.

FABRIZIO: You have to know this, that no Captain encamps near the enemy, unless he is disposed to come to an engagement whenever the enemy wants; and if the others are so disposed, there is no danger except the ordinary, since two parts of the army are organized to make an engagement, while the other part makes the encampment. In cases like this, the Romans assigned this method of fortifying the quarters to the Triari, while the Principi and the Astati remained under arms. They did this, because the Triari, being the last to combat, were in time to leave the work if the enemy came, and take up their arms and take their places. If you want to imitate the Romans, you have to assign the making of the encampment to that company which you would want to put in the place of the Triari in the last part of the army.

But let us return to the discussion of the guards. I do not seem to find in connection with the ancients guarding the camp at night, that they had guards outside, distant from the ditches, as is the custom today, which they call the watch. I believe I should do this, when I think how the army could be easily deceived, because of the difficulty which exists in checking (reviewing) them, for they may be corrupted or attacked by the enemy, so that they judged it dangerous to trust them entirely or in part. And therefore all the power of their protection was within the ditches, which they dug with very great diligence and order, punishing capitally anyone who deviated from such an order. How this was arranged by them, I will not talk to you further in order not to tire you, since you are able to see it by yourselves, if you have not seen it up to now. I will say only briefly what would be done by me. I would regularly have a third of the army remain armed every night, and a fourth of them always on foot, who would be distributed throughout the embankments and all the places of the army, with double guards posted at each of its squares, where a part should remain, and a part continually go from one side of the encampment to the other. And this arrangement I describe, I would also observe by day if I had the enemy near. As to giving it a name, and renewing it every night, and doing the other things that are done in such guarding, since they are things (already) known, I will not talk further of them. I would only remind you of a most important matter, and by observing it do much good, by not observing it do much evil; which is, that great diligence be used as to who does not lodge within the camp at night, and who arrives there anew. And this is an easy matter, to review who is quartered there, with those arrangements we have designated, since every quarter having a predetermined number of men, it is an easy thing to see if there are any men missing or if any are left over; and when they are missing without permission, to punish them as fugitives, and if they are left over, to learn who they are, what they know, and what are their conditions. Such diligence results in the enemy not being able to have correspondence with your Heads, and not to have co-knowledge of your counsels. If this had not been observed with diligence by the Romans, Claudius Nero could not, when he had Hannibal near to him, have departed from the encampment he had in Lucania and go and return from the Marches, without Hannibal having been aware of it. But it is not enough to make these good arrangements, unless they are made to be observed by great security, for there is nothing that wants so much observance as any required in the army. Therefore, the laws for their enforcement should be harsh and hard, and the executor very hard. The Roman punished with the capital penalty whoever was missing from the guard, whoever abandoned the place given him in combat, whoever brought anything concealed from outside the encampment; if anyone should tell of having performed some great act in battle, and should not have done it; if anyone should have fought except at the command of the Captain, if anyone from fear had thrown aside his arms. And if it occurred that an entire Cohort or an entire Legion had made a similar error, in order that they not all be put to death, they put their names in a purse, and drew the tenth part, and those they put to death. Which penalty was so carried out, that if everyone did not hear of it, they at least feared it. And because where there are severe punishments, there also ought to be rewards, so that men should fear and hope at the same time, they proposed rewards for every great deed; such as to him who, during the fighting, saved the life of one of its citizens, to whoever first climbed the walls of enemy towns, to whoever first entered the encampment of the enemy, to whoever in battle wounded or killed an enemy, to whoever had thrown him from his horse. And thus any act of virtue was recognized and rewarded by the Consuls, and publicly praised by everyone: and those who received gifts for any of these things, in addition to the glory and fame they acquired among the soldiers, when they returned to their country, exhibited them with solemn pomp and with great demonstrations among their friends and relatives. It is not to marvel therefore, if that people acquired so much empire, when they had so great an observance of punishment and reward toward them, which operated either for their good or evil, should merit either praise or censure; it behooves us to observe the greater part of these things. And it does not appear proper for me to be silent on a method of punishment observed by them, which was, that as the miscreant was convicted before the Tribune or the Consul, he was struck lightly by him with a rod: after which striking of the criminal, he was allowed to flee, and all the soldiers allowed to kill him, so that immediately each of them threw stones or darts, or hit him with other arms, of a kind from which he went little alive, and rarely returned to camp; and to such that did return to camp, he was not allowed to return home except with so much inconvenience and ignominy, that it was much better for him to die. You see this method almost observed by the Swiss, who have the condemned publicly put to death by the other soldiers. Which is well considered and done for the best, for if it is desired that one be not a defender of a criminal, the better remedy that is found, is to make him the punisher of him (the criminal); for in some respects he favors him while from other desires he longs for his punishment, if he himself is the executioner, than if the execution is carried out by another. If you want, therefore, that one is not to be favored in his mistakes by a people, a good remedy is to see to it that the public judged him. In support of this, the example of Manlius Capitol that can be cited, who, when he was accused by the Senate, was defended so much by the public up to the point where it no longer became the judge: but having become arbiter of his cause, condemned him to death. It is, therefore, a method of punishing this, of doing away with tumults, and of having justice observed. And since in restraining armed men, the fear of laws, or of men, is not enough, the ancients added the authority of God: and, therefore, with very great ceremony, they made their soldiers swear to observe the military discipline, so that if they did the contrary, they not only had to fear the laws and men, but God; and they used every industry to fill them with Religion.

BATTISTA: Did the Romans permit women to be in their armies, or that they indulge in indolent games that are used to day?

FABRIZIO: They prohibited both of them, and this prohibition was not very difficult, because the exercises which they gave each day to the soldiers were so many, sometimes being occupied all together, sometimes individually, that no time was left to them to think either of Venery, or of games, or of other things which make soldiers seditious and useless.

BATTISTA: I like that. But tell me, when the army had to take off, what arrangements did they have?

FABRIZIO: The captain's trumpet was sounded three times: at the first sound the tents were taken down and piled into heaps, at the second they loaded the burdens, and at the third they moved in the manner mentioned above, with the impedimenta behind, the armed men on every side, placing the Legions in the center. And, therefore, you would have to have a battalion of auxiliaries move, and behind it its particular impedimenta, and with those the fourth part of the public impedimenta, which would be all those who should be quartered in one of those (sections of the camp) which we showed a short while back. And, therefore, it would be well to have each one of them assigned to a battalion, so that when the army moved, everyone would know where his place was in marching. And every battalion ought to proceed on its way in this fashion with its own impedimenta, and with a quarter of the public (impedimenta) at its rear, as we showed the Roman army marched.

BATTISTA: In placing the encampment, did they have other considerations than those you mentioned?

FABRIZIO: I tell you again, that in their encampments, the Romans wanted to be able to employ the usual form of their method, in the observance of which, they took no other consideration. But as to other considerations, they had two principal ones: the one, to locate themselves in a healthy place: to locate themselves where the enemy should be unable to besiege them, and cut off their supply of water and provisions. To avoid this weakness, therefore, they avoided marshy places, or exposure to noxious winds. They recognized these, not so much from the characteristics of the site, but from the looks of the inhabitants: and if they saw them with poor color, or short winded, or full of other infections, they did not encamp there. As to the other part of not being besieged, the nature of the place must be considered, where the friends are, and where the enemy, and from these make a conjecture whether or not you can be besieged. And, therefore, the Captain must be very expert concerning sites of the countries, and have around him many others who have the same expertness. They also avoided sickness and hunger so as not to disorganize the army; for if you want to keep it healthy, you must see to it that the soldiers sleep under tents, that they are quartered, where there are trees to create shade, where there is wood to cook the food, and not to march in the heat. You need, therefore, to consider the encampment the day before you arrive there, and in winter guard against marching in the snow and through ice without the convenience of making a fire, and not lack necessary clothing, and not to drink bad water. Those who get sick in the house have them taken care of by doctors; for a captain has no remedy when he has to fight both sickness and the enemy. But nothing is more useful in maintaining an army healthy than exercise: and therefore the ancients made them exercise every day. Whence it is seen how much exercise is of value, for in the quarters it keeps you healthy, and in battle it makes you victorious. As to hunger, not only is it necessary to see that the enemy does not impede your provisions, but to provide whence you are to obtain them, and to see that those you have are not lost. And, therefore, you must always have provisions (on hand) for the army for a month, and beyond that to tax the neighboring friends that they provide you daily, keep the provisions in a strong place, and, above all, dispense it with diligence, giving each one a reasonable measure each day, and so observe this part that they do not become disorganized; for every other thing in war can be overcome with time, this only with time overcomes you. Never make anyone your enemy, who, while seeking to overcome you with the sword (iron), can overcome you by hunger, because if such a victory is not as honorable, it is more secure and more certain. That army, therefore, cannot escape hunger which does not observe justice, and licentiously consume whatever it please, for one evil causes the provisions not to arrive, and the other that when they arrive, they are uselessly consumed: therefore the ancients arranged that what was given was eaten, and in the time they assigned, so that no soldier ate except when the Captain did. Which, as to being observed by the modern armies, everyone does (the contrary), and deservedly they cannot be called orderly and sober as the ancients, but licentious and drunkards.

BATTISTA: You have said in the beginning of arranging the encampment, that you did not want to stay only with two battalions, but took up four, to show how a fair (sized) army was quartered. Therefore I would want you to tell me two things: the one, if I have more or less men, how should I quarter them: the other, what number of soldiers would be enough to fight against any enemy?

FABRIZIO: To the first question, I reply, that if the army has four or six thousand soldiers more or less, rows of quarters are taken away or added as are needed, and in this way it is possible to accommodate more or fewer infinitely. Nonetheless, when the Romans joined together two consular armies, they made two encampments and had the parts of the disarmed men face each other. As to the second question, I reply, that the regular Roman army had about twenty four thousand soldiers: but when a great force pressed them, the most they assembled were fifty thousand. With this number they opposed two hundred thousand Gauls whom they assaulted after the first war which they had with the Carthaginians. With the same number, they opposed

Hannibal. And you have to note that the Romans and Greeks had made war with few (soldiers), strengthened by order and by art; the westerners and easterners had made it with a multitude: but one of these nations serves itself of natural fury, as are the westerners; the other of the great obedience which its men show to their King. But in Greece and Italy, as there is not this natural fury, nor the natural reverence toward their King, it has been necessary to turn to discipline; which is so powerful, that it made the few able to overcome the fury and natural obstinacy of the many. I tell you, therefore, if you want to imitate the Romans and Greeks, the number of fifty thousand soldiers ought not to be exceeded, rather they should actually be less; for the many cause confusion, and do not allow discipline to be observed nor the orders learned. And Pyrrhus used to say that with fifteen thousand men he would assail the world.

But let us pass on to another part. We have made our army win an engagement, and I showed the troubles that can occur in battle; we have made it march, and I have narrated with what impedimenta it can be surrounded while marching: and lastly we have quartered it: where not only a little repose from past hardship ought to be taken, but also to think about how the war ought to be concluded; for in the quarters, many things are discussed, especially if there remain enemies in the field, towns under suspicion, of which it is well to reassure oneself, and to capture those which are hostile. It is necessary, therefore, to come to these demonstrations, and to pass over this difficulty with that (same) glory with which we have fought up to the present. Coming down to particulars, therefore, that if it should happen to you that many men or many peoples should do something, which might be useful to you and very harmful to them, as would be the destruction of the walls of their City, or the sending of many of themselves into exile, it is necessary that you either deceive them in a way that everyone should believe he is affected, so that one not helping the other, all find themselves oppressed without a remedy, or rather, to command everyone what they ought to do on the same day, so that each one believing himself to be alone to whom the command is given, thinks of obeying it, and not of a remedy; and thus, without tumult, your command is executed by everyone. If you should have suspicion of the loyalty of any people, and should want to assure yourself and occupy them without notice, in order to disguise your design more easily, you cannot do better than to communicate to him some of your design, requesting his aid, and indicate to him you want to undertake another enterprise, and to have a mind alien to every thought of his: which will cause him not to think of his defense, as he does not believe you are thinking of attacking him, and he will give you the opportunity which will enable you to satisfy your desire easily. If you should have present in your army someone who keeps the enemy advised of your designs, you cannot do better if you want to avail yourself of his evil intentions, than to communicate to him those things you do not want to do, and keep silent those things you want to do, and tell him you are apprehensive of the things of which you are not apprehensive, and conceal those things of which you are apprehensive: which will cause the enemy to undertake some enterprise, in the belief that he knows your designs, in which you can deceive him and defeat him. If you should design (as did Claudius Nero) to decrease your army, sending aid to some friend, and they should not be aware of it, it is necessary that the encampment be not decreased, but to maintain entire all the signs and arrangements, making the same fires and posting the same guards as for the entire army. Likewise, if you should attach a new force to your army, and do not want the enemy to know you have enlarged it, it is necessary that the encampment be not increased, for it is always most useful to keep your designs secret. Whence Metellus, when he was with the armies in Spain, to one who asked him what he was going to do the next day, answered that if his shirt knew it, he would burn it. Marcus Crassus, to one who asked him when he was going to move his army, said: "Do you believe you are alone in not hearing the trumpets?" If you should desire to learn the secrets of your enemy and know his arrangement, some used to send ambassadors, and with them men expert in war disguised in the clothing of the family, who, taking the opportunity to observe the enemy army, and consideration of his strengths and weaknesses, have given them the occasion to defeat him. Some have sent a close friend of theirs into exile, and through him have learned the designs of their adversary. You may also learn similar secrets from the enemy if you should take prisoners for this purpose. Marius, in the war he waged against Cimbri, in order to learn the loyalty of those Gauls who lived in Lombardy and were leagued with the Roman people, sent them letters, open and sealed: and in the open ones he wrote them that they should not open the sealed ones except at such a time: and before that time, he called for them to be returned, and finding them opened, knew their loyalty was not complete. Some Captains, when they were assaulted have not wanted to go to meet the enemy, but have gone to assail his country, and constrain him to return to defend his home. This often has turned out well, because your soldiers begin to win and fill themselves with booty and confidence, while those of the enemy become dismayed, it appearing to them that from being winners, they have become losers. So that to whoever has made this diversion, it has turned out well. But this can only be done by that man who has his country stronger than that of the enemy, for if it were otherwise, he would go on to lose. It has often been a useful thing for a Captain who finds himself besieged in the quarters of the enemy, to set in motion proceedings for an accord, and to make a truce with him for several days; which only any enemy negligent in every way will do, so that availing yourself of his negligence, you can easily obtain the opportunity to get out of his hands. Sulla twice freed himself from his enemies in this manner, and with this same deceit, Hannibal in Spain got away from the forces of Claudius Nero, who had besieged him.

It also helps one in freeing himself from the enemy to do something in addition to those mentioned, which keeps him at bay. This is done in two ways: either by assaulting him with part of your forces, so that intent on the battle, he gives the rest of your forces the opportunity to be able to save themselves, or to have some new incident spring up, which, by the novelty of the thing, makes him wonder, and for this reason to become apprehensive and stand still, as you know Hannibal did, who, being trapped by Fabius Maximus, at night placed some torches between the horns of many oxen, so that Fabius is suspense over this novelty, did not think further of impeding his passage. A Captain ought, among all the other actions of his, endeavor with every art to divide the forces of the enemy, either by making him suspicious of his men in whom he trusted, or by giving him cause that he has to separate his forces, and, because of this, become weaker. The first method is accomplished by watching the things of some of those whom he has next to him, as exists in war, to save his possessions, maintaining his children or other of his necessities without charge. You know how Hannibal, having burned all the fields around Rome, caused only those of Fabius Maximus to remain safe. You know how Coriolanus, when he came with the army to Rome, saved the possessions of the Nobles, and burned and sacked those of the Plebs. When Metellus led the army against Jugurtha, all me ambassadors, sent to him by Jugurtha, were requested by him to give up Jugurtha as a prisoner; afterwards, writing letters to these same people on the same subject, wrote in such a way that in a little while Jugurtha became suspicious of all his counsellors, and in different ways, dismissed them. Hannibal, having taken refuge with Antiochus, the Roman ambassadors frequented him so much at home, that Antiochus becoming suspicious of him, did not afterwards have any faith in his counsels. As to dividing the enemy forces, there is no more certain way than to have one country assaulted by part of them (your forces), so that being constrained to go to defend it, they (of that country) abandon the war. This is the method employed by Fabius when his Army had encountered the forces of the Gauls, the Tuscans, Umbrians, and Samnites. Titus Didius, having a small force in comparison with those of the enemy, and awaiting a Legion from Rome, the enemy wanted to go out to meet it; so that in order that it should not do so, he gave out by voice throughout his army that he wanted to undertake an engagement with the enemy on the next day; then he took steps that some of the prisoners he had were given the opportunity to escape, who carried back the order of the Consul to fight on the next day, (and) caused the enemy, in order not to diminish his forces, not to go out to meet that Legion: and in this way, kept himself safe. Which method did not serve to divide the forces of the enemy, but to double his own. Some, in order to divide his (the enemy) forces, have employed allowing him to enter their country, and (in proof) allowed him to take many towns so that by placing guards in them, he diminished his forces, and in this manner having made him weak, assaulted and defeated him. Some others, when they wanted to go into one province, feigned making an assault on another, and used so much industry, that as soon as they extended toward that one where there was no fear they would enter, have overcome it before the enemy had time to succor it. For the enemy, as he is not certain whether you are to return back to the place first threatened by you, is constrained not to abandon the one place and succor the other, and thus often he does not defend either. In addition to the matters mentioned, it is important to a Captain when sedition or discord arises among the soldiers, to know how to extinguish it with art. The better way is to castigate the heads of this folly (error); but to do it in a way that you are able to punish them before they are able to become aware of it. The method is, if they are far from you, not to call only the guilty ones, but all the others together with them, so that as they do not believe there is any cause to punish them, they are not disobedient, but provide the opportunity for punishment. When they are present, one ought to strengthen himself with the guiltless, and by their aid, punish them. If there should be discord among them, the best way is to expose them to danger, which fear will always make them united. But, above all, what keeps the Army united, is the reputation of its Captain, which only results from his virtue, for neither blood (birth) nor authority attain it without virtue. And the first thing a Captain is expected to do, is to see to it that the soldiers are paid and punished; for any time payment is missed, punishment must also be dispensed with, because you cannot castigate a soldier you rob, unless you pay him; and as he wants to live, he can abstain from being robbed. But if you pay him but do not punish him, he becomes insolent in every way, because you become of little esteem, and to whomever it happens, he cannot maintain the dignity of his position; and if he does not maintain it, of necessity, tumults and discords follow, which are the ruin of an Army. The Ancient Captains had a molestation from which the present ones are almost free, which was the interpretation of sinister omen to their undertakings; for if an arrow fell in an army, if the Sun or the Moon was obscured, if an earthquake occurred, if the Captain fell while either mounting or dismounting from his horse, it was interpreted in a sinister fashion by the soldiers, and instilled so much fear in them, that when they came to an engagement, they were easily defeated. And, therefore, as soon as such an incident occurred, the ancient Captains either demonstrated the cause of it or reduced it to its natural causes, or interpreted it to (favor) their own purposes. When Caesar went to Africa, and having fallen while he was putting out to sea, said, "Africa, I have taken you": and many have profited from an eclipse of the Moon and from earthquakes: these things cannot happen in our time, as much because our men are not as superstitious, as because our Religion, by itself, entirely takes away such ideas. Yet if it should occur, the orders of the ancients should be imitated. When, either from hunger, or other natural necessity, or human passion, your enemy is brought to extreme desperation, and, driven by it, comes to fight with you, you ought to remain within your quarters, and avoid battle as much as you can. Thus the Lacedemonians did against the Messinians: thus Caesar did against Afranius and Petreius. When Fulvius was Consul against the Cimbri, he had the cavalry assault the enemy continually for many days, and considered how they would issue forth from their quarters in order to pursue them; whence he placed an ambush behind the quarters of the Cimbri, and had them assaulted by the cavalry, and when the Cimbri came out of their quarters to pursue them, Fulvius seized them and plundered them. It has been very effective for a Captain, when his army is in the vicinity of the enemy army, to send his forces with the insignia of the enemy, to rob and burn his own country: whence the enemy, believing they were forces coming to their aid, also ran out to help them plunder, and, because of this, have become disorganized and given the adversary the faculty of overcoming them. Alexander of Epirus used these means fighting against the Illirici, and Leptenus the Syracusan against the Carthaginians, and the design succeeded happily for both. Many have overcome the enemy by giving him the faculty of eating and drinking beyond his means, feigning being afraid, and leaving his quarters full of wine and herds, and when the enemy had filled himself beyond every natural limit, they assaulted him and overcome him with injury to him. Thus Tamirus did against Cyrus, and Tiberius Gracchus against the Spaniards. Some have poisoned the wine and other things to eat in order to be able to overcome them more easily. A little while ago, I said I did not find the ancients had kept a night Watch outside, and I thought they did it to avoid the evils that could happen, for it has been found that sometimes, the sentries posted in the daytime to keep watch for the enemy, have been the ruin of him who posted them; for it has happened often that when they had been taken, and by force had been made to give the signal by which they called their own men, who, coming at the signal, have been either killed or taken. Sometimes it helps to deceive the enemy by changing one of your habits, relying on which, he is ruined: as a Captain had already done, who, when he wanted to have a signal made to his men indicating the coming of the enemy, at night with fire and in the daytime with smoke, commanded that both smoke and flame be made without any intermission; so that when the enemy came, he should remain in the belief that he came without being seen, as he did not see the signals (usually) made to indicate his discovery, made (because of his going disorganized) the victory of his adversary easier. Menno Rodius, when he wanted to draw the enemy from the strong places, sent one in the disguise of a fugitive, who affirmed that his army was full of discord, and that the greater part were deserting, and to give proof of the matter, had certain tumults started among the quarters: whence to the enemy, thinking he was able to break him, assaulted him and was routed.

In addition to the things mentioned, one ought to take care not to bring the enemy to extreme desperation; which Caesar did when he fought the Germans, who, having blocked the way to them, seeing that they were unable to flee, and necessity having made them brave, desired rather to undergo the hardship of pursuing them if they defended themselves. Lucullus, when he saw that some Macedonian cavalry who were with him, had gone over to the side of the enemy, quickly sounded the call to battle, and commanded the other forces to pursue it: whence the enemy, believing that Lucullus did not want to start the battle, went to attack the Macedonians with such fury, that they were constrained to defend themselves, and thus, against their will, they became fighters of the fugitives. Knowing how to make yourself secure of a town when you have doubts of its loyalty once you have conquered it, or before, is also important; which some examples of the ancients teach you. Pompey, when he had doubts of the Catanians, begged them to accept some infirm people he had in his army, and having sent some very robust men in the disguise of infirm ones, occupied the town. Publius Valerius, fearful of the loyalty of the Epidaurians, announced an amnesty to be held, as we will tell you, at a Church outside the town, and when all the public had gone there for the amnesty, he locked the doors, and then let no one out from inside except those whom he trusted. Alexander the Great, when he wanted to go into Asia and secure Thrace for himself, took with him all the chiefs of this province, giving them provisions, and placed lowborn men in charge of the common people of Thrace; and thus he kept the chiefs content by paying them, and the common people quiet by not having Heads who should disquiet them. But among all the things by which Captains gain the people over to themselves, are the examples of chastity and justice, as was that of Scipio in Spain when he returned that girl, beautiful in body, to her husband and father, which did more than arms in gaining over Spain. Caesar, when he paid for the lumber that he used to make the stockades around his army in Gaul, gained such a name for himself of being just, that he facilitated the acquisition of that province for himself. I do not know what else remains for me to talk about regarding such events, and there does not remain any part of this matter that has not been discussed by us. The only thing lacking is to tell of the methods of capturing and defending towns, which I am about to do willingly, if it is not painful for you now.

BATTISTA: Your humaneness is so great, that it makes us pursue our desires without being afraid of being held presumptuous, since you have offered it willingly, that we would be ashamed to ask you. Therefore we say only this to you, that you cannot do a greater or more thankful benefit to us than to furnish us this discussion. But before you pass on to that other matter, resolve a doubt for us: whether it is better to continue the war even in winter, as is done today, or wage it only in the summer, and go into quarters in the winter, as the ancients did.

FABRIZIO: Here, if there had not been the prudence of the questioner, some part that merits consideration would have been omitted. I tell you again that the ancients did everything better and with more prudence than we; and if some error is made in other things, all are made in matters of war. There is nothing more imprudent or more perilous to a Captain than to wage war in winter, and more dangerous to him who brings it, than to him who awaits it. The reason is this: all the industry used in military discipline, is used in order to be organized to undertake an engagement with your enemy, as this is the end toward which a Captain must aim, for the engagement makes you win or lose a war. Therefore, whoever know how to organize it better, and who has his army better disciplined, has the greater advantage in this, and can hope more to win it. On the other hand, there is nothing more inimical to organization than the rough sites, or cold and wet seasons; for the rough side does not allow you to use the plentitude (of your forces) according to discipline, and the cold and wet seasons do not allow you to keep your forces together, and you cannot have them face the enemy united, but of necessity, you must quarter them separately, and without order, having to take into account the castles, hamlets, and farm houses that receive you; so that all the hard work employed by you in disciplining your army is in vain. And do not marvel if they war in winter time today, for as the armies are without discipline, and do not know the harm that is done to them by not being quartered together, for their annoyance does not enable those arrangements to be made and to observe that discipline which they do not have. Yet, the injury caused by campaigning in the field in the winter ought to be observed, remembering that the French in the year one thousand five hundred three (1503) were routed on the Garigliano by the winter, and not by the Spaniards. For, as I have told you, whoever assaults has even greater disadvantage, because weather harms him more when he is in the territory of others, and wants to make war. Whence he is compelled either to withstand the inconveniences of water and cold in order to keep together, or to divide his forces to escape them. But whoever waits, can select the place to his liking, and await him (the enemy) with fresh forces, and can unite them in a moment, and go out to find the enemy forces who cannot withstand their fury. Thus were the French routed, and thus are those always routed who assault an enemy in wintertime, who in itself has prudence. Whoever, therefore, does not want the forces, organization, discipline, and virtue, in some part, to be of value, makes war in the field in the wintertime. And because the Romans wanted to avail themselves of all of these things, into which they put so much industry, avoided not only the wintertime but rough mountains and difficult places, and anything else which could impede their ability to demonstrate their skill and virtue. So this suffices to (answer) your question; and now let us come to treat of the attacking and defending of towns, and of the sites, and of their edifices.

SEVENTH BOOK

You ought to know that towns and fortresses can be strong either by nature or industry. Those are strong by nature which are surrounded by rivers or marshes, as is Mantua or Ferrara, or those situated on a rock or sloping mountain, as Monaco and San Leo; for those situated on mountains which are not difficult to climb, today are (with respect to caves and artillery) very weak. And, therefore, very often today a plain is sought on which to build (a city) to make it strong by industry. The first industry is, to make the walls twisted and full of turned recesses; which pattern results in the enemy not being able to approach them, as they will be able to be attacked easily not only from the front, but on the flanks. If the walls are made too high, they are excessively exposed to the blows of the artillery; if they are made too low, they are very easily scaled. If you dig ditches (moats) in front of them to make it difficult (to employ) ladders, if it should happen that the enemy fills them (which a large army can do easily) the wall becomes prey to the enemy. I believe, therefore, (subject to a better judgment) that if you want to make provision against both evils the wall ought to be made high, with the ditches inside and not outside. This is the strongest way to build that is possible, for it protects you from artillery and ladders, and does not give the enemy the faculty of filling the ditches. The wall, therefore, ought to be as high as occurs to you, and not less than three arm lengths wide, to make it more difficult to be ruined. It ought to have towers placed at intervals of two hundred arm lengths. The ditch inside ought to be at least thirty arm lengths wide and twelve deep, and all the earth that is excavated in making the ditch is thrown toward the city, and is sustained by a wall that is part of the base of the ditch, and extends again as much above the ground, as that a man may take cover behind it: which has the effect of making the depth of the ditch greater. In the base of the ditch, every two hundred arm-lengths, there should be a matted enclosure, which with the artillery causes injury to anyone who should descend into it. The heavy artillery which defends the city, are placed behind the wall enclosing the ditch; for to defend the wall from the front, as it is high, it is not possible to use conveniently anything else other than small or middle sized guns. If the enemy comes to scale your wall, the height of the first wall easily protects you. If he comes with artillery, he must first batter down the first wall: but once it is battered down, because the nature of all batterings is to cause the wall to fall toward the battered side, the ruin of the wall will result (since it does not find a ditch which receives and hides it) in doubling the depth of the ditch, so that it is not possible for you to pass on further as you will find a ruin that holds you back and a ditch which will impede you, and from the wall of the ditch, in safety, the enemy artillery kills you. The only remedy there exists for you, is to fill up the ditch: which is very difficult, as much because its capacity is large, as from the difficulty you have in approaching it, since the walls being winding and recessed, you can enter among them only with difficulty, for the reasons previously mentioned; and then, having to climb over the ruin with the material in hand, causes you a very great difficulty: so that I know a city so organized is completely indestructible.

BATTISTA: If, in addition to the ditch inside, there should be one also on the outside, wouldn't (the encampment) be stronger?

FABRIZIO: It would be, without doubt; but my reasoning is, that if you want to dig one ditch only, it is better inside than outside.

BATTISTA: Would you have water in the ditch, or would you leave them dry?

FABRIZIO: Opinions are different; for ditches full of water protect you from (subterranean) tunnels, the ditches without water make it more difficult for you to fill them in again. But, considering everything, I would have them without water; for they are more secure, and, as it has been observed that in winter time the ditches ice over, the capture of a city is made easy, as happened at Mirandola when Pope Julius besieged it. And to protect yourself from tunnels, I would dig them so deep, that whoever should want to go (tunnel) deeper, should find water. I would also build the fortresses in a way similar to the walls and ditches, so that similar difficulty would be encountered in destroying it I want to call to mind one good thing to anyone who defends a city. This is, that they do not erect bastions outside, and they be distant from its wall. And another to anyone who builds the fortresses: And this is, that he not build any redoubts in them, into which whoever is inside can retire when the wall is lost. What makes me give the first counsel is, that no one ought to do anything, through the medium of which, you begin to lose your reputation without any remedy, the loss of which makes others esteem you less, and dismay those who undertake your defense. And what I say will always happen to you if you erect bastions outside the town you have to defend, for you will always lose them, as you are unable to defend small things when they are placed under the fury of the artillery; so that in losing them, they become the beginning and the cause of your ruin. Genoa, when it rebelled from King Louis of France, erected some bastions on the hills outside the City, which, as soon as they were lost, and they were lost quickly, also caused the city to be lost. As to the second counsel, I affirm there is nothing more dangerous concerning a fortress, than to be able to retire into it, for the hope that men have (lose) when they abandon a place, cause it to be lost, and when it is lost, it then causes the entire fortress to be lost. For an example, there is the recent loss of the fortress of Forli when the Countess Catherine defended it against Caesare Borgia, son of Pope Alexander the Sixth, who had led the army of the King of France. That entire fortress was full of places by both of them: For it was originally a citadel. There was a moat before coming to the fortress, so that it was entered by means of a drawbridge. The fortress was divided into three parts, and each part separated by a ditch, and with water between them; and one passed from one place to another by means of bridges: whence the Duke battered one of those parts of the fortress with artillery, and opened up part of a wall; whence Messer Giovanni Da Casale, who was in charge of the garrison, did not think of defending that opening, but abandoned to retire into the other places; so that the forces of the Duke, having entered that part without opposition, immediately seized all of it, for they became masters of the bridges that connected the members (parts) with each other. He lost the fort which was held to be indestructible because of two mistakes: one, because it had so many redoubts: the other, because no one was made master of his bridges (they were unprotected). The poorly built fortress and the little prudence of the defender, therefore, brought disgrace to the magnanimous enterprise of the Countess, who had the courage to face an army which neither the King of Naples, nor the Duke of Milan, had faced. And although his (the Duke) efforts did not have a good ending, nonetheless, he became noted for those honors which his virtue merited. Which was testified to by the many epigrams made in those times praising him. If I should therefore have to build a fortress, I would make its walls strong, and ditches in the manner we have discussed, nor would I build anything else to live in but houses, and they would be weak and low, so that they would not impede the sight of the walls to anyone who might be in the plaza, so that the Captain should be able to see with (his own) eyes where he could be of help, and that everyone should understand that if the walls and the ditch were lost, the entire fortress would be lost. And even if I should build some redoubts, I would have the bridges so separated, that each part should be master of (protect) the bridge in its own area, arranging that it be buttressed on its pilasters in the middle of the ditch.

BATTISTA: You have said that, today, the little things cannot be defended, and it seems to me I have understood the opposite, that the smaller the thing was, the better it was defended.

FABRIZIO: You have not understood well, for today that place can not be called strong, where he who defends it does not have room to retire among new ditches and ramparts: for such is the fury of the artillery, that he who relies on the protection of only one wall or rampart, deceives himself. And as the bastions (if you want them not to exceed their regular measurements, for then they would be terraces and castles) are not made so that others can retire into them, they are lost quickly. And therefore it is a wise practice to leave these bastions outside, and fortify the entrances of the terraces, and cover their gates with revets, so that one does not go in or out of the gate in a straight line, and there is a ditch with a bridge over it from the revet to the gate. The gates are also fortified with shutters, so as to allow your men to reenter, when, after going out to fight, it happens that the enemy drives them back, and in the ensuing mixing of men, the enemy does not enter with them. And therefore, these things have also been found which the ancients called "cataracts", which, being let down, keep out the enemy but saves one's friends; for in such cases, one can not avail himself of anything else, neither bridges, or the gate, since both are occupied by the crowd.

BATTISTA: I have seen these shutters that you mention, made of small beams, in Germany, in the form of iron grids, while those of ours are made entirely of massive planks. I would want to know whence this difference arises, and which is stronger.

FABRIZIO: I will tell you again, that the methods and organizations of war in all the world, with respect to those of the ancients, are extinct; but in Italy, they are entirely lost, and if there is something more powerful, it results from the examples of the Ultramontanes. You may have heard, and these others can remember, how weakly things were built before King Charles of France crossed into Italy in the year one thousand four hundred ninety four (1494). The battlements were made a half arm length thin (wide), the places for the cross-bowmen and bombardiers (gunners) were made with a small aperture outside and a large one inside, and with many other defects, which I will omit, not to be tedious; for the defenses are easily taken away from slender battlements; the (places for) bombardiers built that way are easily opened (demolished). Now from the French, we have learned to make the battlements wide and large, and also to make the (places of the) bombardiers wide on the inside, and narrow it at the center of the wall, and then again widen it up to the outside edge: and this results in the artillery being able to demolish its defenses only with difficulty, The French, moreover, have many other arrangements such as these, which, because they have not been seen thus, have not been given consideration. Among which, is this method of the shutters made in the form of a grid, which is by far a better method than yours; for if you have to repair the shutters of a gate such as yours, lowering it if you are locked inside, and hence are unable to injure the enemy, so that they can attack it safely either in the dark or with a fire. But if it is made in the shape of a grid, you can, once it is lowered, by those weaves and intervals, to be able to defend it with lances, crossbows, and every other kind of arms.

BATTISTA: I have also seen another Ultramontane custom in Italy, and it is this, making the carriages of the artillery with the spokes of the wheels bent toward the axles. I would like to know why they make them this way, as it seems to me they would be stronger straight, as those of our wheels.

FABRIZIO: Never believe that things which differ from the ordinary are made at home, but if you would believe that I should make them such as to be more beautiful, you would err; for where strength is necessary, no account is taken of beauty; but they all arise from being safer and stronger than ours. The reason is this. When the carriage is loaded, it either goes on a level, or inclines to the right or left side. When it goes level, the wheels equally sustain the weight, which, being divided equally between them, does not burden them much; when it inclines, it comes to have all the weight of the load upon that wheel on which it inclines. If its spokes are straight, they can easily collapse, since the wheel being inclined, the spokes also come to incline, and do not sustain the weight in a straight line. And, thus, when the carriage rides level and when they carry less weight, they come to be stronger; when the carriage rides inclined and when they carry more weight, they are weaker. The contrary happens to the bent spokes of the French carriages; for when the carriage inclines to one side, it points (leans straight) on them, since being ordinarily bent, they then come to be (more) straight (vertical), and can sustain all the weight strongly; and when the carriage goes level and they (the spikes) are bent, they sustain half the weight.

But let us return to our Cities and Fortresses. The French, for the greater security of their towns, and to enable them during sieges to put into and withdraw forces from them more easily, also employ, in addition to the things mentioned, another arrangement, of which I have not yet seen any example in Italy: and it is this, that they erect two pilasters at the outside point of a drawbridge, and upon each of them they balance a beam so that half of it comes over the bridge, and the other half outside. Then they join small beams to the part outside, which are woven together from one beam to another in the shape of a grid, and on the inside they attach a chain to the end of each beam. When they want to close the bridge from the outside, therefore, they release the chains and allow all that gridded part to drop, which closes the bridge when it is lowered, and when they want to open it, they pull on the chains, and they (gridded beams) come to be raised; and they can be raised so that a man can pass under, but not a horse, and also so much that a horse with the man can pass under, and also can be closed entirely, for it is lowered and raised like a lace curtain. This arrangement is more secure than the shutters: for it can be impeded by the enemy so that it cannot come down only with difficulty, (and) it does not come down in a straight line like the shutters which can easily be penetrated. Those who want to build a City, therefore, ought to have all the things mentioned installed; and in addition, they should want at least one mile around the wall where either farming or building would not be allowed, but should be open field where no bushes, embankments, trees, or houses, should exist which would impede the vision, and which should be in the rear of a besieging enemy. It is to be noted that a town which has its ditches outside with its embankments higher than the ground, is very weak; for they provide a refuge for the enemy who assaults you, but does not impede him in attacking you, because they can be easily forced (opened) and give his artillery an emplacement.

But let us pass into the town. I do not want to waste much time in showing you that, in addition to the things mentioned previously, provisions for living and fighting supplies must also be included, for they are the things which everyone needs, and without them, every other provision is in vain. And, generally, two things ought to be done, provision yourself, and deprive the enemy of the opportunity to avail himself of the resources of your country. Therefore, any straw, grain, and cattle, which you cannot receive in your house, ought to be destroyed. Whoever defends a town ought to see to it that nothing is done in a tumultuous and disorganized manner, and have means to let everyone know what he has to do in any incident. The manner is this, that the women, children, aged, and the public stay at home, and leave the town free to the young and the brave: who armed, are distributed for defense, part being on the walls, part at the gates, part in the principal places of the City, in order to remedy those evils which might arise within; another part is not assigned to any place, but is prepared to help anyone requesting their help. And when matters are so organized, only with difficulty can tumults arise which disturb you. I want you to note also that in attacking and defending Cities, nothing gives the enemy hope of being able to occupy a town, than to know the inhabitants are not in the habit of looking for the enemy; for often Cities are lost entirely from fear, without any other action. When one assaults such a City, he should make all his appearances (ostentatious) terrible. On the other hand, he who is assaulted ought to place brave men, who are not afraid of thoughts, but by arms, on the side where the enemy (comes to) fight; for if the attempt proves vain, courage grows in the besieged, and then the enemy is forced to overcome those inside with his virtue and his reputation.

The equipment with which the ancients defended the towns were many, such as, Ballistas, Onagers, Scorpions, Arc-Ballistas, Large Bows, Slingshots; and those with which they assaulted were also many, such as, Battering Rams, Wagons, Hollow Metal Fuses (Muscoli), Trench Covers (Plutei), Siege Machines (Vinee), Scythes, Turtles (somewhat similar to present day tanks). In place of these things, today there is the artillery, which serves both attackers and defenders, and, hence, I will not speak further about it. But let us return to our discussion, and come to the details of the siege (attack). One ought to take care not to be able to be taken by hunger, and not to be forced (to capitulate) by assaults. As to hunger, it has been said that it is necessary, before the siege arrives, to be well provided with food. But when it is lacking during a long siege, some extraordinary means of being provided by friends who want to save you, have been observed to be employed, especially if a river runs in the middle of the besieged City, as were the Romans, when their castle of Casalino was besieged by Hannibal, who, not being able to send them anything else by way of the river, threw great quantities of nuts into it, which being carried by the river without being able to be impeded, fed the Casalinese for some time. Some, when they were besieged, in order to show the enemy they had grain left over, and to make them despair of being able to besiege (defeat) them by hunger, have either thrown bread outside the walls, or have given a calf grain to eat, and then allowed it to be taken, so that when it was killed, and being found full of grain, gave signs of an abundance which they do not have. On the other hand, excellent Captains have used various methods to enfamish the enemy. Fabius allowed the Campanians to sow so that they should lack that grain which they were sowing. Dionysius, when he was besieged at Reggio, feigned wanting to make an accord with them, and while it was being drawn, had himself provided with food, and then when, by this method, had depleted them of grain, pressed them and starved them. Alexander the Great, when he wanted to capture Leucadia, captured all the surrounding castles, and allowed the men from them to take refuge in it (the City), and thus by adding a great multitude, he starved them. As to assaults, it has been said that one ought to guard against the first onrush, with which the Romans often occupied many towns, assaulting them all at once from every side, and they called it *attacking the city by its crown*: as did Scipio when he occupied new Carthage in Spain. If this onrush is withstood, then only with difficulty will you be overcome. And even if it should occur that the enemy had entered inside the city by having forced the walls, even the small terraces give you some remedy if they are not abandoned; for many armies have, once they have entered into a town, been repulsed or slain. The remedy is, that the townspeople keep themselves in high places, and fight them from their houses and towers. Which thing, those who have entered in the City, have endeavored to win in two ways: the one, to open the gates of the City and make a way for the townspeople by which they can escape in safety: the other, to send out a (message) by voice signifying that no one would be harmed unless armed, and whoever would throw his arms on the ground, they would pardon. Which thing has made the winning of many Cities easy. In addition to this, Cities are easy to capture if you fall on them unexpectedly, which you can do when you find yourself with your army far away, so that they do not believe that you either want to assault them, or that you can do it without your presenting yourself, because of the distance from the place. Whence, if you assault them secretly and quickly, it will almost always happen that you will succeed in reporting the victory. I unwillingly discuss those things which have happened in our times, as I would burden you with myself and my (ideas), and I would not know what to say in discussing other things. None the less, concerning this matter, I can not but cite the example of Cesare Borgia, called the Duke Valentine, who, when he was at Nocera with his forces, under the pretext of going to harm Camerino, turned toward the State of Urbino, and occupied a State in one day and without effort, which some other, with great time and expense, would barely have occupied. Those who are besieged must also guard themselves from the deceit and cunning of the enemy, and, therefore, the besieged should not trust anything which they see the enemy doing continuously, but always believe they are being done by deceit, and can change to injure them. When Domitius Calvinus was besieging a town, he undertook habitually to circle the walls of the City every day with a good part of his forces. Whence the townspeople, believing he was doing this for exercise, lightened the guard: when Domitius became aware of this, he assaulted them, and destroyed them. Some Captains, when they heard beforehand that aid was to come to the besieged, have clothed their soldiers with the insignia of those who were to come, and having introduced them inside, have occupied the town. Chimon, the Athenian, one night set fire to a Temple that was outside the town, whence, when the townspeople arrived to succor it, they left the town to the enemy to plunder. Some have put to death those who left the besieged castle to blacksmith (shoe horses), and redressing their soldiers with the clothes of the blacksmiths, who then surrendered the town to him. The ancient Captains also employed various methods to despoil the garrisons of the towns they want to take. Scipio, when he was in Africa, and desiring to occupy several castles in which garrisons had been placed by Carthaginians, feigned several times wanting to assault them, but then from fear not only abstained but drew away from them. Which Hannibal believing to be true, in order to pursue him with a larger force and be able to attack him more easily, withdrew all the garrisons from them: (and) Scipio becoming aware of this, sent Maximus, his Captain, to capture them. Pyrrhus, when he was waging war in Sclavonia, in one of the Chief Cities of that country, where a large force had been brought in to garrison it, feigned to be desperate of being able to capture it, and turning to other places, caused her, in order to succor them, to empty herself of the garrison, so that it became easy to be forced (captured). Many have polluted the water and diverted rivers to take a town, even though they then did not succeed. Sieges and surrenders are also easily accomplished, by dismaying them by pointing out an accomplished victory, or new help which is come to their disfavor. The ancient Captains sought to occupy towns by treachery, corrupting some inside, but have used different methods. Some have sent one of their men under the disguise of a fugitive, who gained authority and confidence with the enemy, which he afterward used for his own benefit. Many by this means have learned the procedures of the guards, and through this knowledge have taken the town. Some have blocked the gate so that it could not be locked with a cart or a beam under some pretext, and by this means, made the entry easy to the enemy. Hannibal persuaded one to give him a castle of the Romans, and that he should feign going on a hunt at night, to show his inability to go by day for fear of the enemy, and when he returned with the game, placed his men inside with it, and killing the guard, captured the gate. You also deceive the besieged by drawing them outside the town and distant from it, by feigning flight when they assault you. And many (among whom was Hannibal) have, in addition, allowed their quarters to be taken in order to have the opportunity of placing them in their midst, and take the town from them. They deceive also by feigning departure, as did Forminus, the Athenian, who having plundered the country of the Calcidians, afterwards received their ambassadors, and filled their City with promises of safety and good will, who, as men of little caution, were shortly after captured by Forminus. The besieged ought to look out for men whom they have among them that are suspect, but sometimes they may want to assure themselves of these by reward, as well as by punishment. Marcellus, recognizing that Lucius Bancius Nolanus had turned to favor Hannibal, employed so much humanity and liberality toward him, that, from an enemy, he made him a very good friend. The besieged ought to use more diligence in their guards when the enemy is distant, than when he is near. And they ought to guard those places better which they think can be attacked less; for many towns have been lost when the enemy assaulted them on a side from which they did not believe they would be assaulted. And this deception occurs for two reasons: either because the place is strong and they believe it is inaccessible, or because the enemy cunningly assaults him on one side with feigned uproars, and on the other silently with the real assaults. And, therefore, the besieged ought to have a great awareness of this, and above all at all times, but especially at night, have good guards at the walls, and place there not only men, but dogs; and keep them ferocious and ready, which by smell, detect the presence of the enemy, and with their baying discover him. And, in addition to dogs, it has been found that geese have also saved a City, as happened to the Romans when the Gauls besieged the Capitol. When Athens was besieged by the Spartans, Alcibiades, in order to see if the guards were awake, arranged that when a light was raised at night, all the guards should rise, and inflicted a penalty on those who did not observe it. Hissicratus, the Athenian, slew a guard who was sleeping, saying he was leaving him as he had found him. Those who are besieged have had various ways of sending news to their friends, and in order not to send embassies by voice, wrote letters in cipher, and concealed them in various ways. The ciphers are according to the desires of whoever arranges them; the method of concealment is varied. Some have written inside the scabbard of a sword. Others have put these letters inside raw bread, and then baked it, and gave it as food to him who brought it. Others have placed them in the most secret places of the body. Others have put them in the collar of a dog known to him who brings it. Others have written ordinary things in a letter, and then have written with water (invisible ink) between one line and another, which afterwards by wetting or scalding (caused) the letter to appear. This method has been very astutely observed in our time, where some wanting to point out a thing which was to be kept secret to their friends who lived inside a town, and not wanting to trust it in person, sent communications written in the customary manner, but interlined as I mentioned above, and had them hung at the gates of a Temple; which were then taken and read by those who recognized them from the countersigns they knew. Which is a very cautious method, because whoever brings it can be deceived by you, and you do not run any danger. There are infinite other ways by which anyone by himself likewise can find and read them. But one writes with more facility to the besieged than the besieged do to friends outside, for the latter can not send out such letters except by one who leaves the town under the guise of a fugitive, which is a doubtful and dangerous exploit when the enemy is cautious to a point. But as to those that are sent inside, he who is sent can, under many pretexts, go into the camp that is besieged, and from here await a convenient opportunity to jump into the town.

But let us come to talk of present captures, and I say that, if they occur when you are being fought in your City, which is not arranged with ditches inside, as we pointed out a little while ago, when you do not want the enemy to enter by the breaks in the wall made by artillery (as there is no remedy for the break which it makes), it is necessary for you, while the artillery is battering, to dig a ditch inside the wall that is being hit, at least thirty arm lengths wide, and throw all (the earth) that is excavated toward the town, which makes embankments and the ditch deeper: and you must do this quickly, so that if the wall falls, the ditch will be excavated at least five or six arm lengths deep. While this ditch is being excavated, it is necessary that it be closed on each side by a blockhouse. And if the wall is so strong that it gives you time to dig the ditches and erect the block houses, that part which is battered comes to be stronger than the rest of the City, for such a repair comes to have the form that we gave to inside ditches. But if the wall is weak and does not give you time, then there is need to show virtue, and oppose them with armed forces, and with all your strength. This method of repair was observed by the Pisans when you went to besiege them, and they were able to do this because they had strong walls which gave them time, and the ground firm and most suitable for erecting ramparts and making repairs. Which, had they not had this benefit, would have been lost. It would always be prudent, therefore, first to prepare yourself, digging the ditches inside your City and throughout all its circuit, as we devised a little while ago; for in this case, as the defenses have been made, the enemy is awaited with leisure and safety. The ancients often occupied towns with tunnels in two ways: either they dug a secret tunnel which came out inside the town, and through which they entered it, in the way in which the Romans took the City of the Veienti: or, by tunneling they undermined a wall, and caused it to be ruined. This last method is more effective today, and causes Cities located high up to be weaker, for they can be undermined more easily, and then when that powder which ignites in an instant is placed inside those tunnels, it not only ruins the wall, but the mountains are opened, and the fortresses are entirely disintegrated into several parts. The remedy for this is to build on a plain, and make the ditch which girds your City so deep, that the enemy can not excavate further below it without finding water, which is the only enemy of these excavations. And even if you find a knoll within the town that you defend, you cannot remedy it otherwise than to dig many deep wells within your walls, which are as outlets to those excavations which the enemy might be able to arrange against it. Another remedy is to make an excavation opposite to where you learn he is excavating: which method readily impedes him, but is very difficult to foresee when you are besieged by a cautious enemy. Whoever is besieged, above all, ought to take care not to be attacked in times of repose, as after having engaged in battle, after having stood guard, that is, at dawn, the evening between night and day, and, above all, at dinner time, in which times many towns have been captured, and many armies ruined by those inside. One ought, therefore, to be always on guard with diligence on every side, and in good part well armed. I do not want to miss telling you that what makes defending a City or an encampment difficult, is to have to keep all the forces you have in them disunited; for the enemy being able all together to assault you at his discretion, you must keep every place guarded on all sides, and thus he assaults you with his entire force, and you defend it with part of yours. The besieged can also be completely overcome, while those outside cannot unless repulsed; whence many who have been besieged either in their encampment or in a town, although inferior in strength, have suddenly issued forth with all their forces, and have overcome the enemy. Marcellus did this at Nola, and Caesar did this in Gaul, where his encampment being assaulted by a great number of Gauls, and seeing he could not defend it without having to divide this forces into several parts, and unable to stay within the stockade with the driving attack of the enemy, opened the encampment on one side, and turning to that side with all his forces, attacked them with such fury, and with such virtue, that he overcame and defeated them. The constancy of the besieged has also often displeased and dismayed the besieger. And when Pompey was affronting Caesar, and Caesar's army was suffering greatly from hunger, some of his bread was brought to Pompey, who, seeing it made of grass, commanded it not be shown to his army in order not to frighten it, seeing what kind of enemies he had to encounter. Nothing gave the Romans more honor in the war against Hannibal, as their constancy; for, in whatever more inimical and adverse fortune, they never asked for peace, (and) never gave any sign of fear: rather, when Hannibal was around Rome, those fields on which he had situated his quarters were sold at a higher price than they would ordinarily have been sold in other times; and they were so obstinate in their enterprises, that to defend Rome, they did not leave off attacking Capua, which was being besieged by the Romans at the same time Rome was being besieged.

I know that I have spoken to you of many things, which you have been able to understand and consider by yourselves; none the less, I have done this (as I also told you today) to be able to show you, through them, the better kind of training, and also to satisfy those, if there should be any, who had not had that opportunity to learn, as you have. Nor does it appear to me there is anything left for me to tell you other than some general rules, with which you should be very familiar: which are these. What benefits the enemy, harms you; and what benefits you, harm the enemy. Whoever is more vigilant in observing the designs of the enemy in war, and endures much hardship in training his army, will incur fewer dangers, and can have greater hope for victory. Never lead your soldiers into an engagement unless you are assured of their courage, know they are without fear, and are organized, and never make an attempt unless you see they hope for victory. It is better to defeat the enemy by hunger than with steel; in such victory fortune counts more than virtue. No proceeding is better than that which you have concealed from the enemy until the time you have executed it. To know how to recognize an opportunity in war, and take it, benefits you more than anything else. Nature creates few men brave; industry and training makes many. Discipline in war counts more than fury. If some on the side of the enemy desert to come to your service, if they be loyal, they will always make you a great acquisition; for the forces of the adversary diminish more with the loss of those who flee, than with those who are killed, even though the name of the fugitives is suspect to the new friends, and odious to the old. It is better in organizing an engagement to reserve great aid behind the front line, than to spread out your soldiers to make a greater front. He is overcome with difficulty, who knows how to recognize his forces and those of the enemy. The virtue of the soldiers is worth more than a multitude, and the site is often of more benefit than virtue. New and speedy things frighten armies, while the customary and slow things are esteemed little by them: you will therefore make your army experienced, and learn (the strength) of a new enemy by skirmishes, before you come to an engagement with him. Whoever pursues a routed enemy in a disorganized manner, does nothing but become vanquished from having been a victor. Whoever does not make provisions necessary to live (eat), is overcome without steel. Whoever trusts more in cavalry than in infantry, or more in infantry than in cavalry, must settle for the location. If you want to see whether any spy has come into the camp during the day, have no one go to his quarters. Change your proceeding when you become aware that the enemy has foreseen it. Counsel with many on the things you ought to do, and confer with few on what you do afterwards. When soldiers are confined to their quarters, they are kept there by fear or punishment; then when they are led by war, (they are led) by hope and reward. Good Captains never come to an engagement unless necessity compels them, or the opportunity calls them. Act so your enemies do not know how you want to organize your army for battle, and in whatever way you organize them, arrange it so that the first line can be received by the second and by the third. In a battle, never use a company for some other purpose than what you have assigned it to, unless you want to cause disorder. Accidents are remedied with difficulty, unless you quickly take the facility of thinking. Men, steel, money, and bread, are the sinews of war; but of these four, the first two are more necessary, for men and steel find money and bread, but money and bread do not find men and steel. The unarmed rich man is the prize of the poor soldier. Accustom your soldiers to despise delicate living and luxurious clothing.

This is as much as occurs to me generally to remind you, and I know I could have told you of many other things in my discussion, as for example, how and in how many ways the ancients organized their ranks, how they dressed, and how they trained in many other things; and to give you many other particulars, which I have not judged necessary to narrate, as much because you are able to see them, as because my intention has not been to show you in detail how the ancient army was created, but how an army should be organized in these times, which should have more virtue than they now have. Whence it does not please me to discuss the ancient matters further than those I have judged necessary to such an introduction. I know I should have enlarged more on the cavalry, and also on naval warfare; for whoever defines the military, says, that it is an army on land and on the sea, on foot and on horseback. Of naval matters, I will not presume to talk, not because of not being informed, but because I should leave the talk to the Genoese and Venetians, who have made much study of it, and have done great things in the past. Of the cavalry, I also do not want to say anything other than what I have said above, this part being (as I said) less corrupted. In addition to this, if the infantry, who are the nerve of the army, are well organized, of necessity it happens that good cavalry be created. I would only remind you that whoever organizes the military in his country, so as to fill (the quota) of cavalry, should make two provisions: the one, that he should distribute horses of good breed throughout his countryside, and accustom his men to make a round-up of fillies, as you do in this country with calves and mules: the other, (so that the round-up men find a buyer) I would prohibit anyone to keep mules who did not keep a horse; so that whoever wanted to keep a mount only, would also be constrained to keep a horse; and, in addition, none should be able to dress in silk, except whoever keeps a horse. I understand this arrangement has been done by some Princes of our times, and to have resulted in an excellent cavalry being produced in their countries in a very brief time. About other things, how much should be expected from the cavalry, I will go back to what I said to you today, and to that which is the custom. Perhaps you will also desire to learn what parts a Captain ought to have. In this, I will satisfy you in a brief manner; for I would not knowingly select any other man than one who should know how to do all those things which we have discussed today. And these would still not be enough for him if he did not know how to find them out by himself, for no one without imagination was ever very great in his profession; and if imagination makes for honor in other things, it will, above all, honor you in this one. And it is to be observed, that every creation (imagination), even though minor, is celebrated by the writers, as is seen where they praised Alexander the Great, who, in order to break camp more secretly, did not give the signal with the trumpet, but with a hat on the end of a lance. He is also praised for having ordered his soldiers, when coming to battle with the enemy, to kneel with the left foot (knee) so that they could more strongly withstand the attack (of the enemy); which not only gave him victory, but also so much praise that all the statues erected in his honor show him in that pose.

But as it is time to finish this discussion, I want to return to the subject, and so, in part, escape that penalty which, in this town, custom decrees for those who do not return. If you remember well, Cosimo, you said to me that I was, on the one hand, an exalter of antiquity, and a censurer of those who did not imitate them in serious matters, and, on the other (hand), in matters of war in which I worked very hard, I did not imitate them, you were unable to discover the reason: to that I replied, that men who want to do something must first prepare themselves to know how to do it in order to be able afterwards to do it when the occasion permits it. Whether or not I would know how to bring the army to the ancient ways, I would rather you be the judge, who have heard me discuss on this subject at length; whence you have been able to know how much time I have consumed on these thoughts, and I also believe you should be able to imagine how much desire there is in me to put them into effect. Which you can guess, if I was ever able to do it, or if ever the opportunity was given to me. Yet, to make you more certain, and for my greater justification, I would like also to cite you the reasons, and in part, will observe what I promised you, to show you the ease and the difficulty that are present in such imitation. I say to you, therefore, that no activity among men today is easier to restore to its ancient ways than the military; but for those only who are Princes of so large a State, that they are able to assemble fifteen or twenty thousand young men from among their own subjects. On the other hand, nothing is more difficult than this to those who do not have such a convenience. And, because I want you to understand this part better, you have to know that Captains who are praised are of two kinds. The one includes those, who, with an army (well) ordered through its own natural discipline, have done great things, such as were the greater part of the Roman Citizens, and others, who have led armies, who have not had any hardship in maintaining them good, and to see to it that they were safely led. The other includes those who not only had to overcome the enemy but before they came to this, had been compelled to make their army good and well ordered, (and) who, without doubt, deserve greater praise that those others merited who with a army which was (naturally) good have acted with so much virtue. Such as these were Pelopidas, Epaminondas, Tullus Hostilius, Phillip of Macedonia father of Alexander, Cyrus King of the Persians, and Gracchus the Roman. All these had first to make the army good, and then fight with it. All of these were able to do so, as much by their prudence, as by having subjects capable of being directed in such practices. Nor would it have been possible for any of them to accomplish any praiseworthy deed, no matter how good and excellent they might have been, should they have been in an alien country, full of corrupt men, and not accustomed to sincere obedience. It is not enough, therefore, in Italy, to govern an army already trained, but it is necessary first to know how to do it, and then how to command it. And of these, there need to be those Princes, who because they have a large State and many subjects, have the opportunity to accomplish this. Of whom, I cannot be one, for I have never commanded, nor can I command except armies of foreigners, and men obligated to others and not to me. Whether or not it is possible to introduce into them (those Princes) some of the things we discussed today, I want to leave to your judgment. Would I make one of these soldiers who practice today carry more arms than is customary, and in addition, food for two or three days, and a shovel? Should I make him dig, or keep him many hours every day under arms in feigned exercises, so that in real (battles) afterward he could be of value to me? Would they abstain from gambling, lasciviousness, swearing, and insolence, which they do daily? Would they be brought to so much discipline, obedience, and respect, that a tree full of apples which should be found in the middle of an encampment, would be left intact, as is read happened many times in the ancient armies? What can I promise them, by which they well respect, love, or fear me, when, with a war ended, they no longer must come to me for anything? Of what can I make them ashamed, who are born and brought up without shame? By what Deity or Saints do I make them take an oath? By those they adore, or by those they curse? I do not know any whom they adore; but I well know that they curse them all. How can I believe they will observe the promises to those men, for whom they show their contempt hourly? How can those who deprecate God, have reverence for men? What good customs, therefore, is it possible to instill in such people? And if you should tell me the Swiss and the Spaniards are good, I should confess they are far better than the Italians: but if you will note my discussion, and the ways in which both proceeded, you will see that there are still many things missing among them (the Swiss and Spaniards) to bring them up to the perfection of the ancients. And the Swiss have been good from their natural customs, for the reasons I told you today, and the others (Spaniards) from necessity; for when they fight in a foreign country, it seems to them they are constrained to win or die, and as no place appeared to them where they might flee, they became good. But it is a goodness defective in many parts, for there is nothing good in them except that they are accustomed to await the enemy up to the point of the pike and of the sword. Nor would there be anyone suitable to teach them what they lack, and much less anyone who does not (speak) their language.

But let us turn to the Italians, who, because they have not wise Princes, have not produced any good army; and because they did not have the necessity that the Spaniards had, have not undertaken it by themselves, so that they remain the shame of the world. And the people are not to blame, but their Princes are, who have been castigated, and by their ignorance have received a just punishment, ignominiously losing the State, (and) without any show of virtue. Do you want to see if what I tell you is true? Consider how many wars have been waged in Italy, from the passage of King Charles (of France) until today; and wars usually make men warlike and acquire reputations; these, as much as they have been great (big) and cruel, so much more have caused its members and its leaders to lose reputation. This necessarily points out, that the customary orders were not, and are not, good, and there is no one who know how to take up the new orders. Nor do you ever believe that reputation will be acquired by Italian arms, except in the manner I have shown, and by those who have large States in Italy, for this custom can be instilled in men who are simple, rough, and your own, but not to men who are malignant, have bad habits, and are foreigners. And a good sculptor will never be found who believes he can make a beautiful statue from a piece of marble poorly shaped, even though it may be a rough one. Our Italian Princes, before they tasted the blows of the ultramontane wars, believed it was enough for them to know what was written, think of a cautious reply, write a beautiful letter, show wit and promptness in his sayings and in his words, know how to weave a deception, ornament himself with gems and gold, sleep and eat with greater splendor than others, keep many lascivious persons around, conduct himself avariciously and haughtily toward his subjects, become rotten with idleness, hand out military ranks at his will, express contempt for anyone who may have demonstrated any praiseworthy manner, want their words should be the responses of oracles; nor were these little men aware that they were preparing themselves to be the prey of anyone who assaulted them. From this, then, in the year one thousand four hundred ninety four (1494), there arose the great frights, the sudden flights, and the miraculous (stupendous) losses: and those most powerful States of Italy were several times sacked and despoiled in this manner. But what is worse is, that those who remained persist in the same error, and exist in the same disorder: and they do not consider that those who held the State anciently, had done all those things we discussed, and that they concentrated on preparing the body for hardships and the mind not to be afraid of danger. Whence it happened that Caesar, Alexander, and all those excellent men and Princes, were the first among the combatants, went around on foot, and even if they did lose their State, wanted also to lose their lives; so that they lived and died with virtue. And if they, or part of them, could be accused of having too much ambition to rule, there never could be found in them any softness or anything to condemn, which makes men delicate and cowardly. If these things were to be read and believed by these Princes, it would be impossible that they would not change their way of living, and their countries not change in fortune. And as, in the beginning of our discussion, you complained of your organization, I tell you, if you had organized it as we discussed above, and it did not give a good account for itself, then you have reason to complain; but if it is not organized and trained as I have said, (the Army) it can have reason to complain of you, who have made an abortion, and not a perfect figure (organization). The Venetians also, and the Duke of Ferrara, begun it, but did not pursue it; which was due to their fault, and not of their men. And I affirm to now, that any of them who have States in Italy today, will begin in this way, he will be the Lord higher than any other in this Province; and it will happen to his State as happened to the Kingdom of the Macedonians, which, coming under Phillip, who had learned the manner of organizing the armies from Epaminondas, the Theban, became, with these arrangements and practices (while the rest of

Greece was in idleness, and attended to reciting comedies) so powerful, that in a few years, he was able to occupy it completely, and leave such a foundation to his son, that he was able to make himself Prince of the entire world. Whoever disparages these thoughts, therefore, if he be a Prince, disparages his Principality, and if he be a Citizen, his City. And I complain of nature, which either ought to make me a recognizer of this, or ought to have given me the faculty to be able to pursue it. Nor, even today when I am old, do I think I can have the opportunity: and because of this, I have been liberal with you, who, being young and qualified, when the things I have said please you, could, at the proper time, in favor of your Princes, aid and counsel them. I do not want you to be afraid or mistrustful of this, because this country appears to be born (to be destined) to resuscitate the things which are dead, as has been observed with Poetry, Painting, and Sculpture. But as for waiting for me, because of my years, do not rely on it. And, truly, if in the past fortune had conceded to me what would have sufficed for such an enterprise, I believe I would, in a very brief time, have shown the world how much the ancient institutions were of value, and, without doubt, I would have enlarged it with glory, or would have lost it without shame.

THE PRINCE

INTRODUCTION

Nicolo Machiavelli was born at Florence on 3rd May 1469. He was the second son of Bernardo di Nicolo Machiavelli, a lawyer of some repute, and of Bartolommea di Stefano Nelli, his wife. Both parents were members of the old Florentine nobility.

His life falls naturally into three periods, each of which singularly enough constitutes a distinct and important era in the history of Florence. His youth was concurrent with the greatness of Florence as an Italian power under the guidance of Lorenzo de' Medici, Il Magnifico. The downfall of the Medici in Florence occurred in 1494, in which year Machiavelli entered the public service. During his official career Florence was free under the government of a Republic, which lasted until 1512, when the Medici returned to power, and Machiavelli lost his office. The Medici again ruled Florence from 1512 until 1527, when they were once more driven out. This was the period of Machiavelli's literary activity and increasing influence; but he died, within a few weeks of the expulsion of the Medici, on 22nd June 1527, in his fifty-eighth year, without having regained office.

YOUTH — Aet. 1-25—1469-94

Although there is little recorded of the youth of Machiavelli, the Florence of those days is so well known that the early environment of this representative citizen may be easily imagined. Florence has been described as a city with two opposite currents of life, one directed by the fervent and austere Savonarola, the other by the splendour-loving Lorenzo. Savonarola's influence upon the young Machiavelli must have been slight, for although at one time he wielded immense power over the fortunes of Florence, he only furnished Machiavelli with a subject of a gibe in "The Prince," where he is cited as an example of an unarmed prophet who came to a bad end. Whereas the magnificence of the Medicean rule during the life of Lorenzo appeared to have impressed Machiavelli strongly, for he frequently recurs to it in his writings, and it is to Lorenzo's grandson that he dedicates "The Prince."

Machiavelli, in his "History of Florence," gives us a picture of the young men among whom his youth was passed. He writes: "They were freer than their forefathers in dress and living, and spent more in other kinds of excesses, consuming their time and money in idleness, gaming, and women; their chief aim was to appear well dressed and to speak with wit and acuteness, whilst he who could wound others the most cleverly was thought the wisest." In a letter to his son Guido, Machiavelli shows why youth should avail itself of its opportunities for study, and leads us to infer that his own youth had been so occupied. He writes: "I have received your letter, which has given me the greatest pleasure, especially because you tell me you are quite restored in health, than which I could have no better news; for if God grant life to you, and to me, I hope to make a good man of you if you are willing to do your share." Then, writing of a new patron, he continues: "This will turn out well for you, but it is necessary for you to study; since, then, you have no longer the excuse of illness, take pains to study letters and music, for you see what honour is done to me for the little skill I have. Therefore, my son, if you wish to please me, and to bring success and honour to yourself, do right and study, because others will help you if you help yourself."

OFFICE — Aet. 25-43—1494-1512

The second period of Machiavelli's life was spent in the service of the free Republic of Florence, which flourished, as stated above, from the expulsion of the Medici in 1494 until their return in 1512. After serving four years in one of the public offices he was appointed Chancellor and Secretary to the Second Chancery, the Ten of Liberty and Peace. Here we are on firm ground when dealing with the events of Machiavelli's life, for during this time he took a leading part in the affairs of the Republic, and we have its decrees, records, and dispatches to guide us, as well as his own writings. A mere recapitulation of a few of his transactions with the statesmen and soldiers of his time gives a fair indication of his activities, and supplies the sources from which he drew the experiences and characters which illustrate "The Prince."

His first mission was in 1499 to Catherina Sforza, "my lady of Forli" of "The Prince," from whose conduct and fate he drew the moral that it is far better to earn the confidence of the people than to rely on fortresses. This is a very noticeable principle in Machiavelli, and is urged by him in many ways as a matter of vital importance to princes.

In 1500 he was sent to France to obtain terms from Louis XII for continuing the war against Pisa: this king it was who, in his conduct of affairs in Italy, committed the five capital errors in statecraft summarized in "The Prince," and was consequently driven out. He, also, it was who made the dissolution of his marriage a condition of support to Pope Alexander VI; which leads Machiavelli to refer those who urge that such promises should be kept to what he has written concerning the faith of princes.

Machiavelli's public life was largely occupied with events arising out of the ambitions of Pope Alexander VI and his son, Cesare Borgia, the Duke Valentino, and these characters fill a large space of "The Prince." Machiavelli never hesitates to cite the actions of the duke for the benefit of usurpers who wish to keep the states they have seized; he can, indeed, find no precepts to offer so good as the pattern of Cesare Borgia's conduct, insomuch that Cesare is acclaimed by some critics as the "hero" of "The Prince." Yet in "The Prince" the duke is in point of fact cited as a type of the man who rises on the fortune of others, and falls with them; who takes every course that might be expected from a prudent man but the course which will save him; who is prepared for all eventualities but the one which happens; and who, when all his abilities fail to carry him through, exclaims that it was not his fault, but an extraordinary and unforeseen fatality.

On the death of Pius III, in 1503, Machiavelli was sent to Rome to watch the election of his successor, and there he saw Cesare Borgia cheated into allowing the choice of the College to fall on Giuliano delle Rovere (Julius II), who was one of the cardinals that had most reason to fear the duke. Machiavelli, when commenting on this election, says that he who thinks new favours will cause great personages to forget old injuries deceives himself. Julius did not rest until he had ruined Cesare.

It was to Julius II that Machiavelli was sent in 1506, when that pontiff was commencing his enterprise against Bologna; which he brought to a successful issue, as he did many of his other adventures, owing chiefly to his impetuous character. It is in reference to Pope Julius that Machiavelli moralizes on the resemblance between Fortune and women, and concludes that it is the bold rather than the cautious man that will win and hold them both.

It is impossible to follow here the varying fortunes of the Italian states, which in 1507 were controlled by France, Spain, and Germany, with results that have lasted to our day; we are concerned with those events, and with the three great actors in them, so far only as they impinge on the personality of Machiavelli. He had several meetings with Louis XII of France, and his estimate of that monarch's character has already been alluded to. Machiavelli has painted Ferdinand of Aragon as the man who accomplished great things under the cloak of religion, but who in reality had no mercy, faith, humanity, or integrity; and who, had he allowed himself to be influenced by such motives, would have been ruined. The Emperor Maximilian was one of the most interesting men of the age, and his character has been drawn by many hands; but Machiavelli, who was an envoy at his court in 1507-8, reveals the secret of his many failures when he describes him as a secretive man, without force of character—ignoring the human agencies necessary to carry his schemes into effect, and never insisting on the fulfillment of his wishes.

The remaining years of Machiavelli's official career were filled with events arising out of the League of Cambrai, made in 1508 between the three great European powers already mentioned and the pope, with the object of crushing the Venetian Republic. This result was attained in the battle of Vaila, when Venice lost in one day all that she had won in eight hundred years. Florence had a difficult part to play during these events, complicated as they were by the feud which broke out between the pope and the French, because friendship with France had dictated the entire policy of the Republic. When, in 1511, Julius II finally formed the Holy League against France, and with the assistance of the Swiss drove the French out of Italy, Florence lay at the mercy of the Pope, and had to submit to his terms, one of which was that the Medici should be restored. The return of the Medici to Florence on 1st September 1512, and the consequent fall of the Republic, was the signal for the dismissal of Machiavelli and his friends, and thus put an end to his public career, for, as we have seen, he died without regaining office.

LITERATURE AND DEATH — Aet. 43-58—1512-27

On the return of the Medici, Machiavelli, who for a few weeks had vainly hoped to retain his office under the new masters of Florence, was dismissed by decree dated 7th November 1512. Shortly after this he was accused of complicity in an abortive conspiracy against the Medici, imprisoned, and put to the question by torture. The new Medicean people, Leo X, procured his release, and he retired to his small property at San Casciano, near Florence, where he devoted himself to literature. In a letter to Francesco Vettori, dated 13th December 1513, he has left a very interesting description of his life at this period, which elucidates his methods and his motives in writing "The Prince." After describing his daily occupations with his family and neighbours, he writes: "The evening being come, I return home and go to my study; at the entrance I pull off my peasant-clothes, covered with dust and dirt, and put on my noble court dress, and thus becomingly re-clothed I pass into the ancient courts of the men of old, where, being lovingly received by them, I am fed with that food which is mine alone; where I do not hesitate to speak with them, and to ask for the reason of their actions, and they in their benignity answer me; and for four hours I feel no weariness, I forget every trouble, poverty does not dismay, death does not terrify me; I am possessed entirely by those great men. And because Dante says:

Knowledge doth come of learning well retained,
Unfruitful else,

I have noted down what I have gained from their conversation, and have composed a small work on 'Principalities,' where I pour myself out as fully as I can in meditation on the subject, discussing what a principality is, what kinds there are, how they can be acquired, how they can be kept, why they are lost: and if any of my fancies ever pleased you, this ought not to displease you: and to a prince, especially to a new one, it should be welcome: therefore I dedicate it to his Magnificence Giuliano. Filippo Casavecchio has seen it; he will be able to tell you what is in it, and of the discourses I have had with him; nevertheless, I am still enriching and polishing it."

The "little book" suffered many vicissitudes before attaining the form in which it has reached us. Various mental influences were at work during its composition; its title and patron were changed; and for some unknown reason it was finally dedicated to Lorenzo de' Medici. Although Machiavelli discussed with Casavecchio whether it should be sent or presented in person to the patron, there is no evidence that Lorenzo ever received or even read it: he certainly never gave Machiavelli any employment. Although it was plagiarized during Machiavelli's lifetime, "The Prince" was never published by him and its text is still disputable.

Machiavelli concludes his letter to Vettori thus: "And as to this little thing [his book], when it has been read it will be seen that during the fifteen years I have given to the study of statecraft I have neither slept nor idled; and men ought ever to desire to be served by one who has reaped experience at the expense of others. And of my loyalty none could doubt, because having always kept faith I could not now learn how to break it; for he who has been faithful and honest, as I have, cannot change his nature; and my poverty is a witness to my honesty."

Before Machiavelli had got "The Prince" off his hands he commenced his "Discourse on the First Decade of Titus Livius," which should be read concurrently with "The Prince." These and several minor works occupied him until the year 1518, when he accepted a small commission to look after the affairs of some Florentine merchants at Genoa. In 1519 the Medicean rulers of Florence granted a few political concessions to her citizens, and Machiavelli with others was consulted upon a new constitution under which the Great Council was to be restored; but on one pretext or another it was not promulgated.

In 1520 the Florentine merchants again had recourse to Machiavelli to settle their difficulties with Lucca, but this year was chiefly remarkable for his re-entry into Florentine literary society, where he was much sought after, and also for the production of his "Art of War." It was in the same year that he received a commission at the instance of Cardinal de' Medici to write the "History of Florence," a task which occupied him until 1525. His return to popular favour may have determined the Medici to give him this employment, for an old writer observes that "an able statesman out of work, like a huge whale, will endeavour to overturn the ship unless he has an empty cask to play with."

When the "History of Florence" was finished, Machiavelli took it to Rome for presentation to his patron, Giuliano de' Medici, who had in the meanwhile become pope under the title of Clement VII. It is somewhat remarkable that, as, in 1513, Machiavelli had written "The Prince" for the instruction of the Medici after they had just regained power in Florence, so, in 1525, he dedicated the "History of Florence" to the head of the family when its ruin was now at hand. In that year the battle of Pavia destroyed the French rule in Italy, and left Francis I a prisoner in the hands of his great rival, Charles V. This was followed by the sack of Rome, upon the news of which the popular party at Florence threw off the yoke of the Medici, who were once more banished.

Machiavelli was absent from Florence at this time, but hastened his return, hoping to secure his former office of secretary to the "Ten of Liberty and Peace." Unhappily he was taken ill soon after he reached Florence, where he died on 22nd June 1527.

THE MAN AND HIS WORKS

No one can say where the bones of Machiavelli rest, but modern Florence has decreed him a stately cenotaph in Santa Croce, by the side of her most famous sons; recognizing that, whatever other nations may have found in his works, Italy found in them the idea of her unity and the germs of her renaissance among the nations of Europe. Whilst it is idle to protest against the world-wide and evil signification of his name, it may be pointed out that the harsh construction of his doctrine which this sinister reputation implies was unknown to his own day, and that the researches of recent times have enabled us to interpret him more reasonably. It is due to these inquiries that the shape of an "unholy necromancer," which so long haunted men's vision, has begun to fade.

Machiavelli was undoubtedly a man of great observation, acuteness, and industry; noting with appreciative eye whatever passed before him, and with his supreme literary gift turning it to account in his enforced retirement from affairs. He does not present himself, nor is he depicted by his contemporaries, as a type of that rare combination, the successful statesman and author, for he appears to have been only moderately prosperous in his several embassies and political employments. He was misled by Catherina Sforza, ignored by Louis XII, overawed by Cesare Borgia; several of his embassies were quite barren of results; his attempts to fortify Florence failed, and the soldiery that he raised astonished everybody by their cowardice. In the conduct of his own affairs he was timid and time-serving; he dared not appear by the side of Soderini, to whom he owed so much, for fear of compromising himself; his connection with the Medici was open to suspicion, and Giuliano appears to have recognized his real forte when he set him to write the "History of Florence," rather than employ him in the state. And it is on the literary side of his character, and there alone that we find no weakness and no failure.

Although the light of almost four centuries has been focused on "The Prince," its problems are still debatable and interesting, because they are the eternal problems between the ruled and their rulers. Such as they are, its ethics are those of Machiavelli's contemporaries; yet they cannot be said to be out of date so long as the governments of Europe rely on material rather than on moral forces. Its historical incidents and personages become interesting by reason of the uses which Machiavelli makes of them to illustrate his theories of government and conduct.

Leaving out of consideration those maxims of state which still furnish some European and eastern statesmen with principles of action, "The Prince" is bestrewn with truths that can be proved at every turn. Men are still the dupes of their simplicity and greed, as they were in the days of Alexander VI. The cloak of religion still conceals the vices which Machiavelli laid bare in the character of Ferdinand of Aragon. Men will not look at things as they really are, but as they wish them to be—and are ruined. In politics there are no perfectly safe courses; prudence consists in choosing the least dangerous ones. Then—to pass to a higher plane— Machiavelli reiterates that, although crimes may win an empire, they do not win glory. Necessary wars are just wars, and the arms of a nation are hallowed when it has no other resource but to fight.

It is the cry of a far later day than Machiavelli's that government should be elevated into a living moral force, capable of inspiring the people with a just recognition of the fundamental principles of society; to this "high argument" "The Prince" contributes but little. Machiavelli always refused to write either of men or of governments otherwise than as he found them, and he writes with such skill and insight that his work is of abiding value. But what invests "The Prince" with more than a merely artistic or historical interest is the incontrovertible truth that it deals with the great principles which still guide nations and rulers in their relationship with each other and their neighbours.

In translating "The Prince" my aim has been to achieve at all costs an exact literal rendering of the original, rather than a fluent paraphrase adapted to the modern notions of style and expression. Machiavelli was no facile phrasemonger; the conditions under which he wrote obliged him to weigh every word; his themes were lofty, his substance grave, his manner nobly plain and serious. "Quis eo fuit unquam in partiundis rebus, in definiendis, in explanandis pressior?" In "The Prince," it may be truly said, there is reason assignable, not only for every word, but for the position of every word. To an Englishman of Shakespeare's time the translation of such a treatise was in some ways a comparatively easy task, for in those times the genius of the English more nearly resembled that of the Italian language; to the Englishman of today it is not so simple. To take a single example: the word "intrattenere," employed by Machiavelli to indicate the policy adopted by the Roman Senate towards the weaker states of Greece, would by an Elizabethan be correctly rendered "entertain," and every contemporary reader would understand what was meant by saying that "Rome entertained the Aetolians and the Achaeans without augmenting their power." But today such a phrase would seem obsolete and ambiguous, if not unmeaning: we are compelled to say that "Rome maintained friendly relations with the Aetolians," etc., using four words to do the work of one. I have tried to preserve the pithy brevity of the Italian so far as was consistent with an absolute fidelity to the sense. If the result be an occasional asperity I can only hope that the reader, in his eagerness to reach the author's meaning, may overlook the roughness of the road that leads him to it.

The following is a list of the works of Machiavelli:

Principal works. Discorso sopra le cose di Pisa, 1499; Del modo di trattare i popoli della Valdichiana ribellati, 1502; Del modo tenuto dal duca Valentino nell' ammazzare Vitellozzo Vitelli, Oliverotto da Fermo, etc., 1502; Discorso sopra la provisione del danaro, 1502; Decennale primo (poem in terza rima), 1506; Ritratti delle cose dell' Alemagna, 1508-12; Decennale secondo, 1509; Ritratti delle cose di Francia, 1510; Discorsi sopra la prima deca di T. Livio, 3 vols., 1512-17; Il Principe, 1513; Andria, comedy translated from Terence, 1513 (?); Mandragola, prose comedy in five acts, with prologue in verse, 1513; Della lingua (dialogue), 1514; Clizia, comedy in prose, 1515 (?); Belfagor arcidiavolo (novel), 1515; Asino d'oro (poem in terza rima), 1517; Dell' arte della guerra, 1519-20; Discorso sopra il riformare lo stato di Firenze, 1520; Sommario delle cose della citta di Lucca, 1520; Vita di Castruccio Castracani da Lucca, 1520; Istorie fiorentine, 8 books, 1521-5; Frammenti storici, 1525.

Other poems include Sonetti, Canzoni, Ottave, and Canti carnascialeschi.

Editions. Aldo, Venice, 1546; della Tertina, 1550; Cambiagi, Florence, 6 vols., 1782-5; dei Classici, Milan, 10 1813; Silvestri, 9 vols., 1820-2; Passerini, Fanfani, Milanesi, 6 vols. only published, 1873-7.

Minor works. Ed. F. L. Polidori, 1852; Lettere familiari, ed. E. Alvisi, 1883, 2 editions, one with excisions; Credited Writings, ed. G. Canestrini, 1857; Letters to F. Vettori, see A. Ridolfi, Pensieri intorno allo scopo di N. Machiavelli nel libro Il Principe, etc.; D. Ferrara, The Private Correspondence of Nicolo Machiavelli, 1929.

DEDICATION

To the Magnificent Lorenzo Di Piero De' Medici:

Those who strive to obtain the good graces of a prince are accustomed to come before him with such things as they hold most precious, or in which they see him take most delight; whence one often sees horses, arms, cloth of gold, precious stones, and similar ornaments presented to princes, worthy of their greatness.

Desiring therefore to present myself to your Magnificence with some testimony of my devotion towards you, I have not found among my possessions anything which I hold more dear than, or value so much as, the knowledge of the actions of great men, acquired by long experience in contemporary affairs, and a continual study of antiquity; which, having reflected upon it with great and prolonged diligence, I now send, digested into a little volume, to your Magnificence.

And although I may consider this work unworthy of your countenance, nevertheless I trust much to your benignity that it may be acceptable, seeing that it is not possible for me to make a better gift than to offer you the opportunity of understanding in the shortest time all that I have learnt in so many years, and with so many troubles and dangers; which work I have not embellished with swelling or magnificent words, nor stuffed with rounded periods, nor with any extrinsic allurements or adornments whatever, with which so many are accustomed to embellish their works; for I have wished either that no honour should be given it, or else that the truth of the matter and the weightiness of the theme shall make it acceptable.

Nor do I hold with those who regard it as a presumption if a man of low and humble condition dare to discuss and settle the concerns of princes; because, just as those who draw landscapes place themselves below in the plain to contemplate the nature of the mountains and of lofty places, and in order to contemplate the plains place themselves upon high mountains, even so to understand the nature of the people it needs to be a prince, and to understand that of princes it needs to be of the people.

Take then, your Magnificence, this little gift in the spirit in which I send it; wherein, if it be diligently read and considered by you, you will learn my extreme desire that you should attain that greatness which fortune and your other attributes promise. And if your Magnificence from the summit of your greatness will sometimes turn your eyes to these lower regions, you will see how unmeritedly I suffer a great and continued malignity of fortune.

CHAPTER I — HOW MANY KINDS OF PRINCIPALITIES THERE ARE, AND BY WHAT MEANS THEY ARE ACQUIRED

All states, all powers, that have held and hold rule over men have been and are either republics or principalities.

Principalities are either hereditary, in which the family has been long established; or they are new.

The new are either entirely new, as was Milan to Francesco Sforza, or they are, as it were, members annexed to the hereditary state of the prince who has acquired them, as was the kingdom of Naples to that of the King of Spain.

Such dominions thus acquired are either accustomed to live under a prince, or to live in freedom; and are acquired either by the arms of the prince himself, or of others, or else by fortune or by ability.

CHAPTER II — CONCERNING HEREDITARY PRINCIPALITIES

I will leave out all discussion on republics, inasmuch as in another place I have written of them at length, and will address myself only to principalities. In doing so I will keep to the order indicated above, and discuss how such principalities are to be ruled and preserved.

I say at once there are fewer difficulties in holding hereditary states, and those long accustomed to the family of their prince, than new ones; for it is sufficient only not to transgress the customs of his ancestors, and to deal prudently with circumstances as they arise, for a prince of average powers to maintain himself in his state, unless he be deprived of it by some extraordinary and excessive force; and if he should be so deprived of it, whenever anything sinister happens to the usurper, he will regain it.

We have in Italy, for example, the Duke of Ferrara, who could not have withstood the attacks of the Venetians in '84, nor those of Pope Julius in '10, unless he had been long established in his dominions. For the hereditary prince has less cause and less necessity to offend; hence it happens that he will be more loved; and unless extraordinary vices cause him to be hated, it is reasonable to expect that his subjects will be naturally well disposed towards him; and in the antiquity and duration of his rule the memories and motives that make for change are lost, for one change always leaves the toothing for another.

CHAPTER III — CONCERNING MIXED PRINCIPALITIES

But the difficulties occur in a new principality. And firstly, if it be not entirely new, but is, as it were, a member of a state which, taken collectively, may be called composite, the changes arise chiefly from an inherent difficulty which there is in all new principalities; for men change their rulers willingly, hoping to better themselves, and this hope induces them to take up arms against him who rules: wherein they are deceived, because they afterwards find by experience they have gone from bad to worse. This follows also on another natural and common necessity, which always causes a new prince to burden those who have submitted to him with his soldiery and with infinite other hardships which he must put upon his new acquisition.

In this way you have enemies in all those whom you have injured in seizing that principality, and you are not able to keep those friends who put you there because of your not being able to satisfy them in the way they expected, and you cannot take strong measures against them, feeling bound to them. For, although one may be very strong in armed forces, yet in entering a province one has always need of the goodwill of the natives. For these reasons Louis the Twelfth, King of France, quickly occupied Milan, and as quickly lost it; and to turn him out the first time it only needed Lodovico's own forces; because those who had opened the gates to him, finding themselves deceived in their hopes of future benefit, would not endure the ill-treatment of the new prince. It is very true that, after acquiring rebellious provinces a second time, they are not so lightly lost afterwards, because the prince, with little reluctance, takes the opportunity of the rebellion to punish the delinquents, to clear out the suspects, and to strengthen himself in the weakest places. Thus to cause France to lose Milan the first time it was enough for the Duke Lodovico[1] to raise insurrections on the borders; but to cause him to lose it a second time it was necessary to bring the whole world against him, and that his armies should be defeated and driven out of Italy; which followed from the causes above mentioned.

Nevertheless Milan was taken from France both the first and the second time. The general reasons for the first have been discussed; it remains to name those for the second, and to see what resources he had, and what any one in his situation would have had for maintaining himself more securely in his acquisition than did the King of France.

Now I say that those dominions which, when acquired, are added to an ancient state by him who acquires them, are either of the same country and language, or they are not. When they are, it is easier to hold them, especially when they have not been accustomed to self-government; and to hold them securely it is enough to have destroyed the family of the prince who was ruling them; because the two peoples, preserving in other things the old conditions, and not being unlike in customs, will live quietly together, as one has seen in Brittany, Burgundy, Gascony, and Normandy, which have been bound to France for so long a time: and, although there may be some difference in language, nevertheless the customs are alike, and the people will easily be able to get on amongst themselves. He who has annexed them, if he wishes to hold them, has only to bear in mind two considerations: the one, that the family of their former lord is extinguished; the other, that neither their laws nor their taxes are altered, so that in a very short time they will become entirely one body with the old principality.

But when states are acquired in a country differing in language, customs, or laws, there are difficulties, and good fortune and great energy are needed to hold them, and one of the greatest and most real helps would be that he who has acquired them should go and reside there. This would make his position more secure and durable, as it has made that of the Turk in Greece, who, notwithstanding all the other measures taken by him for holding that state, if he had not settled there, would not have been able to keep it. Because, if one is on the spot, disorders are seen as they spring up, and one can quickly remedy them; but if one is not at hand, they are heard of only when they are great, and then one can no longer remedy them. Besides this, the country is not pillaged by your officials; the subjects are satisfied by prompt recourse to the prince; thus, wishing to be good, they have more cause to love him, and wishing to be otherwise, to fear him. He who would attack that state from the outside must have the utmost caution; as long as the prince resides there it can only be wrested from him with the greatest difficulty.

The other and better course is to send colonies to one or two places, which may be as keys to that state, for it is necessary either to do this or else to keep there a great number of cavalry and infantry. A prince does not spend much on colonies, for with little or no expense he can send them out and keep them there, and he offends a minority only of the citizens from whom he takes lands and houses to give them to the new inhabitants; and those whom he offends, remaining poor and scattered, are never able to injure him; whilst the rest being uninjured are easily kept quiet, and at the same time are anxious not to err for fear it should happen to them as it has to those who have been despoiled. In conclusion, I say that these colonies are not costly, they are more faithful, they injure less, and the injured, as has been said, being poor and scattered, cannot hurt. Upon this, one has to remark that men ought either to be well treated or crushed, because they can avenge

---

1 Duke Lodovico was Lodovico Moro, a son of Francesco Sforza, who married Beatrice d'Este. He ruled over Milan from 1494 to 1500, and died in 1510

themselves of lighter injuries, of more serious ones they cannot; therefore the injury that is to be done to a man ought to be of such a kind that one does not stand in fear of revenge.

But in maintaining armed men there in place of colonies one spends much more, having to consume on the garrison all the income from the state, so that the acquisition turns into a loss, and many more are exasperated, because the whole state is injured; through the shifting of the garrison up and down all become acquainted with hardship, and all become hostile, and they are enemies who, whilst beaten on their own ground, are yet able to do hurt. For every reason, therefore, such guards are as useless as a colony is useful.

Again, the prince who holds a country differing in the above respects ought to make himself the head and defender of his less powerful neighbours, and to weaken the more powerful amongst them, taking care that no foreigner as powerful as himself shall, by any accident, get a footing there; for it will always happen that such a one will be introduced by those who are discontented, either through excess of ambition or through fear, as one has seen already. The Romans were brought into Greece by the Aetolians, and in every other country where they obtained a footing they were brought in by the inhabitants. And the usual course of affairs is that, as soon as a powerful foreigner enters a country, all the subject states are drawn to him, moved by the hatred which they feel against the ruling power. So that in respect to those subject states he has not to take any trouble to gain them over to himself, for the whole of them quickly rally to the state which he has acquired there. He has only to take care that they do not get hold of too much power and too much authority, and then with his own forces, and with their goodwill, he can easily keep down the more powerful of them, so as to remain entirely master in the country. And he who does not properly manage this business will soon lose what he has acquired, and whilst he does hold it he will have endless difficulties and troubles.

The Romans, in the countries which they annexed, observed closely these measures; they sent colonies and maintained friendly relations with[2] the minor powers, without increasing their strength; they kept down the greater, and did not allow any strong foreign powers to gain authority. Greece appears to me sufficient for an example. The Achaeans and Aetolians were kept friendly by them, the kingdom of Macedonia was humbled, Antiochus was driven out; yet the merits of the Achaeans and Aetolians never secured for them permission to increase their power, nor did the persuasions of Philip ever induce the Romans to be his friends without first humbling him, nor did the influence of Antiochus make them agree that he should retain any lordship over the country. Because the Romans did in these instances what all prudent princes ought to do, who have to regard not only present troubles, but also future ones, for which they must prepare with every energy, because, when foreseen, it is easy to remedy them; but if you wait until they approach, the medicine is no longer in time because the malady has become incurable; for it happens in this, as the physicians say it happens in hectic fever, that in the beginning of the malady it is easy to cure but difficult to detect, but in the course of time, not having been either detected or treated in the beginning, it becomes easy to detect but difficult to cure. This it happens in affairs of state, for when the evils that arise have been foreseen (which it is only given to a wise man to see), they can be quickly redressed, but when, through not having been foreseen, they have been permitted to grow in a way that every one can see them, there is no longer a remedy. Therefore, the Romans, foreseeing troubles, dealt with them at once, and, even to avoid a war, would not let them come to a head, for they knew that war is not to be avoided, but is only to be put off to the advantage of others; moreover they wished to fight with Philip and Antiochus in Greece so as not to have to do it in Italy; they could have avoided both, but this they did not wish; nor did that ever please them which is for ever in the mouths of the wise ones of our time: Let us enjoy the benefits of the time—but rather the benefits of their own valour and prudence, for time drives everything before it, and is able to bring with it good as well as evil, and evil as well as good.

---

2 See remark in the introduction on the word "intrattenere."

But let us turn to France and inquire whether she has done any of the things mentioned. I will speak of Louis [3] (and not of Charles) [4] as the one whose conduct is the better to be observed, he having held possession of Italy for the longest period; and you will see that he has done the opposite to those things which ought to be done to retain a state composed of diverse elements.

King Louis was brought into Italy by the ambition of the Venetians, who desired to obtain half the state of Lombardy by his intervention. I will not blame the course taken by the king, because, wishing to get a foothold in Italy, and having no friends there—seeing rather that every door was shut to him owing to the conduct of Charles—he was forced to accept those friendships which he could get, and he would have succeeded very quickly in his design if in other matters he had not made some mistakes. The king, however, having acquired Lombardy, regained at once the authority which Charles had lost: Genoa yielded; the Florentines became his friends; the Marquess of Mantua, the Duke of Ferrara, the Bentivogli, my lady of Forli, the Lords of Faenza, of Pesaro, of Rimini, of Camerino, of Piombino, the Lucchese, the Pisans, the Sienese—everybody made advances to him to become his friend. Then could the Venetians realize the rashness of the course taken by them, which, in order that they might secure two towns in Lombardy, had made the king master of two-thirds of Italy.

Let any one now consider with what little difficulty the king could have maintained his position in Italy had he observed the rules above laid down, and kept all his friends secure and protected; for although they were numerous they were both weak and timid, some afraid of the Church, some of the Venetians, and thus they would always have been forced to stand in with him, and by their means he could easily have made himself secure against those who remained powerful. But he was no sooner in Milan than he did the contrary by assisting Pope Alexander to occupy the Romagna. It never occurred to him that by this action he was weakening himself, depriving himself of friends and of those who had thrown themselves into his lap, whilst he aggrandized the Church by adding much temporal power to the spiritual, thus giving it greater authority. And having committed this prime error, he was obliged to follow it up, so much so that, to put an end to the ambition of Alexander, and to prevent his becoming the master of Tuscany, he was himself forced to come into Italy.

And as if it were not enough to have aggrandized the Church, and deprived himself of friends, he, wishing to have the kingdom of Naples, divides it with the King of Spain, and where he was the prime arbiter in Italy he takes an associate, so that the ambitious of that country and the malcontents of his own should have somewhere to shelter; and whereas he could have left in the kingdom his own pensioner as king, he drove him out, to put one there who was able to drive him, Louis, out in turn.

The wish to acquire is in truth very natural and common, and men always do so when they can, and for this they will be praised not blamed; but when they cannot do so, yet wish to do so by any means, then there is folly and blame. Therefore, if France could have attacked Naples with her own forces, she ought to have done so; if she could not, then she ought not to have divided it. And if the partition which she made with the Venetians in Lombardy was justified by the excuse that by it she got a foothold in Italy, this other partition merited blame, for it had not the excuse of that necessity.

Therefore Louis made these five errors: he destroyed the minor powers, he increased the strength of one of the greater powers in Italy, he brought in a foreign power, he did not settle in the country, he did not send colonies. Which errors, had he lived, were not enough to injure him had he not made a sixth by taking away their dominions from the Venetians; because, had he not aggrandized the Church, nor brought Spain into Italy, it would have been very reasonable and necessary to humble them; but having first taken these steps, he ought never to have consented to their ruin, for they, being powerful, would always have kept off others from

---

3 Louis XII, King of France, "The Father of the People," born 1462, died 1515.
4 Charles VIII, King of France, born 1470, died 1498.

designs on Lombardy, to which the Venetians would never have consented except to become masters themselves there; also because the others would not wish to take Lombardy from France in order to give it to the Venetians, and to run counter to both they would not have had the courage.

And if any one should say: "King Louis yielded the Romagna to Alexander and the kingdom to Spain to avoid war," I answer for the reasons given above that a blunder ought never to be perpetrated to avoid war, because it is not to be avoided, but is only deferred to your disadvantage. And if another should allege the pledge which the king had given to the Pope that he would assist him in the enterprise, in exchange for the dissolution of his marriage[5] and for the cap to Rouen[6], to that I reply what I shall write later on concerning the faith of princes, and how it ought to be kept.

Thus King Louis lost Lombardy by not having followed any of the conditions observed by those who have taken possession of countries and wished to retain them. Nor is there any miracle in this, but much that is reasonable and quite natural. And on these matters I spoke at Nantes with Rouen, when Valentino, as Cesare Borgia, the son of Pope Alexander, was usually called, occupied the Romagna, and on Cardinal Rouen observing to me that the Italians did not understand war, I replied to him that the French did not understand statecraft, meaning that otherwise they would not have allowed the Church to reach such greatness. And in fact is has been seen that the greatness of the Church and of Spain in Italy has been caused by France, and her ruin may be attributed to them. From this a general rule is drawn which never or rarely fails: that he who is the cause of another becoming powerful is ruined; because that predominancy has been brought about either by astuteness or else by force, and both are distrusted by him who has been raised to power.

CHAPTER IV — WHY THE KINGDOM OF DARIUS, CONQUERED BY ALEXANDER, DID NOT REBEL AGAINST THE SUCCESSORS OF ALEXANDER AT HIS DEATH

Considering the difficulties which men have had to hold to a newly acquired state, some might wonder how, seeing that Alexander the Great became the master of Asia in a few years, and died whilst it was scarcely settled (whence it might appear reasonable that the whole empire would have rebelled), nevertheless his successors maintained themselves, and had to meet no other difficulty than that which arose among themselves from their own ambitions.

I answer that the principalities of which one has record are found to be governed in two different ways; either by a prince, with a body of servants, who assist him to govern the kingdom as ministers by his favour and permission; or by a prince and barons, who hold that dignity by antiquity of blood and not by the grace of the prince. Such barons have states and their own subjects, who recognize them as lords and hold them in natural affection. Those states that are governed by a prince and his servants hold their prince in more consideration, because in all the country there is no one who is recognized as superior to him, and if they yield obedience to another they do it as to a minister and official, and they do not bear him any particular affection.

The examples of these two governments in our time are the Turk and the King of France. The entire monarchy of the Turk is governed by one lord, the others are his servants; and, dividing his kingdom into sanjaks, he sends there different administrators, and shifts and changes them as he chooses. But the King of France is placed in the midst of an ancient body of lords, acknowledged by their own subjects, and beloved by them; they have their own prerogatives, nor can the king take these away except at his peril. Therefore, he who considers both of these states will recognize great difficulties in seizing the state of the Turk, but, once it is conquered, great ease in holding it. The causes of the difficulties in seizing the kingdom of the Turk are

---

5 Louis XII divorced his wife, Jeanne, daughter of Louis XI, and married in 1499 Anne of Brittany, widow of Charles VIII, in order to retain the Duchy of Brittany for the crown.
6 The Archbishop of Rouen. He was Georges d'Amboise, created a cardinal by Alexander VI. Born 1460, died 1510.

that the usurper cannot be called in by the princes of the kingdom, nor can he hope to be assisted in his designs by the revolt of those whom the lord has around him. This arises from the reasons given above; for his ministers, being all slaves and bondmen, can only be corrupted with great difficulty, and one can expect little advantage from them when they have been corrupted, as they cannot carry the people with them, for the reasons assigned. Hence, he who attacks the Turk must bear in mind that he will find him united, and he will have to rely more on his own strength than on the revolt of others; but, if once the Turk has been conquered, and routed in the field in such a way that he cannot replace his armies, there is nothing to fear but the family of this prince, and, this being exterminated, there remains no one to fear, the others having no credit with the people; and as the conqueror did not rely on them before his victory, so he ought not to fear them after it.

The contrary happens in kingdoms governed like that of France, because one can easily enter there by gaining over some baron of the kingdom, for one always finds malcontents and such as desire a change. Such men, for the reasons given, can open the way into the state and render the victory easy; but if you wish to hold it afterwards, you meet with infinite difficulties, both from those who have assisted you and from those you have crushed. Nor is it enough for you to have exterminated the family of the prince, because the lords that remain make themselves the heads of fresh movements against you, and as you are unable either to satisfy or exterminate them, that state is lost whenever time brings the opportunity.

Now if you will consider what was the nature of the government of Darius, you will find it similar to the kingdom of the Turk, and therefore it was only necessary for Alexander, first to overthrow him in the field, and then to take the country from him. After which victory, Darius being killed, the state remained secure to Alexander, for the above reasons. And if his successors had been united they would have enjoyed it securely and at their ease, for there were no tumults raised in the kingdom except those they provoked themselves.

But it is impossible to hold with such tranquility states constituted like that of France. Hence arose those frequent rebellions against the Romans in Spain, France, and Greece, owing to the many principalities there were in these states, of which, as long as the memory of them endured, the Romans always held an insecure possession; but with the power and long continuance of the empire the memory of them passed away, and the Romans then became secure possessors. And when fighting afterwards amongst themselves, each one was able to attach to himself his own parts of the country, according to the authority he had assumed there; and the family of the former lord being exterminated, none other than the Romans were acknowledged.

When these things are remembered no one will marvel at the ease with which Alexander held the Empire of Asia, or at the difficulties which others have had to keep an acquisition, such as Pyrrhus and many more; this is not occasioned by the little or abundance of ability in the conqueror, but by the want of uniformity in the subject state.

CHAPTER V — CONCERNING THE WAY TO GOVERN CITIES OR PRINCIPALITIES WHICH LIVED UNDER THEIR OWN LAWS BEFORE THEY WERE ANNEXED

Whenever those states which have been acquired as stated have been accustomed to live under their own laws and in freedom, there are three courses for those who wish to hold them: the first is to ruin them, the next is to reside there in person, the third is to permit them to live under their own laws, drawing a tribute, and establishing within it an oligarchy which will keep it friendly to you. Because such a government, being created by the prince, knows that it cannot stand without his friendship and interest, and does it utmost to support him; and therefore he who would keep a city accustomed to freedom will hold it more easily by the means of its own citizens than in any other way.

CHAPTER V — CONCERNING THE WAY TO GOVERN CITIES OR PRINCIPALITIES WHICH LIVED UNDER THEIR OWN LAWS BEFORE THEY WERE ANNEXED

There are, for example, the Spartans and the Romans. The Spartans held Athens and Thebes, establishing there an oligarchy; nevertheless they lost them. The Romans, in order to hold Capua, Carthage, and Numantia, dismantled them, and did not lose them. They wished to hold Greece as the Spartans held it, making it free and permitting its laws, and did not succeed. So to hold it they were compelled to dismantle many cities in the country, for in truth there is no safe way to retain them otherwise than by ruining them. And he who becomes master of a city accustomed to freedom and does not destroy it, may expect to be destroyed by it, for in rebellion it has always the watchword of liberty and its ancient privileges as a rallying point, which neither time nor benefits will ever cause it to forget. And whatever you may do or provide against, they never forget that name or their privileges unless they are disunited or dispersed, but at every chance they immediately rally to them, as Pisa after the hundred years she had been held in bondage by the Florentines.

But when cities or countries are accustomed to live under a prince, and his family is exterminated, they, being on the one hand accustomed to obey and on the other hand not having the old prince, cannot agree in making one from amongst themselves, and they do not know how to govern themselves. For this reason they are very slow to take up arms, and a prince can gain them to himself and secure them much more easily. But in republics there is more vitality, greater hatred, and more desire for vengeance, which will never permit them to allow the memory of their former liberty to rest; so that the safest way is to destroy them or to reside there.

CHAPTER VI — CONCERNING NEW PRINCIPALITIES WHICH ARE ACQUIRED BY ONE'S OWN ARMS AND ABILITY

Let no one be surprised if, in speaking of entirely new principalities as I shall do, I adduce the highest examples both of prince and of state; because men, walking almost always in paths beaten by others, and following by imitation their deeds, are yet unable to keep entirely to the ways of others or attain to the power of those they imitate. A wise man ought always to follow the paths beaten by great men, and to imitate those who have been supreme, so that if his ability does not equal theirs, at least it will savour of it. Let him act like the clever archers who, designing to hit the mark which yet appears too far distant, and knowing the limits to which the strength of their bow attains, take aim much higher than the mark, not to reach by their strength or arrow to so great a height, but to be able with the aid of so high an aim to hit the mark they wish to reach.

I say, therefore, that in entirely new principalities, where there is a new prince, more or less difficulty is found in keeping them, accordingly as there is more or less ability in him who has acquired the state. Now, as the fact of becoming a prince from a private station presupposes either ability or fortune, it is clear that one or other of these things will mitigate in some degree many difficulties. Nevertheless, he who has relied least on fortune is established the strongest. Further, it facilitates matters when the prince, having no other state, is compelled to reside there in person.

But to come to those who, by their own ability and not through fortune, have risen to be princes, I say that Moses, Cyrus, Romulus, Theseus, and such like are the most excellent examples. And although one may not discuss Moses, he having been a mere executor of the will of God, yet he ought to be admired, if only for that favour which made him worthy to speak with God. But in considering Cyrus and others who have acquired or founded kingdoms, all will be found admirable; and if their particular deeds and conduct shall be considered, they will not be found inferior to those of Moses, although he had so great a preceptor. And in examining their actions and lives one cannot see that they owed anything to fortune beyond opportunity, which brought them the material to mould into the form which seemed best to them. Without that opportunity their powers of mind would have been extinguished, and without those powers the opportunity would have come in vain. It was necessary, therefore, to Moses that he should find the people of Israel in Egypt enslaved and oppressed by the Egyptians, in order that they should be disposed to follow him so as to be delivered out of bondage. It was necessary that Romulus should not remain in Alba, and that he should be abandoned at his birth, in order that he should become King of Rome and founder of the fatherland. It was necessary that Cyrus should find the Persians discontented with the government of the Medes, and the Medes soft and effeminate through their long peace. Theseus could not have shown his ability had he not found the Athenians dispersed. These opportunities, therefore, made those men fortunate, and their high ability enabled them to recognize the opportunity whereby their country was ennobled and made famous.

Those who by valorous ways become princes, like these men, acquire a principality with difficulty, but they keep it with ease. The difficulties they have in acquiring it rise in part from the new rules and methods which they are forced to introduce to establish their government and its security. And it ought to be remembered that there is nothing more difficult to take in hand, more perilous to conduct, or more uncertain in its success, then to take the lead in the introduction of a new order of things. Because the innovator has for enemies all those who have done well under the old conditions, and lukewarm defenders in those who may do well under the new. This coolness arises partly from fear of the opponents, who have the laws on their side, and partly from the incredulity of men, who do not readily believe in new things until they have had a long experience of them. Thus it happens that whenever those who are hostile have the opportunity to attack they do it like partisans, whilst the others defend lukewarmly, in such wise that the prince is endangered along with them.

It is necessary, therefore, if we desire to discuss this matter thoroughly, to inquire whether these innovators can rely on themselves or have to depend on others: that is to say, whether, to consummate their enterprise, have they to use prayers or can they use force? In the first instance they always succeed badly, and never compass anything; but when they can rely on themselves and use force, then they are rarely endangered. Hence it is that all armed prophets have conquered, and the unarmed ones have been destroyed. Besides the reasons mentioned, the nature of the people is variable, and whilst it is easy to persuade them, it is difficult to fix them in that persuasion. And thus it is necessary to take such measures that, when they believe no longer, it may be possible to make them believe by force.

If Moses, Cyrus, Theseus, and Romulus had been unarmed they could not have enforced their constitutions for long—as happened in our time to Fra Girolamo Savonarola, who was ruined with his new order of things immediately the multitude believed in him no longer, and he had no means of keeping steadfast those who believed or of making the unbelievers to believe. Therefore such as these have great difficulties in consummating their enterprise, for all their dangers are in the ascent, yet with ability they will overcome them; but when these are overcome, and those who envied them their success are exterminated, they will begin to be respected, and they will continue afterwards powerful, secure, honoured, and happy.

To these great examples I wish to add a lesser one; still it bears some resemblance to them, and I wish it to suffice me for all of a like kind: it is Hiero the Syracusan[7]. This man rose from a private station to be Prince of Syracuse, nor did he, either, owe anything to fortune but opportunity; for the Syracusans, being oppressed, chose him for their captain, afterwards he was rewarded by being made their prince. He was of so great ability, even as a private citizen, that one who writes of him says he wanted nothing but a kingdom to be a king. This man abolished the old soldiery, organized the new, gave up old alliances, made new ones; and as he had his own soldiers and allies, on such foundations he was able to build any edifice: thus, whilst he had endured much trouble in acquiring, he had but little in keeping.

---

7 Hiero II, born about 307 B.C., died 216 B.C.

CHAPTER VII — CONCERNING NEW PRINCIPALITIES WHICH ARE ACQUIRED EITHER BY THE ARMS OF OTHERS OR BY GOOD FORTUNE

Those who solely by good fortune become princes from being private citizens have little trouble in rising, but much in keeping atop; they have not any difficulties on the way up, because they fly, but they have many when they reach the summit. Such are those to whom some state is given either for money or by the favour of him who bestows it; as happened to many in Greece, in the cities of Ionia and of the Hellespont, where princes were made by Darius, in order that they might hold the cities both for his security and his glory; as also were those emperors who, by the corruption of the soldiers, from being citizens came to empire. Such stand simply elevated upon the goodwill and the fortune of him who has elevated them—two most inconstant and unstable things. Neither have they the knowledge requisite for the position; because, unless they are men of great worth and ability, it is not reasonable to expect that they should know how to command, having always lived in a private condition; besides, they cannot hold it because they have not forces which they can keep friendly and faithful.

States that rise unexpectedly, then, like all other things in nature which are born and grow rapidly, cannot leave their foundations and correspondencies[8] fixed in such a way that the first storm will not overthrow them; unless, as is said, those who unexpectedly become princes are men of so much ability that they know they have to be prepared at once to hold that which fortune has thrown into their laps, and that those foundations, which others have laid BEFORE they became princes, they must lay AFTERWARDS.

Concerning these two methods of rising to be a prince by ability or fortune, I wish to adduce two examples within our own recollection, and these are Francesco Sforza[9] and Cesare Borgia. Francesco, by proper means and with great ability, from being a private person rose to be Duke of Milan, and that which he had acquired with a thousand anxieties he kept with little trouble. On the other hand, Cesare Borgia, called by the people Duke Valentino, acquired his state during the ascendancy of his father, and on its decline he lost it, notwithstanding that he had taken every measure and done all that ought to be done by a wise and able man to fix firmly his roots in the states which the arms and fortunes of others had bestowed on him.

Because, as is stated above, he who has not first laid his foundations may be able with great ability to lay them afterwards, but they will be laid with trouble to the architect and danger to the building. If, therefore, all the steps taken by the duke be considered, it will be seen that he laid solid foundations for his future power, and I do not consider it superfluous to discuss them, because I do not know what better precepts to give a new prince than the example of his actions; and if his dispositions were of no avail, that was not his fault, but the extraordinary and extreme malignity of fortune.

Alexander the Sixth, in wishing to aggrandize the duke, his son, had many immediate and prospective difficulties. Firstly, he did not see his way to make him master of any state that was not a state of the Church; and if he was willing to rob the Church he knew that the Duke of Milan and the Venetians would not consent, because Faenza and Rimini were already under the protection of the Venetians. Besides this, he saw the arms

8 "Le radici e corrispondenze," their roots (i.e. foundations) and correspondencies or relations with other states—a common meaning of "correspondence" and "correspondency" in the sixteenth and seventeenth centuries.
9 Francesco Sforza, born 1401, died 1466. He married Bianca Maria Visconti, a natural daughter of Filippo Visconti, the Duke of Milan, on whose death he procured his own elevation to the duchy. Machiavelli was the accredited agent of the Florentine Republic to Cesare Borgia (1478- 1507) during the transactions which led up to the assassinations of the Orsini and Vitelli at Sinigalia, and along with his letters to his chiefs in Florence he has left an account, written ten years before "The Prince," of the proceedings of the duke in his "Descritione del modo tenuto dal duca Valentino nello ammazzare Vitellozzo Vitelli," etc., a translation of which is appended to the present work.

of Italy, especially those by which he might have been assisted, in hands that would fear the aggrandizement of the Pope, namely, the Orsini and the Colonnesi and their following. It behooved him, therefore, to upset this state of affairs and embroil the powers, so as to make himself securely master of part of their states. This was easy for him to do, because he found the Venetians, moved by other reasons, inclined to bring back the French into Italy; he would not only not oppose this, but he would render it more easy by dissolving the former marriage of King Louis. Therefore the king came into Italy with the assistance of the Venetians and the consent of Alexander. He was no sooner in Milan than the Pope had soldiers from him for the attempt on the Romagna, which yielded to him on the reputation of the king. The duke, therefore, having acquired the Romagna and beaten the Colonnesi, while wishing to hold that and to advance further, was hindered by two things: the one, his forces did not appear loyal to him, the other, the goodwill of France: that is to say, he feared that the forces of the Orsini, which he was using, would not stand to him, that not only might they hinder him from winning more, but might themselves seize what he had won, and that the king might also do the same. Of the Orsini he had a warning when, after taking Faenza and attacking Bologna, he saw them go very unwillingly to that attack. And as to the king, he learned his mind when he himself, after taking the Duchy of Urbino, attacked Tuscany, and the king made him desist from that undertaking; hence the duke decided to depend no more upon the arms and the luck of others.

For the first thing he weakened the Orsini and Colonnesi parties in Rome, by gaining to himself all their adherents who were gentlemen, making them his gentlemen, giving them good pay, and, according to their rank, honouring them with office and command in such a way that in a few months all attachment to the factions was destroyed and turned entirely to the duke. After this he awaited an opportunity to crush the Orsini, having scattered the adherents of the Colonna house. This came to him soon and he used it well; for the Orsini, perceiving at length that the aggrandizement of the duke and the Church was ruin to them, called a meeting of the Magione in Perugia. From this sprung the rebellion at Urbino and the tumults in the Romagna, with endless dangers to the duke, all of which he overcame with the help of the French. Having restored his authority, not to leave it at risk by trusting either to the French or other outside forces, he had recourse to his wiles, and he knew so well how to conceal his mind that, by the mediation of Signor Pagolo—whom the duke did not fail to secure with all kinds of attention, giving him money, apparel, and horses—the Orsini were reconciled, so that their simplicity brought them into his power at Sinigalia[10]. Having exterminated the leaders, and turned their partisans into his friends, the duke laid sufficiently good foundations to his power, having all the Romagna and the Duchy of Urbino; and the people now beginning to appreciate their prosperity, he gained them all over to himself. And as this point is worthy of notice, and to be imitated by others, I am not willing to leave it out.

When the duke occupied the Romagna he found it under the rule of weak masters, who rather plundered their subjects than ruled them, and gave them more cause for disunion than for union, so that the country was full of robbery, quarrels, and every kind of violence; and so, wishing to bring back peace and obedience to authority, he considered it necessary to give it a good governor. Thereupon he promoted Messer Ramiro d'Orco[11], a swift and cruel man, to whom he gave the fullest power. This man in a short time restored peace and unity with the greatest success. Afterwards the duke considered that it was not advisable to confer such excessive authority, for he had no doubt but that he would become odious, so he set up a court of judgment in the country, under a most excellent president, wherein all cities had their advocates. And because he knew that the past severity had caused some hatred against himself, so, to clear himself in the minds of the people, and gain them entirely to himself, he desired to show that, if any cruelty had been practised, it had not

---

10 Sinigalia, 31st December 1502.
11 Ramiro d'Orco. Ramiro de Lorqua.

originated with him, but in the natural sternness of the minister. Under this pretence he took Ramiro, and one morning caused him to be executed and left on the piazza at Cesena with the block and a bloody knife at his side. The barbarity of this spectacle caused the people to be at once satisfied and dismayed.

But let us return whence we started. I say that the duke, finding himself now sufficiently powerful and partly secured from immediate dangers by having armed himself in his own way, and having in a great measure crushed those forces in his vicinity that could injure him if he wished to proceed with his conquest, had next to consider France, for he knew that the king, who too late was aware of his mistake, would not support him. And from this time he began to seek new alliances and to temporize with France in the expedition which she was making towards the kingdom of Naples against the Spaniards who were besieging Gaeta. It was his intention to secure himself against them, and this he would have quickly accomplished had Alexander lived.

Such was his line of action as to present affairs. But as to the future he had to fear, in the first place, that a new successor to the Church might not be friendly to him and might seek to take from him that which Alexander had given him, so he decided to act in four ways. Firstly, by exterminating the families of those lords whom he had despoiled, so as to take away that pretext from the Pope. Secondly, by winning to himself all the gentlemen of Rome, so as to be able to curb the Pope with their aid, as has been observed. Thirdly, by converting the college more to himself. Fourthly, by acquiring so much power before the Pope should die that he could by his own measures resist the first shock. Of these four things, at the death of Alexander, he had accomplished three. For he had killed as many of the dispossessed lords as he could lay hands on, and few had escaped; he had won over the Roman gentlemen, and he had the most numerous party in the college. And as to any fresh acquisition, he intended to become master of Tuscany, for he already possessed Perugia and Piombino, and Pisa was under his protection. And as he had no longer to study France (for the French were already driven out of the kingdom of Naples by the Spaniards, and in this way both were compelled to buy his goodwill), he pounced down upon Pisa. After this, Lucca and Siena yielded at once, partly through hatred and partly through fear of the Florentines; and the Florentines would have had no remedy had he continued to prosper, as he was prospering the year that Alexander died, for he had acquired so much power and reputation that he would have stood by himself, and no longer have depended on the luck and the forces of others, but solely on his own power and ability.

But Alexander died five years after he had first drawn the sword. He left the duke with the state of Romagna alone consolidated, with the rest in the air, between two most powerful hostile armies, and sick unto death. Yet there were in the duke such boldness and ability, and he knew so well how men are to be won or lost, and so firm were the foundations which in so short a time he had laid, that if he had not had those armies on his back, or if he had been in good health, he would have overcome all difficulties. And it is seen that his foundations were good, for the Romagna awaited him for more than a month. In Rome, although but half alive, he remained secure; and whilst the Baglioni, the Vitelli, and the Orsini might come to Rome, they could not effect anything against him. If he could not have made Pope him whom he wished, at least the one whom he did not wish would not have been elected. But if he had been in sound health at the death of Alexander[12], everything would have been different to him. On the day that Julius the Second[13] was elected, he told me that he had thought of everything that might occur at the death of his father, and had provided a remedy for all, except that he had never anticipated that, when the death did happen, he himself would be on the point to die.

When all the actions of the duke are recalled, I do not know how to blame him, but rather it appears to be, as I have said, that I ought to offer him for imitation to all those who, by the fortune or the arms of others, are raised to government. Because he, having a lofty spirit and far-reaching aims, could not have regulated his

---

12 Alexander VI died of fever, 18th August 1503.
13 Julius II was Giuliano della Rovere, Cardinal of San Pietro ad Vincula, born 1443, died 1513.

conduct otherwise, and only the shortness of the life of Alexander and his own sickness frustrated his designs. Therefore, he who considers it necessary to secure himself in his new principality, to win friends, to overcome either by force or fraud, to make himself beloved and feared by the people, to be followed and revered by the soldiers, to exterminate those who have power or reason to hurt him, to change the old order of things for new, to be severe and gracious, magnanimous and liberal, to destroy a disloyal soldiery and to create new, to maintain friendship with kings and princes in such a way that they must help him with zeal and offend with caution, cannot find a more lively example than the actions of this man.

Only can he be blamed for the election of Julius the Second, in whom he made a bad choice, because, as is said, not being able to elect a Pope to his own mind, he could have hindered any other from being elected Pope; and he ought never to have consented to the election of any cardinal whom he had injured or who had cause to fear him if they became pontiffs. For men injure either from fear or hatred. Those whom he had injured, amongst others, were San Pietro ad Vincula, Colonna, San Giorgio, and Ascanio[14]. The rest, in becoming Pope, had to fear him, Rouen and the Spaniards excepted; the latter from their relationship and obligations, the former from his influence, the kingdom of France having relations with him. Therefore, above everything, the duke ought to have created a Spaniard Pope, and, failing him, he ought to have consented to Rouen and not San Pietro ad Vincula. He who believes that new benefits will cause great personages to forget old injuries is deceived. Therefore, the duke erred in his choice, and it was the cause of his ultimate ruin.

CHAPTER VIII — CONCERNING THOSE WHO HAVE OBTAINED A PRINCIPALITY BY WICKEDNESS

Although a prince may rise from a private station in two ways, neither of which can be entirely attributed to fortune or genius, yet it is manifest to me that I must not be silent on them, although one could be more copiously treated when I discuss republics. These methods are when, either by some wicked or nefarious ways, one ascends to the principality, or when by the favour of his fellow-citizens a private person becomes the prince of his country. And speaking of the first method, it will be illustrated by two examples—one ancient, the other modern—and without entering further into the subject, I consider these two examples will suffice those who may be compelled to follow them.

Agathocles, the Sicilian[15], became King of Syracuse not only from a private but from a low and abject position. This man, the son of a potter, through all the changes in his fortunes always led an infamous life. Nevertheless, he accompanied his infamies with so much ability of mind and body that, having devoted himself to the military profession, he rose through its ranks to be Praetor of Syracuse. Being established in that position, and having deliberately resolved to make himself prince and to seize by violence, without obligation to others, that which had been conceded to him by assent, he came to an understanding for this purpose with Amilcar, the Carthaginian, who, with his army, was fighting in Sicily. One morning he assembled the people and the senate of Syracuse, as if he had to discuss with them things relating to the Republic, and at a given signal the soldiers killed all the senators and the richest of the people; these dead, he seized and held the princedom of that city without any civil commotion. And although he was twice routed by the Carthaginians, and ultimately besieged, yet not only was he able to defend his city, but leaving part of his men for its defence, with the others he attacked Africa, and in a short time raised the siege of Syracuse. The Carthaginians, reduced to extreme necessity, were compelled to come to terms with Agathocles, and, leaving

---

14 San Giorgio is Raffaello Riario. Ascanio is Ascanio Sforza.
15 Agathocles the Sicilian, born 361 B.C., died 289 B.C.

Sicily to him, had to be content with the possession of Africa.

Therefore, he who considers the actions and the genius of this man will see nothing, or little, which can be attributed to fortune, inasmuch as he attained pre-eminence, as is shown above, not by the favour of any one, but step by step in the military profession, which steps were gained with a thousand troubles and perils, and were afterwards boldly held by him with many hazardous dangers. Yet it cannot be called talent to slay fellow-citizens, to deceive friends, to be without faith, without mercy, without religion; such methods may gain empire, but not glory. Still, if the courage of Agathocles in entering into and extricating himself from dangers be considered, together with his greatness of mind in enduring and overcoming hardships, it cannot be seen why he should be esteemed less than the most notable captain. Nevertheless, his barbarous cruelty and inhumanity with infinite wickedness do not permit him to be celebrated among the most excellent men. What he achieved cannot be attributed either to fortune or genius.

In our times, during the rule of Alexander the Sixth, Oliverotto da Fermo, having been left an orphan many years before, was brought up by his maternal uncle, Giovanni Fogliani, and in the early days of his youth sent to fight under Pagolo Vitelli, that, being trained under his discipline, he might attain some high position in the military profession. After Pagolo died, he fought under his brother Vitellozzo, and in a very short time, being endowed with wit and a vigorous body and mind, he became the first man in his profession. But it appearing a paltry thing to serve under others, he resolved, with the aid of some citizens of Fermo, to whom the slavery of their country was dearer than its liberty, and with the help of the Vitelleschi, to seize Fermo. So he wrote to Giovanni Fogliani that, having been away from home for many years, he wished to visit him and his city, and in some measure to look upon his patrimony; and although he had not laboured to acquire anything except honour, yet, in order that the citizens should see he had not spent his time in vain, he desired to come honourably, so would be accompanied by one hundred horsemen, his friends and retainers; and he entreated Giovanni to arrange that he should be received honourably by the Fermians, all of which would be not only to his honour, but also to that of Giovanni himself, who had brought him up.

Giovanni, therefore, did not fail in any attentions due to his nephew, and he caused him to be honourably received by the Fermians, and he lodged him in his own house, where, having passed some days, and having arranged what was necessary for his wicked designs, Oliverotto gave a solemn banquet to which he invited Giovanni Fogliani and the chiefs of Fermo. When the viands and all the other entertainments that are usual in such banquets were finished, Oliverotto artfully began certain grave discourses, speaking of the greatness of Pope Alexander and his son Cesare, and of their enterprises, to which discourse Giovanni and others answered; but he rose at once, saying that such matters ought to be discussed in a more private place, and he betook himself to a chamber, whither Giovanni and the rest of the citizens went in after him. No sooner were they seated than soldiers issued from secret places and slaughtered Giovanni and the rest. After these murders Oliverotto, mounted on horseback, rode up and down the town and besieged the chief magistrate in the palace, so that in fear the people were forced to obey him, and to form a government, of which he made himself the prince. He killed all the malcontents who were able to injure him, and strengthened himself with new civil and military ordinances, in such a way that, in the year during which he held the principality, not only was he secure in the city of Fermo, but he had become formidable to all his neighbours. And his destruction would have been as difficult as that of Agathocles if he had not allowed himself to be overreached by Cesare Borgia, who took him with the Orsini and Vitelli at Sinigalia, as was stated above. Thus one year after he had committed this parricide, he was strangled, together with Vitellozzo, whom he had made his leader in valour and wickedness.

Some may wonder how it can happen that Agathocles, and his like, after infinite treacheries and cruelties, should live for long secure in his country, and defend himself from external enemies, and never be conspired against by his own citizens; seeing that many others, by means of cruelty, have never been able even in peaceful times to hold the state, still less in the doubtful times of war. I believe that this follows from severities[16] being badly or properly used. Those may be called properly used, if of evil it is possible to speak well, that are applied at one blow and are necessary to one's security, and that are not persisted in afterwards unless they can be turned to the advantage of the subjects. The badly employed are those which, notwithstanding they may be few in the commencement, multiply with time rather than decrease. Those who practise the first system are able, by aid of God or man, to mitigate in some degree their rule, as Agathocles did. It is impossible for those who follow the other to maintain themselves.

Hence it is to be remarked that, in seizing a state, the usurper ought to examine closely into all those injuries which it is necessary for him to inflict, and to do them all at one stroke so as not to have to repeat them daily; and thus by not unsettling men he will be able to reassure them, and win them to himself by benefits. He who does otherwise, either from timidity or evil advice, is always compelled to keep the knife in his hand; neither can he rely on his subjects, nor can they attach themselves to him, owing to their continued and repeated wrongs. For injuries ought to be done all at one time, so that, being tasted less, they offend less; benefits ought to be given little by little, so that the flavour of them may last longer.

And above all things, a prince ought to live amongst his people in such a way that no unexpected circumstances, whether of good or evil, shall make him change; because if the necessity for this comes in troubled times, you are too late for harsh measures; and mild ones will not help you, for they will be considered as forced from you, and no one will be under any obligation to you for them.

CHAPTER IX — CONCERNING A CIVIL PRINCIPALITY

But coming to the other point—where a leading citizen becomes the prince of his country, not by wickedness or any intolerable violence, but by the favour of his fellow citizens—this may be called a civil principality: nor is genius or fortune altogether necessary to attain to it, but rather a happy shrewdness. I say then that such a principality is obtained either by the favour of the people or by the favour of the nobles. Because in all cities these two distinct parties are found, and from this it arises that the people do not wish to be ruled nor oppressed by the nobles, and the nobles wish to rule and oppress the people; and from these two opposite desires there arises in cities one of three results, either a principality, self-government, or anarchy.

A principality is created either by the people or by the nobles, accordingly as one or other of them has the opportunity; for the nobles, seeing they cannot withstand the people, begin to cry up the reputation of one of themselves, and they make him a prince, so that under his shadow they can give vent to their ambitions. The people, finding they cannot resist the nobles, also cry up the reputation of one of themselves, and make him a prince so as to be defended by his authority. He who obtains sovereignty by the assistance of the nobles maintains himself with more difficulty than he who comes to it by the aid of the people, because the former finds himself with many around him who consider themselves his equals, and because of this he can neither rule nor manage them to his liking. But he who reaches sovereignty by popular favour finds himself alone, and has none around him, or few, who are not prepared to obey him.

Besides this, one cannot by fair dealing, and without injury to others, satisfy the nobles, but you can satisfy the people, for their object is more righteous than that of the nobles, the latter wishing to oppress, while the former only desire not to be oppressed. It is to be added also that a prince can never secure himself against a hostile people, because of their being too many, whilst from the nobles he can secure himself, as they are few in number. The worst that a prince may expect from a hostile people is to be abandoned by them; but from hostile nobles he has not only to fear abandonment, but also that they will rise against him; for they, being in

---

16 Mr Burd suggests that this word probably comes near the modern equivalent of Machiavelli's thought when he speaks of "crudelta" than the more obvious "cruelties."

these affairs more far-seeing and astute, always come forward in time to save themselves, and to obtain favours from him whom they expect to prevail. Further, the prince is compelled to live always with the same people, but he can do well without the same nobles, being able to make and unmake them daily, and to give or take away authority when it pleases him.

Therefore, to make this point clearer, I say that the nobles ought to be looked at mainly in two ways: that is to say, they either shape their course in such a way as binds them entirely to your fortune, or they do not. Those who so bind themselves, and are not rapacious, ought to be honoured and loved; those who do not bind themselves may be dealt with in two ways; they may fail to do this through pusillanimity and a natural want of courage, in which case you ought to make use of them, especially of those who are of good counsel; and thus, whilst in prosperity you honour them, in adversity you do not have to fear them. But when for their own ambitious ends they shun binding themselves, it is a token that they are giving more thought to themselves than to you, and a prince ought to guard against such, and to fear them as if they were open enemies, because in adversity they always help to ruin him.

Therefore, one who becomes a prince through the favour of the people ought to keep them friendly, and this he can easily do seeing they only ask not to be oppressed by him. But one who, in opposition to the people, becomes a prince by the favour of the nobles, ought, above everything, to seek to win the people over to himself, and this he may easily do if he takes them under his protection. Because men, when they receive good from him of whom they were expecting evil, are bound more closely to their benefactor; thus the people quickly become more devoted to him than if he had been raised to the principality by their favours; and the prince can win their affections in many ways, but as these vary according to the circumstances one cannot give fixed rules, so I omit them; but, I repeat, it is necessary for a prince to have the people friendly, otherwise he has no security in adversity.

Nabis[17], Prince of the Spartans, sustained the attack of all Greece, and of a victorious Roman army, and against them he defended his country and his government; and for the overcoming of this peril it was only necessary for him to make himself secure against a few, but this would not have been sufficient had the people been hostile. And do not let any one impugn this statement with the trite proverb that "He who builds on the people, builds on the mud," for this is true when a private citizen makes a foundation there, and persuades himself that the people will free him when he is oppressed by his enemies or by the magistrates; wherein he would find himself very often deceived, as happened to the Gracchi in Rome and to Messer Giorgio Scali[18] in Florence. But granted a prince who has established himself as above, who can command, and is a man of courage, undismayed in adversity, who does not fail in other qualifications, and who, by his resolution and energy, keeps the whole people encouraged—such a one will never find himself deceived in them, and it will be shown that he has laid his foundations well.

These principalities are liable to danger when they are passing from the civil to the absolute order of government, for such princes either rule personally or through magistrates. In the latter case their government is weaker and more insecure, because it rests entirely on the goodwill of those citizens who are raised to the magistracy, and who, especially in troubled times, can destroy the government with great ease, either by intrigue or open defiance; and the prince has not the chance amid tumults to exercise absolute authority, because the citizens and subjects, accustomed to receive orders from magistrates, are not of a mind to obey him amid these confusions, and there will always be in doubtful times a scarcity of men whom he can trust. For such a prince cannot rely upon what he observes in quiet times, when citizens have need of the state, because then every one agrees with him; they all promise, and when death is far distant they all wish to die for him; but in troubled times, when the state has need of its citizens, then he finds but few. And so much the

---

17 Nabis, tyrant of Sparta, conquered by the Romans under Flamininus in 195 B.C.; killed 192 B.C.
18 Messer Giorgio Scali. This event is to be found in Machiavelli's "Florentine History," Book III.

more is this experiment dangerous, inasmuch as it can only be tried once. Therefore a wise prince ought to adopt such a course that his citizens will always in every sort and kind of circumstance have need of the state and of him, and then he will always find them faithful.

CHAPTER X — CONCERNING THE WAY IN WHICH THE STRENGTH OF ALL PRINCIPALITIES OUGHT TO BE MEASURED

It is necessary to consider another point in examining the character of these principalities: that is, whether a prince has such power that, in case of need, he can support himself with his own resources, or whether he has always need of the assistance of others. And to make this quite clear I say that I consider those who are able to support themselves by their own resources who can, either by abundance of men or money, raise a sufficient army to join battle against any one who comes to attack them; and I consider those always to have need of others who cannot show themselves against the enemy in the field, but are forced to defend themselves by sheltering behind walls. The first case has been discussed, but we will speak of it again should it recur. In the second case one can say nothing except to encourage such princes to provision and fortify their towns, and not on any account to defend the country. And whoever shall fortify his town well, and shall have managed the other concerns of his subjects in the way stated above, and to be often repeated, will never be attacked without great caution, for men are always adverse to enterprises where difficulties can be seen, and it will be seen not to be an easy thing to attack one who has his town well fortified, and is not hated by his people.

The cities of Germany are absolutely free, they own but little country around them, and they yield obedience to the emperor when it suits them, nor do they fear this or any other power they may have near them, because they are fortified in such a way that every one thinks the taking of them by assault would be tedious and difficult, seeing they have proper ditches and walls, they have sufficient artillery, and they always keep in public depots enough for one year's eating, drinking, and firing. And beyond this, to keep the people quiet and without loss to the state, they always have the means of giving work to the community in those labours that are the life and strength of the city, and on the pursuit of which the people are supported; they also hold military exercises in repute, and moreover have many ordinances to uphold them.

Therefore, a prince who has a strong city, and had not made himself odious, will not be attacked, or if any one should attack he will only be driven off with disgrace; again, because that the affairs of this world are so changeable, it is almost impossible to keep an army a whole year in the field without being interfered with. And whoever should reply: If the people have property outside the city, and see it burnt, they will not remain patient, and the long siege and self-interest will make them forget their prince; to this I answer that a powerful and courageous prince will overcome all such difficulties by giving at one time hope to his subjects that the evil will not be for long, at another time fear of the cruelty of the enemy, then preserving himself adroitly from those subjects who seem to him to be too bold.

Further, the enemy would naturally on his arrival at once burn and ruin the country at the time when the spirits of the people are still hot and ready for the defence; and, therefore, so much the less ought the prince to hesitate; because after a time, when spirits have cooled, the damage is already done, the ills are incurred, and there is no longer any remedy; and therefore they are so much the more ready to unite with their prince, he appearing to be under obligations to them now that their houses have been burnt and their possessions ruined in his defence. For it is the nature of men to be bound by the benefits they confer as much as by those they receive. Therefore, if everything is well considered, it will not be difficult for a wise prince to keep the minds of his citizens steadfast from first to last, when he does not fail to support and defend them.

CHAPTER XI — CONCERNING ECCLESIASTICAL PRINCIPALITIES

It only remains now to speak of ecclesiastical principalities, touching which all difficulties are prior to getting possession, because they are acquired either by capacity or good fortune, and they can be held without either; for they are sustained by the ancient ordinances of religion, which are so all-powerful, and of such a character that the principalities may be held no matter how their princes behave and live. These princes alone have states and do not defend them; and they have subjects and do not rule them; and the states, although unguarded, are not taken from them, and the subjects, although not ruled, do not care, and they have neither the desire nor the ability to alienate themselves. Such principalities only are secure and happy. But being upheld by powers, to which the human mind cannot reach, I shall speak no more of them, because, being exalted and maintained by God, it would be the act of a presumptuous and rash man to discuss them.

Nevertheless, if any one should ask of me how comes it that the Church has attained such greatness in temporal power, seeing that from Alexander backwards the Italian potentates (not only those who have been called potentates, but every baron and lord, though the smallest) have valued the temporal power very slightly —yet now a king of France trembles before it, and it has been able to drive him from Italy, and to ruin the Venetians—although this may be very manifest, it does not appear to me superfluous to recall it in some measure to memory.

Before Charles, King of France, passed into Italy[19], this country was under the dominion of the Pope, the Venetians, the King of Naples, the Duke of Milan, and the Florentines. These potentates had two principal anxieties: the one, that no foreigner should enter Italy under arms; the other, that none of themselves should seize more territory. Those about whom there was the most anxiety were the Pope and the Venetians. To restrain the Venetians the union of all the others was necessary, as it was for the defence of Ferrara; and to keep down the Pope they made use of the barons of Rome, who, being divided into two factions, Orsini and Colonnesi, had always a pretext for disorder, and, standing with arms in their hands under the eyes of the Pontiff, kept the pontificate weak and powerless. And although there might arise sometimes a courageous pope, such as Sixtus, yet neither fortune nor wisdom could rid him of these annoyances. And the short life of a pope is also a cause of weakness; for in the ten years, which is the average life of a pope, he can with difficulty lower one of the factions; and if, so to speak, one people should almost destroy the Colonnesi, another would arise hostile to the Orsini, who would support their opponents, and yet would not have time to ruin the Orsini. This was the reason why the temporal powers of the pope were little esteemed in Italy.

Alexander the Sixth arose afterwards, who of all the pontiffs that have ever been showed how a pope with both money and arms was able to prevail; and through the instrumentality of the Duke Valentino, and by reason of the entry of the French, he brought about all those things which I have discussed above in the actions of the duke. And although his intention was not to aggrandize the Church, but the duke, nevertheless, what he did contributed to the greatness of the Church, which, after his death and the ruin of the duke, became the heir to all his labours.

Pope Julius came afterwards and found the Church strong, possessing all the Romagna, the barons of Rome reduced to impotence, and, through the chastisements of Alexander, the factions wiped out; he also found the way open to accumulate money in a manner such as had never been practised before Alexander's time. Such things Julius not only followed but improved upon, and he intended to gain Bologna, to ruin the Venetians, and to drive the French out of Italy. All of these enterprises prospered with him, and so much the more to his credit, inasmuch as he did everything to strengthen the Church and not any private person. He kept also the Orsini and Colonnesi factions within the bounds in which he found them; and although there was among them some mind to make disturbance, nevertheless he held two things firm: the one, the greatness of the

---

19 Charles VIII invaded Italy in 1494.

Church, with which he terrified them; and the other, not allowing them to have their own cardinals, who caused the disorders among them. For whenever these factions have their cardinals they do not remain quiet for long, because cardinals foster the factions in Rome and out of it, and the barons are compelled to support them, and thus from the ambitions of prelates arise disorders and tumults among the barons. For these reasons his Holiness Pope Leo[20] found the pontificate most powerful, and it is to be hoped that, if others made it great in arms, he will make it still greater and more venerated by his goodness and infinite other virtues.

CHAPTER XII — HOW MANY KINDS OF SOLDIERY THERE ARE, AND CONCERNING MERCENARIES

Having discoursed particularly on the characteristics of such principalities as in the beginning I proposed to discuss, and having considered in some degree the causes of their being good or bad, and having shown the methods by which many have sought to acquire them and to hold them, it now remains for me to discuss generally the means of offence and defence which belong to each of them.

We have seen above how necessary it is for a prince to have his foundations well-laid, otherwise it follows of necessity he will go to ruin. The chief foundations of all states, new as well as old or composite, are good laws and good arms; and as there cannot be good laws where the state is not well armed, it follows that where they are well armed they have good laws. I shall leave the laws out of the discussion and shall speak of the arms.

I say, therefore, that the arms with which a prince defends his state are either his own, or they are mercenaries, auxiliaries, or mixed. Mercenaries and auxiliaries are useless and dangerous; and if one holds his state based on these arms, he will stand neither firm nor safe; for they are disunited, ambitious, and without discipline, unfaithful, valiant before friends, cowardly before enemies; they have neither the fear of God nor fidelity to men, and destruction is deferred only so long as the attack is; for in peace one is robbed by them, and in war by the enemy. The fact is, they have no other attraction or reason for keeping the field than a trifle of stipend, which is not sufficient to make them willing to die for you. They are ready enough to be your soldiers whilst you do not make war, but if war comes they take themselves off or run from the foe; which I should have little trouble to prove, for the ruin of Italy has been caused by nothing else than by resting all her hopes for many years on mercenaries, and although they formerly made some display and appeared valiant amongst themselves, yet when the foreigners came they showed what they were. Thus it was that Charles, King of France, was allowed to seize Italy with chalk in hand[21]; and he who told us that our sins were the cause of it told the truth, but they were not the sins he imagined, but those which I have related. And as they were the sins of princes, it is the princes who have also suffered the penalty.

I wish to demonstrate further the infelicity of these arms. The mercenary captains are either capable men or they are not; if they are, you cannot trust them, because they always aspire to their own greatness, either by oppressing you, who are their master, or others contrary to your intentions; but if the captain is not skilful, you are ruined in the usual way.

And if it be urged that whoever is armed will act in the same way, whether mercenary or not, I reply that

---

20 Pope Leo X was the Cardinal de' Medici.

21 "With chalk in hand," "col gesso." This is one of the bons mots of Alexander VI, and refers to the ease with which Charles VIII seized Italy, implying that it was only necessary for him to send his quartermasters to chalk up the billets for his soldiers to conquer the country. Cf. "The History of Henry VII," by Lord Bacon: "King Charles had conquered the realm of Naples, and lost it again, in a kind of a felicity of a dream. He passed the whole length of Italy without resistance: so that it was true what Pope Alexander was wont to say: That the Frenchmen came into Italy with chalk in their hands, to mark up their lodgings, rather than with swords to fight."

when arms have to be resorted to, either by a prince or a republic, then the prince ought to go in person and perform the duty of a captain; the republic has to send its citizens, and when one is sent who does not turn out satisfactorily, it ought to recall him, and when one is worthy, to hold him by the laws so that he does not leave the command. And experience has shown princes and republics, single-handed, making the greatest progress, and mercenaries doing nothing except damage; and it is more difficult to bring a republic, armed with its own arms, under the sway of one of its citizens than it is to bring one armed with foreign arms. Rome and Sparta stood for many ages armed and free. The Switzers are completely armed and quite free.

Of ancient mercenaries, for example, there are the Carthaginians, who were oppressed by their mercenary soldiers after the first war with the Romans, although the Carthaginians had their own citizens for captains. After the death of Epaminondas, Philip of Macedon was made captain of their soldiers by the Thebans, and after victory he took away their liberty.

Duke Filippo being dead, the Milanese enlisted Francesco Sforza against the Venetians, and he, having overcome the enemy at Caravaggio[22], allied himself with them to crush the Milanese, his masters. His father, Sforza, having been engaged by Queen Johanna[23] of Naples, left her unprotected, so that she was forced to throw herself into the arms of the King of Aragon, in order to save her kingdom. And if the Venetians and Florentines formerly extended their dominions by these arms, and yet their captains did not make themselves princes, but have defended them, I reply that the Florentines in this case have been favoured by chance, for of the able captains, of whom they might have stood in fear, some have not conquered, some have been opposed, and others have turned their ambitions elsewhere. One who did not conquer was Giovanni Acuto[24], and since he did not conquer his fidelity cannot be proved; but every one will acknowledge that, had he conquered, the Florentines would have stood at his discretion. Sforza had the Bracceschi always against him, so they watched each other. Francesco turned his ambition to Lombardy; Braccio against the Church and the kingdom of Naples. But let us come to that which happened a short while ago. The Florentines appointed as their captain Pagolo Vitelli, a most prudent man, who from a private position had risen to the greatest renown. If this man had taken Pisa, nobody can deny that it would have been proper for the Florentines to keep in with him, for if he became the soldier of their enemies they had no means of resisting, and if they held to him they must obey him. The Venetians, if their achievements are considered, will be seen to have acted safely and gloriously so long as they sent to war their own men, when with armed gentlemen and plebians they did valiantly. This was before they turned to enterprises on land, but when they began to fight on land they forsook this virtue and followed the custom of Italy. And in the beginning of their expansion on land, through not having much territory, and because of their great reputation, they had not much to fear from their captains; but when they expanded, as under Carmignuola[25], they had a taste of this mistake; for, having found him a most valiant man (they beat the Duke of Milan under his leadership), and, on the other hand, knowing how lukewarm he was in the war, they feared they would no longer conquer under him, and for this reason they were not willing, nor were they able, to let him go; and so, not to lose again that which they had acquired, they were compelled, in order to secure themselves, to murder him. They had afterwards for their captains Bartolomeo da Bergamo, Roberto da San Severino, the count of Pitigliano[26], and the like, under

---

22 Battle of Caravaggio, 15th September 1448.

23 Johanna II of Naples, the widow of Ladislao, King of Naples.

24 Giovanni Acuto. An English knight whose name was Sir John Hawkwood. He fought in the English wars in France, and was knighted by Edward III; afterwards he collected a body of troops and went into Italy. These became the famous "White Company." He took part in many wars, and died in Florence in 1394. He was born about 1320 at Sible Hedingham, a village in Essex. He married Domnia, a daughter of Bernabo Visconti.

25 Carmignuola. Francesco Bussone, born at Carmagnola about 1390, executed at Venice, 5th May 1432.

26 Bartolomeo Colleoni of Bergamo; died 1457. Roberto of San Severino; died fighting for Venice against Sigismund, Duke of Austria, in 1487. "Primo capitano in Italia."— Machiavelli. Count of Pitigliano; Nicolo Orsini, born 1442, died

whom they had to dread loss and not gain, as happened afterwards at Vaila[27], where in one battle they lost that which in eight hundred years they had acquired with so much trouble. Because from such arms conquests come but slowly, long delayed and inconsiderable, but the losses sudden and portentous.

And as with these examples I have reached Italy, which has been ruled for many years by mercenaries, I wish to discuss them more seriously, in order that, having seen their rise and progress, one may be better prepared to counteract them. You must understand that the empire has recently come to be repudiated in Italy, that the Pope has acquired more temporal power, and that Italy has been divided up into more states, for the reason that many of the great cities took up arms against their nobles, who, formerly favoured by the emperor, were oppressing them, whilst the Church was favouring them so as to gain authority in temporal power: in many others their citizens became princes. From this it came to pass that Italy fell partly into the hands of the Church and of republics, and, the Church consisting of priests and the republic of citizens unaccustomed to arms, both commenced to enlist foreigners.

The first who gave renown to this soldiery was Alberigo da Conio[28], the Romagnian. From the school of this man sprang, among others, Braccio and Sforza, who in their time were the arbiters of Italy. After these came all the other captains who till now have directed the arms of Italy; and the end of all their valour has been, that she has been overrun by Charles, robbed by Louis, ravaged by Ferdinand, and insulted by the Switzers. The principle that has guided them has been, first, to lower the credit of infantry so that they might increase their own. They did this because, subsisting on their pay and without territory, they were unable to support many soldiers, and a few infantry did not give them any authority; so they were led to employ cavalry, with a moderate force of which they were maintained and honoured; and affairs were brought to such a pass that, in an army of twenty thousand soldiers, there were not to be found two thousand foot soldiers. They had, besides this, used every art to lessen fatigue and danger to themselves and their soldiers, not killing in the fray, but taking prisoners and liberating without ransom. They did not attack towns at night, nor did the garrisons of the towns attack encampments at night; they did not surround the camp either with stockade or ditch, nor did they campaign in the winter. All these things were permitted by their military rules, and devised by them to avoid, as I have said, both fatigue and dangers; thus they have brought Italy to slavery and contempt.

CHAPTER XIII — CONCERNING AUXILIARIES, MIXED SOLDIERY, AND ONE'S OWN

Auxiliaries, which are the other useless arm, are employed when a prince is called in with his forces to aid and defend, as was done by Pope Julius in the most recent times; for he, having, in the enterprise against Ferrara, had poor proof of his mercenaries, turned to auxiliaries, and stipulated with Ferdinand, King of Spain[29], for his assistance with men and arms. These arms may be useful and good in themselves, but for him who calls them in they are always disadvantageous; for losing, one is undone, and winning, one is their captive.

And although ancient histories may be full of examples, I do not wish to leave this recent one of Pope Julius the Second, the peril of which cannot fail to be perceived; for he, wishing to get Ferrara, threw himself entirely into the hands of the foreigner. But his good fortune brought about a third event, so that he did not

---

1510.

27 Battle of Vaila in 1509.

28 Alberigo da Conio. Alberico da Barbiano, Count of Cunio in Romagna. He was the leader of the famous "Company of St George," composed entirely of Italian soldiers. He died in 1409.

29 Ferdinand V (F. II of Aragon and Sicily, F. III of Naples), surnamed "The Catholic," born 1542, died 1516.

reap the fruit of his rash choice; because, having his auxiliaries routed at Ravenna, and the Switzers having risen and driven out the conquerors (against all expectation, both his and others), it so came to pass that he did not become prisoner to his enemies, they having fled, nor to his auxiliaries, he having conquered by other arms than theirs.

The Florentines, being entirely without arms, sent ten thousand Frenchmen to take Pisa, whereby they ran more danger than at any other time of their troubles.

The Emperor of Constantinople[30], to oppose his neighbours, sent ten thousand Turks into Greece, who, on the war being finished, were not willing to quit; this was the beginning of the servitude of Greece to the infidels.

Therefore, let him who has no desire to conquer make use of these arms, for they are much more hazardous than mercenaries, because with them the ruin is ready made; they are all united, all yield obedience to others; but with mercenaries, when they have conquered, more time and better opportunities are needed to injure you; they are not all of one community, they are found and paid by you, and a third party, which you have made their head, is not able all at once to assume enough authority to injure you. In conclusion, in mercenaries dastardy is most dangerous; in auxiliaries, valour. The wise prince, therefore, has always avoided these arms and turned to his own; and has been willing rather to lose with them than to conquer with the others, not deeming that a real victory which is gained with the arms of others.

I shall never hesitate to cite Cesare Borgia and his actions. This duke entered the Romagna with auxiliaries, taking there only French soldiers, and with them he captured Imola and Forli; but afterwards, such forces not appearing to him reliable, he turned to mercenaries, discerning less danger in them, and enlisted the Orsini and Vitelli; whom presently, on handling and finding them doubtful, unfaithful, and dangerous, he destroyed and turned to his own men. And the difference between one and the other of these forces can easily be seen when one considers the difference there was in the reputation of the duke, when he had the French, when he had the Orsini and Vitelli, and when he relied on his own soldiers, on whose fidelity he could always count and found it ever increasing; he was never esteemed more highly than when every one saw that he was complete master of his own forces.

I was not intending to go beyond Italian and recent examples, but I am unwilling to leave out Hiero, the Syracusan, he being one of those I have named above. This man, as I have said, made head of the army by the Syracusans, soon found out that a mercenary soldiery, constituted like our Italian condottieri, was of no use; and it appearing to him that he could neither keep them not let them go, he had them all cut to pieces, and afterwards made war with his own forces and not with aliens.

I wish also to recall to memory an instance from the Old Testament applicable to this subject. David offered himself to Saul to fight with Goliath, the Philistine champion, and, to give him courage, Saul armed him with his own weapons; which David rejected as soon as he had them on his back, saying he could make no use of them, and that he wished to meet the enemy with his sling and his knife. In conclusion, the arms of others either fall from your back, or they weigh you down, or they bind you fast.

Charles the Seventh[31], the father of King Louis the Eleventh[32], having by good fortune and valour liberated France from the English, recognized the necessity of being armed with forces of his own, and he established in his kingdom ordinances concerning men-at-arms and infantry. Afterwards his son, King Louis, abolished the infantry and began to enlist the Switzers, which mistake, followed by others, is, as is now seen, a source of peril to that kingdom; because, having raised the reputation of the Switzers, he has entirely diminished the value of his own arms, for he has destroyed the infantry altogether; and his men-at-arms he has subordinated to others, for, being as they are so accustomed to fight along with Switzers, it does not appear that they can

---

30 Joannes Cantacuzenus, born 1300, died 1383.
31 Charles VII of France, surnamed "The Victorious," born 1403, died 1461.
32 Louis XI, son of the above, born 1423, died 1483.

now conquer without them. Hence it arises that the French cannot stand against the Switzers, and without the Switzers they do not come off well against others. The armies of the French have thus become mixed, partly mercenary and partly national, both of which arms together are much better than mercenaries alone or auxiliaries alone, but much inferior to one's own forces. And this example proves it, for the kingdom of France would be unconquerable if the ordinance of Charles had been enlarged or maintained.

But the scanty wisdom of man, on entering into an affair which looks well at first, cannot discern the poison that is hidden in it, as I have said above of hectic fevers. Therefore, if he who rules a principality cannot recognize evils until they are upon him, he is not truly wise; and this insight is given to few. And if the first disaster to the Roman Empire[33] should be examined, it will be found to have commenced only with the enlisting of the Goths; because from that time the vigour of the Roman Empire began to decline, and all that valour which had raised it passed away to others.

I conclude, therefore, that no principality is secure without having its own forces; on the contrary, it is entirely dependent on good fortune, not having the valour which in adversity would defend it. And it has always been the opinion and judgment of wise men that nothing can be so uncertain or unstable as fame or power not founded on its own strength. And one's own forces are those which are composed either of subjects, citizens, or dependents; all others are mercenaries or auxiliaries. And the way to make ready one's own forces will be easily found if the rules suggested by me shall be reflected upon, and if one will consider how Philip, the father of Alexander the Great, and many republics and princes have armed and organized themselves, to which rules I entirely commit myself.

CHAPTER XIV — THAT WHICH CONCERNS A PRINCE ON THE SUBJECT OF THE ART OF WAR

A prince ought to have no other aim or thought, nor select anything else for his study, than war and its rules and discipline; for this is the sole art that belongs to him who rules, and it is of such force that it not only upholds those who are born princes, but it often enables men to rise from a private station to that rank. And, on the contrary, it is seen that when princes have thought more of ease than of arms they have lost their states. And the first cause of your losing it is to neglect this art; and what enables you to acquire a state is to be master of the art. Francesco Sforza, through being martial, from a private person became Duke of Milan; and the sons, through avoiding the hardships and troubles of arms, from dukes became private persons. For among other evils which being unarmed brings you, it causes you to be despised, and this is one of those ignominies against which a prince ought to guard himself, as is shown later on. Because there is nothing proportionate between the armed and the unarmed; and it is not reasonable that he who is armed should yield obedience willingly to him who is unarmed, or that the unarmed man should be secure among armed servants. Because, there being in the one disdain and in the other suspicion, it is not possible for them to work well together. And therefore a prince who does not understand the art of war, over and above the other misfortunes already mentioned, cannot be respected by his soldiers, nor can he rely on them. He ought never, therefore, to have out of his thoughts this subject of war, and in peace he should addict himself more to its

33 "Many speakers to the House the other night in the debate on the reduction of armaments seemed to show a most lamentable ignorance of the conditions under which the   British Empire maintains its existence. When Mr Balfour replied to the allegations that the Roman Empire sank under   the weight of its military obligations, he said that this was 'wholly unhistorical.' He might well have added that the   Roman power was at its zenith when every citizen acknowledged his liability to fight for the State, but that   it began to decline as soon as this obligation was no longer recognized."—Pall Mall Gazette, 15th May 1906.

exercise than in war; this he can do in two ways, the one by action, the other by study.

As regards action, he ought above all things to keep his men well organized and drilled, to follow incessantly the chase, by which he accustoms his body to hardships, and learns something of the nature of localities, and gets to find out how the mountains rise, how the valleys open out, how the plains lie, and to understand the nature of rivers and marshes, and in all this to take the greatest care. Which knowledge is useful in two ways: Firstly, he learns to know his country, and is better able to undertake its defence; afterwards, by means of the knowledge and observation of that locality, he understands with ease any other which it may be necessary for him to study hereafter; because the hills, valleys, and plains, and rivers and marshes that are, for instance, in Tuscany, have a certain resemblance to those of other countries, so that with a knowledge of the aspect of one country one can easily arrive at a knowledge of others. And the prince that lacks this skill lacks the essential which it is desirable that a captain should possess, for it teaches him to surprise his enemy, to select quarters, to lead armies, to array the battle, to besiege towns to advantage.

Philopoemen[34], Prince of the Achaeans, among other praises which writers have bestowed on him, is commended because in time of peace he never had anything in his mind but the rules of war; and when he was in the country with friends, he often stopped and reasoned with them: "If the enemy should be upon that hill, and we should find ourselves here with our army, with whom would be the advantage? How should one best advance to meet him, keeping the ranks? If we should wish to retreat, how ought we to pursue?" And he would set forth to them, as he went, all the chances that could befall an army; he would listen to their opinion and state his, confirming it with reasons, so that by these continual discussions there could never arise, in time of war, any unexpected circumstances that he could not deal with.

But to exercise the intellect the prince should read histories, and study there the actions of illustrious men, to see how they have borne themselves in war, to examine the causes of their victories and defeat, so as to avoid the latter and imitate the former; and above all do as an illustrious man did, who took as an exemplar one who had been praised and famous before him, and whose achievements and deeds he always kept in his mind, as it is said Alexander the Great imitated Achilles, Caesar Alexander, Scipio Cyrus. And whoever reads the life of Cyrus, written by Xenophon, will recognize afterwards in the life of Scipio how that imitation was his glory, and how in chastity, affability, humanity, and liberality Scipio conformed to those things which have been written of Cyrus by Xenophon. A wise prince ought to observe some such rules, and never in peaceful times stand idle, but increase his resources with industry in such a way that they may be available to him in adversity, so that if fortune chances it may find him prepared to resist her blows.

CHAPTER XV — CONCERNING THINGS FOR WHICH MEN, AND ESPECIALLY PRINCES, ARE PRAISED OR BLAMED

It remains now to see what ought to be the rules of conduct for a prince towards subject and friends. And as I know that many have written on this point, I expect I shall be considered presumptuous in mentioning it again, especially as in discussing it I shall depart from the methods of other people. But, it being my intention to write a thing which shall be useful to him who apprehends it, it appears to me more appropriate to follow up the real truth of the matter than the imagination of it; for many have pictured republics and principalities which in fact have never been known or seen, because how one lives is so far distant from how one ought to live, that he who neglects what is done for what ought to be done, sooner effects his ruin than his preservation; for a man who wishes to act entirely up to his professions of virtue soon meets with what destroys him among so much that is evil.

Hence it is necessary for a prince wishing to hold his own to know how to do wrong, and to make use of it or

---

34 Philopoemen, "the last of the Greeks," born 252 B.C.,died 183 B.C.

not according to necessity. Therefore, putting on one side imaginary things concerning a prince, and discussing those which are real, I say that all men when they are spoken of, and chiefly princes for being more highly placed, are remarkable for some of those qualities which bring them either blame or praise; and thus it is that one is reputed liberal, another miserly, using a Tuscan term (because an avaricious person in our language is still he who desires to possess by robbery, whilst we call one miserly who deprives himself too much of the use of his own); one is reputed generous, one rapacious; one cruel, one compassionate; one faithless, another faithful; one effeminate and cowardly, another bold and brave; one affable, another haughty; one lascivious, one chaste; one sincere, another cunning; one hard, another easy; one grave, another frivolous; one religious, another unbelieving, and the like. And I know that every one will confess that it would be most praiseworthy in a prince to exhibit all the above qualities that are considered good; but because they can neither be entirely possessed nor observed, for human conditions do not permit it, it is necessary for him to be sufficiently prudent that he may know how to avoid the reproach of those vices which would lose him his state; and also to keep himself, if it be possible, from those which would not lose him it; but this not being possible, he may with less hesitation abandon himself to them. And again, he need not make himself uneasy at incurring a reproach for those vices without which the state can only be saved with difficulty, for if everything is considered carefully, it will be found that something which looks like virtue, if followed, would be his ruin; whilst something else, which looks like vice, yet followed brings him security and prosperity.

CHAPTER XVI — CONCERNING LIBERALITY AND MEANNESS

Commencing then with the first of the above-named characteristics, I say that it would be well to be reputed liberal. Nevertheless, liberality exercised in a way that does not bring you the reputation for it, injures you; for if one exercises it honestly and as it should be exercised, it may not become known, and you will not avoid the reproach of its opposite. Therefore, any one wishing to maintain among men the name of liberal is obliged to avoid no attribute of magnificence; so that a prince thus inclined will consume in such acts all his property, and will be compelled in the end, if he wish to maintain the name of liberal, to unduly weigh down his people, and tax them, and do everything he can to get money. This will soon make him odious to his subjects, and becoming poor he will be little valued by any one; thus, with his liberality, having offended many and rewarded few, he is affected by the very first trouble and imperiled by whatever may be the first danger; recognizing this himself, and wishing to draw back from it, he runs at once into the reproach of being miserly.

Therefore, a prince, not being able to exercise this virtue of liberality in such a way that it is recognized, except to his cost, if he is wise he ought not to fear the reputation of being mean, for in time he will come to be more considered than if liberal, seeing that with his economy his revenues are enough, that he can defend himself against all attacks, and is able to engage in enterprises without burdening his people; thus it comes to pass that he exercises liberality towards all from whom he does not take, who are numberless, and meanness towards those to whom he does not give, who are few.

We have not seen great things done in our time except by those who have been considered mean; the rest have failed. Pope Julius the Second was assisted in reaching the papacy by a reputation for liberality, yet he did not strive afterwards to keep it up, when he made war on the King of France; and he made many wars without imposing any extraordinary tax on his subjects, for he supplied his additional expenses out of his long thriftiness. The present King of Spain would not have undertaken or conquered in so many enterprises if he had been reputed liberal. A prince, therefore, provided that he has not to rob his subjects, that he can defend himself, that he does not become poor and abject, that he is not forced to become rapacious, ought to hold of little account a reputation for being mean, for it is one of those vices which will enable him to govern.

And if any one should say: Caesar obtained empire by liberality, and many others have reached the highest positions by having been liberal, and by being considered so, I answer: Either you are a prince in fact, or in a way to become one. In the first case this liberality is dangerous, in the second it is very necessary to be considered liberal; and Caesar was one of those who wished to become pre-eminent in Rome; but if he had survived after becoming so, and had not moderated his expenses, he would have destroyed his government.

And if any one should reply: Many have been princes, and have done great things with armies, who have been considered very liberal, I reply: Either a prince spends that which is his own or his subjects' or else that of others. In the first case he ought to be sparing, in the second he ought not to neglect any opportunity for liberality. And to the prince who goes forth with his army, supporting it by pillage, sack, and extortion, handling that which belongs to others, this liberality is necessary, otherwise he would not be followed by soldiers. And of that which is neither yours nor your subjects' you can be a ready giver, as were Cyrus, Caesar, and Alexander; because it does not take away your reputation if you squander that of others, but adds to it; it is only squandering your own that injures you.

And there is nothing wastes so rapidly as liberality, for even whilst you exercise it you lose the power to do so, and so become either poor or despised, or else, in avoiding poverty, rapacious and hated. And a prince should guard himself, above all things, against being despised and hated; and liberality leads you to both. Therefore it is wiser to have a reputation for meanness which brings reproach without hatred, than to be compelled through seeking a reputation for liberality to incur a name for rapacity which begets reproach with hatred.

CHAPTER XVII — CONCERNING CRUELTY AND CLEMENCY, AND WHETHER IT IS BETTER TO BE LOVED THAN FEARED

Coming now to the other qualities mentioned above, I say that every prince ought to desire to be considered clement and not cruel. Nevertheless he ought to take care not to misuse this clemency. Cesare Borgia was considered cruel; notwithstanding, his cruelty reconciled the Romagna, unified it, and restored it to peace and loyalty. And if this be rightly considered, he will be seen to have been much more merciful than the Florentine people, who, to avoid a reputation for cruelty, permitted Pistoia to be destroyed[35]. Therefore a prince, so long as he keeps his subjects united and loyal, ought not to mind the reproach of cruelty; because with a few examples he will be more merciful than those who, through too much mercy, allow disorders to arise, from which follow murders or robberies; for these are wont to injure the whole people, whilst those executions which originate with a prince offend the individual only.

And of all princes, it is impossible for the new prince to avoid the imputation of cruelty, owing to new states being full of dangers. Hence Virgil, through the mouth of Dido, excuses the inhumanity of her reign owing to its being new, saying:

"Res dura, et regni novitas me talia cogunt
Moliri, et late fines custode tueri[36]."

---

35 During the rioting between the Cancellieri and Panciatichi factions in 1502 and 1503.
36 . . . against my will, my fate
A throne unsettled, and an infant state,
Bid me defend my realms with all my pow'rs,
And guard with these severities my shores.

Nevertheless he ought to be slow to believe and to act, nor should he himself show fear, but proceed in a temperate manner with prudence and humanity, so that too much confidence may not make him incautious and too much distrust render him intolerable.

Upon this a question arises: whether it be better to be loved than feared or feared than loved? It may be answered that one should wish to be both, but, because it is difficult to unite them in one person, it is much safer to be feared than loved, when, of the two, either must be dispensed with. Because this is to be asserted in general of men, that they are ungrateful, fickle, false, cowardly, covetous, and as long as you succeed they are yours entirely; they will offer you their blood, property, life, and children, as is said above, when the need is far distant; but when it approaches they turn against you. And that prince who, relying entirely on their promises, has neglected other precautions, is ruined; because friendships that are obtained by payments, and not by greatness or nobility of mind, may indeed be earned, but they are not secured, and in time of need cannot be relied upon; and men have less scruple in offending one who is beloved than one who is feared, for love is preserved by the link of obligation which, owing to the baseness of men, is broken at every opportunity for their advantage; but fear preserves you by a dread of punishment which never fails.

Nevertheless a prince ought to inspire fear in such a way that, if he does not win love, he avoids hatred; because he can endure very well being feared whilst he is not hated, which will always be as long as he abstains from the property of his citizens and subjects and from their women. But when it is necessary for him to proceed against the life of someone, he must do it on proper justification and for manifest cause, but above all things he must keep his hands off the property of others, because men more quickly forget the death of their father than the loss of their patrimony. Besides, pretexts for taking away the property are never wanting; for he who has once begun to live by robbery will always find pretexts for seizing what belongs to others; but reasons for taking life, on the contrary, are more difficult to find and sooner lapse. But when a prince is with his army, and has under control a multitude of soldiers, then it is quite necessary for him to disregard the reputation of cruelty, for without it he would never hold his army united or disposed to its duties.

Among the wonderful deeds of Hannibal this one is enumerated: that having led an enormous army, composed of many various races of men, to fight in foreign lands, no dissensions arose either among them or against the prince, whether in his bad or in his good fortune. This arose from nothing else than his inhuman cruelty, which, with his boundless valour, made him revered and terrible in the sight of his soldiers, but without that cruelty, his other virtues were not sufficient to produce this effect. And shortsighted writers admire his deeds from one point of view and from another condemn the principal cause of them. That it is true his other virtues would not have been sufficient for him may be proved by the case of Scipio, that most excellent man, not only of his own times but within the memory of man, against whom, nevertheless, his army rebelled in Spain; this arose from nothing but his too great forbearance, which gave his soldiers more license than is consistent with military discipline. For this he was upbraided in the Senate by Fabius Maximus, and called the corrupter of the Roman soldiery. The Locrians were laid waste by a legate of Scipio, yet they were not avenged by him, nor was the insolence of the legate punished, owing entirely to his easy nature. Insomuch that someone in the Senate, wishing to excuse him, said there were many men who knew much better how not to err than to correct the errors of others. This disposition, if he had been continued in the command, would have destroyed in time the fame and glory of Scipio; but, he being under the control of the Senate, this injurious characteristic not only concealed itself, but contributed to his glory.

Returning to the question of being feared or loved, I come to the conclusion that, men loving according to their own will and fearing according to that of the prince, a wise prince should establish himself on that which

---

Christopher Pitt.

is in his own control and not in that of others; he must endeavour only to avoid hatred, as is noted.

CHAPTER XVIII[37] — CONCERNING THE WAY IN WHICH PRINCES SHOULD KEEP FAITH

Every one admits how praiseworthy it is in a prince to keep faith, and to live with integrity and not with craft. Nevertheless our experience has been that those princes who have done great things have held good faith of little account, and have known how to circumvent the intellect of men by craft, and in the end have overcome those who have relied on their word. You must know there are two ways of contesting[38], the one by the law, the other by force; the first method is proper to men, the second to beasts, but because the first is frequently not sufficient, it is necessary to have recourse to the second. Therefore it is necessary for a prince to understand how to avail himself of the beast and the man. This has been figuratively taught to princes by ancient writers, who describe how Achilles and many other princes of old were given to the Centaur Chiron to nurse, who brought them up in his discipline; which means solely that, as they had for a teacher one who was half beast and half man, so it is necessary for a prince to know how to make use of both natures, and that one without the other is not durable. A prince, therefore, being compelled knowingly to adopt the beast, ought to choose the fox and the lion; because the lion cannot defend himself against snares and the fox cannot defend himself against wolves. Therefore, it is necessary to be a fox to discover the snares and a lion to terrify the wolves. Those who rely simply on the lion do not understand what they are about. Therefore a wise lord cannot, nor ought he to, keep faith when such observance may be turned against him, and when the reasons that caused him to pledge it exist no longer. If men were entirely good this precept would not hold, but because they are bad, and will not keep faith with you, you too are not bound to observe it with them. Nor will there ever be wanting to a prince legitimate reasons to excuse this non-observance. Of this endless modern examples could be given, showing how many treaties and engagements have been made void and of no effect through the faithlessness of princes; and he who has known best how to employ the fox has succeeded best.

But it is necessary to know well how to disguise this characteristic, and to be a great pretender and dissembler; and men are so simple, and so subject to present necessities, that he who seeks to deceive will always find someone who will allow himself to be deceived. One recent example I cannot pass over in silence. Alexander the Sixth did nothing else but deceive men, nor ever thought of doing otherwise, and he always found victims; for there never was a man who had greater power in asserting, or who with greater oaths would affirm a thing, yet would observe it less; nevertheless his deceits always succeeded according to his wishes,[39] because he well understood this side of mankind.

Therefore it is unnecessary for a prince to have all the good qualities I have enumerated, but it is very necessary to appear to have them. And I shall dare to say this also, that to have them and always to observe them is injurious, and that to appear to have them is useful; to appear merciful, faithful, humane, religious,

---

37 "The present chapter has given greater offence than any other portion of Machiavelli's writings." Burd, "Il Principe," p. 297.

38 "Contesting," i.e. "striving for mastery." Mr Burd points out that this passage is imitated directly from Cicero's "De Officiis": "Nam cum sint duo genera decertandi, unum per disceptationem, alterum per vim; cumque illud   proprium sit hominis, hoc beluarum; confugiendum est ad posterius, si uti non licet superiore."

39 "Nondimanco sempre gli succederono gli inganni (ad votum)." The words "ad votum" are omitted in the Testina addition, 1550.

Alexander never did what he said, cesare never said what he did.
Italian Proverb.

upright, and to be so, but with a mind so framed that should you require not to be so, you may be able and know how to change to the opposite.

And you have to understand this, that a prince, especially a new one, cannot observe all those things for which men are esteemed, being often forced, in order to maintain the state, to act contrary to fidelity[40], friendship, humanity, and religion. Therefore it is necessary for him to have a mind ready to turn itself accordingly as the winds and variations of fortune force it, yet, as I have said above, not to diverge from the good if he can avoid doing so, but, if compelled, then to know how to set about it.

For this reason a prince ought to take care that he never lets anything slip from his lips that is not replete with the above-named five qualities, that he may appear to him who sees and hears him altogether merciful, faithful, humane, upright, and religious. There is nothing more necessary to appear to have than this last quality, inasmuch as men judge generally more by the eye than by the hand, because it belongs to everybody to see you, to few to come in touch with you. Every one sees what you appear to be, few really know what you are, and those few dare not oppose themselves to the opinion of the many, who have the majesty of the state to defend them; and in the actions of all men, and especially of princes, which it is not prudent to challenge, one judges by the result.

For that reason, let a prince have the credit of conquering and holding his state, the means will always be considered honest, and he will be praised by everybody; because the vulgar are always taken by what a thing seems to be and by what comes of it; and in the world there are only the vulgar, for the few find a place there only when the many have no ground to rest on.

One prince[41] of the present time, whom it is not well to name, never preaches anything else but peace and good faith, and to both he is most hostile, and either, if he had kept it, would have deprived him of reputation and kingdom many a time.

CHAPTER XIX — THAT ONE SHOULD AVOID BEING DESPISED AND HATED

Now, concerning the characteristics of which mention is made above, I have spoken of the more important ones, the others I wish to discuss briefly under this generality, that the prince must consider, as has been in part said before, how to avoid those things which will make him hated or contemptible; and as often as he shall have succeeded he will have fulfilled his part, and he need not fear any danger in other reproaches.

It makes him hated above all things, as I have said, to be rapacious, and to be a violator of the property and women of his subjects, from both of which he must abstain. And when neither their property nor their honor is touched, the majority of men live content, and he has only to contend with the ambition of a few, whom he can curb with ease in many ways.

It makes him contemptible to be considered fickle, frivolous, effeminate, mean-spirited, irresolute, from all of which a prince should guard himself as from a rock; and he should endeavour to show in his actions

---

40 "Contrary to fidelity" or "faith," "contro alla fede," and "tutto fede," "altogether faithful," in the next paragraph. It is noteworthy that these two phrases, "contro alla fede" and "tutto fede," were omitted in the Testina edition, which was published with the sanction of the papal authorities. It may be that the meaning attached to the word "fede" was "the faith," i.e. the Catholic creed, and not as rendered here "fidelity" and "faithful." Observe that the word "religione" was suffered to stand in the text of the Testina, being used to signify indifferently every shade of belief, as witness "the religion," a phrase inevitably employed to designate the Huguenot heresy. South in his Sermon IX, p. 69, ed. 1843, comments on this passage as follows: "That great patron and Coryphaeus of this tribe, Nicolo Machiavel, laid down this for a master rule in his political scheme: 'That the show of religion was helpful to the politician, but the reality of it hurtful and pernicious.'"

41 Ferdinand of Aragon. "When Machiavelli was writing 'Prince' it would have been clearly impossible to mention Ferdinand's name here without giving offence." Burd's "Il Principe," p. 308.

greatness, courage, gravity, and fortitude; and in his private dealings with his subjects let him show that his judgments are irrevocable, and maintain himself in such reputation that no one can hope either to deceive him or to get round him.

That prince is highly esteemed who conveys this impression of himself, and he who is highly esteemed is not easily conspired against; for, provided it is well known that he is an excellent man and revered by his people, he can only be attacked with difficulty. For this reason a prince ought to have two fears, one from within, on account of his subjects, the other from without, on account of external powers. From the latter he is defended by being well armed and having good allies, and if he is well armed he will have good friends, and affairs will always remain quiet within when they are quiet without, unless they should have been already disturbed by conspiracy; and even should affairs outside be disturbed, if he has carried out his preparations and has lived as I have said, as long as he does not despair, he will resist every attack, as I said Nabis the Spartan did.

But concerning his subjects, when affairs outside are disturbed he has only to fear that they will conspire secretly, from which a prince can easily secure himself by avoiding being hated and despised, and by keeping the people satisfied with him, which it is most necessary for him to accomplish, as I said above at length. And one of the most efficacious remedies that a prince can have against conspiracies is not to be hated and despised by the people, for he who conspires against a prince always expects to please them by his removal; but when the conspirator can only look forward to offending them, he will not have the courage to take such a course, for the difficulties that confront a conspirator are infinite. And as experience shows, many have been the conspiracies, but few have been successful; because he who conspires cannot act alone, nor can he take a companion except from those whom he believes to be malcontents, and as soon as you have opened your mind to a malcontent you have given him the material with which to content himself, for by denouncing you he can look for every advantage; so that, seeing the gain from this course to be assured, and seeing the other to be doubtful and full of dangers, he must be a very rare friend, or a thoroughly obstinate enemy of the prince, to keep faith with you.

And, to reduce the matter into a small compass, I say that, on the side of the conspirator, there is nothing but fear, jealousy, prospect of punishment to terrify him; but on the side of the prince there is the majesty of the principality, the laws, the protection of friends and the state to defend him; so that, adding to all these things the popular goodwill, it is impossible that any one should be so rash as to conspire. For whereas in general the conspirator has to fear before the execution of his plot, in this case he has also to fear the sequel to the crime; because on account of it he has the people for an enemy, and thus cannot hope for any escape.

Endless examples could be given on this subject, but I will be content with one, brought to pass within the memory of our fathers. Messer Annibale Bentivogli, who was prince in Bologna (grandfather of the present Annibale), having been murdered by the Canneschi, who had conspired against him, not one of his family survived but Messer Giovanni[42], who was in childhood: immediately after his assassination the people rose and murdered all the Canneschi. This sprung from the popular goodwill which the house of Bentivogli enjoyed in those days in Bologna; which was so great that, although none remained there after the death of Annibale who was able to rule the state, the Bolognese, having information that there was one of the Bentivogli family in Florence, who up to that time had been considered the son of a blacksmith, sent to Florence for him and gave him the government of their city, and it was ruled by him until Messer Giovanni came in due course to the government.

For this reason I consider that a prince ought to reckon conspiracies of little account when his people hold him in esteem; but when it is hostile to him, and bears hatred towards him, he ought to fear everything and

---

42 Giovanni Bentivogli, born in Bologna 1438, died at Milan 1508. He ruled Bologna from 1462 to 1506. Machiavelli's strong condemnation of conspiracies may get its edge from his own very recent experience (February 1513), when he had been arrested and tortured for his alleged complicity in the Boscoli conspiracy.

everybody. And well-ordered states and wise princes have taken every care not to drive the nobles to desperation, and to keep the people satisfied and contented, for this is one of the most important objects a prince can have.

Among the best ordered and governed kingdoms of our times is France, and in it are found many good institutions on which depend the liberty and security of the king; of these the first is the parliament and its authority, because he who founded the kingdom, knowing the ambition of the nobility and their boldness, considered that a bit to their mouths would be necessary to hold them in; and, on the other side, knowing the hatred of the people, founded in fear, against the nobles, he wished to protect them, yet he was not anxious for this to be the particular care of the king; therefore, to take away the reproach which he would be liable to from the nobles for favouring the people, and from the people for favouring the nobles, he set up an arbiter, who should be one who could beat down the great and favour the lesser without reproach to the king. Neither could you have a better or a more prudent arrangement, or a greater source of security to the king and kingdom. From this one can draw another important conclusion that princes ought to leave affairs of reproach to the management of others, and keep those of grace in their own hands. And further, I consider that a prince ought to cherish the nobles, but not so as to make himself hated by the people.

It may appear, perhaps, to some who have examined the lives and deaths of the Roman emperors that many of them would be an example contrary to my opinion, seeing that some of them lived nobly and showed great qualities of soul, nevertheless they have lost their empire or have been killed by subjects who have conspired against them. Wishing, therefore, to answer these objections, I will recall the characters of some of the emperors, and will show that the causes of their ruin were not different to those alleged by me; at the same time I will only submit for consideration those things that are noteworthy to him who studies the affairs of those times.

It seems to me sufficient to take all those emperors who succeeded to the empire from Marcus the philosopher down to Maximinus; they were Marcus and his son Commodus, Pertinax, Julian, Severus and his son Antoninus Caracalla, Macrinus, Heliogabalus, Alexander, and Maximinus.

There is first to note that, whereas in other principalities the ambition of the nobles and the insolence of the people only have to be contended with, the Roman emperors had a third difficulty in having to put up with the cruelty and avarice of their soldiers, a matter so beset with difficulties that it was the ruin of many; for it was a hard thing to give satisfaction both to soldiers and people; because the people loved peace, and for this reason they loved the unaspiring prince, whilst the soldiers loved the warlike prince who was bold, cruel, and rapacious, which qualities they were quite willing he should exercise upon the people, so that they could get double pay and give vent to their own greed and cruelty. Hence it arose that those emperors were always overthrown who, either by birth or training, had no great authority, and most of them, especially those who came new to the principality, recognizing the difficulty of these two opposing humours, were inclined to give satisfaction to the soldiers, caring little about injuring the people. Which course was necessary, because, as princes cannot help being hated by someone, they ought, in the first place, to avoid being hated by every one, and when they cannot compass this, they ought to endeavour with the utmost diligence to avoid the hatred of the most powerful. Therefore, those emperors who through inexperience had need of special favour adhered more readily to the soldiers than to the people; a course which turned out advantageous to them or not, accordingly as the prince knew how to maintain authority over them.

From these causes it arose that Marcus, Pertinax, and Alexander, being all men of modest life, lovers of justice, enemies to cruelty, humane, and benignant, came to a sad end except Marcus; he alone lived and died honoured, because he had succeeded to the throne by hereditary title, and owed nothing either to the soldiers or the people; and afterwards, being possessed of many virtues which made him respected, he always kept both orders in their places whilst he lived, and was neither hated nor despised.

But Pertinax was created emperor against the wishes of the soldiers, who, being accustomed to live licentiously under Commodus, could not endure the honest life to which Pertinax wished to reduce them; thus, having given cause for hatred, to which hatred there was added contempt for his old age, he was overthrown at the very beginning of his administration. And here it should be noted that hatred is acquired as much by good works as by bad ones, therefore, as I said before, a prince wishing to keep his state is very often forced to do evil; for when that body is corrupt whom you think you have need of to maintain yourself —it may be either the people or the soldiers or the nobles—you have to submit to its humours and to gratify them, and then good works will do you harm.

But let us come to Alexander, who was a man of such great goodness, that among the other praises which are accorded him is this, that in the fourteen years he held the empire no one was ever put to death by him unjudged; nevertheless, being considered effeminate and a man who allowed himself to be governed by his mother, he became despised, the army conspired against him, and murdered him.

Turning now to the opposite characters of Commodus, Severus, Antoninus Caracalla, and Maximinus, you will find them all cruel and rapacious-men who, to satisfy their soldiers, did not hesitate to commit every kind of iniquity against the people; and all, except Severus, came to a bad end; but in Severus there was so much valour that, keeping the soldiers friendly, although the people were oppressed by him, he reigned successfully; for his valour made him so much admired in the sight of the soldiers and people that the latter were kept in a way astonished and awed and the former respectful and satisfied. And because the actions of this man, as a new prince, were great, I wish to show briefly that he knew well how to counterfeit the fox and the lion, which natures, as I said above, it is necessary for a prince to imitate.

Knowing the sloth of the Emperor Julian, he persuaded the army in Sclavonia, of which he was captain, that it would be right to go to Rome and avenge the death of Pertinax, who had been killed by the praetorian soldiers; and under this pretext, without appearing to aspire to the throne, he moved the army on Rome, and reached Italy before it was known that he had started. On his arrival at Rome, the Senate, through fear, elected him emperor and killed Julian. After this there remained for Severus, who wished to make himself master of the whole empire, two difficulties; one in Asia, where Niger, head of the Asiatic army, had caused himself to be proclaimed emperor; the other in the west where Albinus was, who also aspired to the throne. And as he considered it dangerous to declare himself hostile to both, he decided to attack Niger and to deceive Albinus. To the latter he wrote that, being elected emperor by the Senate, he was willing to share that dignity with him and sent him the title of Caesar; and, moreover, that the Senate had made Albinus his colleague; which things were accepted by Albinus as true. But after Severus had conquered and killed Niger, and settled oriental affairs, he returned to Rome and complained to the Senate that Albinus, little recognizing the benefits that he had received from him, had by treachery sought to murder him, and for this ingratitude he was compelled to punish him. Afterwards he sought him out in France, and took from him his government and life. He who will, therefore, carefully examine the actions of this man will find him a most valiant lion and a most cunning fox; he will find him feared and respected by every one, and not hated by the army; and it need not be wondered at that he, a new man, was able to hold the empire so well, because his supreme renown always protected him from that hatred which the people might have conceived against him for his violence.

But his son Antoninus was a most eminent man, and had very excellent qualities, which made him admirable in the sight of the people and acceptable to the soldiers, for he was a warlike man, most enduring of fatigue, a despiser of all delicate food and other luxuries, which caused him to be beloved by the armies. Nevertheless, his ferocity and cruelties were so great and so unheard of that, after endless single murders, he killed a large number of the people of Rome and all those of Alexandria. He became hated by the whole world, and also feared by those he had around him, to such an extent that he was murdered in the midst of his army by a centurion. And here it must be noted that such-like deaths, which are deliberately inflicted with a resolved and desperate courage, cannot be avoided by princes, because any one who does not fear to die can inflict them; but a prince may fear them the less because they are very rare; he has only to be careful not to do any grave injury to those whom he employs or has around him in the service of the state. Antoninus had not taken this care, but had contumeliously killed a brother of that centurion, whom also he daily threatened, yet retained in his bodyguard; which, as it turned out, was a rash thing to do, and proved the emperor's ruin.

But let us come to Commodus, to whom it should have been very easy to hold the empire, for, being the son of Marcus, he had inherited it, and he had only to follow in the footsteps of his father to please his people and soldiers; but, being by nature cruel and brutal, he gave himself up to amusing the soldiers and corrupting them, so that he might indulge his rapacity upon the people; on the other hand, not maintaining his dignity, often descending to the theatre to compete with gladiators, and doing other vile things, little worthy of the imperial majesty, he fell into contempt with the soldiers, and being hated by one party and despised by the other, he was conspired against and was killed.

It remains to discuss the character of Maximinus. He was a very warlike man, and the armies, being disgusted with the effeminacy of Alexander, of whom I have already spoken, killed him and elected Maximinus to the throne. This he did not possess for long, for two things made him hated and despised; the one, his having kept sheep in Thrace, which brought him into contempt (it being well known to all, and considered a great indignity by every one), and the other, his having at the accession to his dominions deferred going to Rome and taking possession of the imperial seat; he had also gained a reputation for the utmost ferocity by having, through his prefects in Rome and elsewhere in the empire, practised many cruelties, so that the whole world was moved to anger at the meanness of his birth and to fear at his barbarity. First Africa rebelled, then the Senate with all the people of Rome, and all Italy conspired against him, to which may be added his own army; this latter, besieging Aquileia and meeting with difficulties in taking it, were disgusted with his cruelties, and fearing him less when they found so many against him, murdered him.

I do not wish to discuss Heliogabalus, Macrinus, or Julian, who, being thoroughly contemptible, were quickly wiped out; but I will bring this discourse to a conclusion by saying that princes in our times have this difficulty of giving inordinate satisfaction to their soldiers in a far less degree, because, notwithstanding one has to give them some indulgence, that is soon done; none of these princes have armies that are veterans in the governance and administration of provinces, as were the armies of the Roman Empire; and whereas it was then more necessary to give satisfaction to the soldiers than to the people, it is now more necessary to all princes, except the Turk and the Soldan, to satisfy the people rather the soldiers, because the people are the more powerful.

From the above I have excepted the Turk, who always keeps round him twelve thousand infantry and fifteen thousand cavalry on which depend the security and strength of the kingdom, and it is necessary that, putting aside every consideration for the people, he should keep them his friends. The kingdom of the Soldan is similar; being entirely in the hands of soldiers, it follows again that, without regard to the people, he must keep them his friends. But you must note that the state of the Soldan is unlike all other principalities, for the reason that it is like the Christian pontificate, which cannot be called either an hereditary or a newly formed principality; because the sons of the old prince are not the heirs, but he who is elected to that position by those who have authority, and the sons remain only noblemen. And this being an ancient custom, it cannot be called a new principality, because there are none of those difficulties in it that are met with in new ones; for although the prince is new, the constitution of the state is old, and it is framed so as to receive him as if he were its hereditary lord.

But returning to the subject of our discourse, I say that whoever will consider it will acknowledge that either hatred or contempt has been fatal to the above-named emperors, and it will be recognized also how it happened that, a number of them acting in one way and a number in another, only one in each way came to a happy end and the rest to unhappy ones. Because it would have been useless and dangerous for Pertinax and Alexander, being new princes, to imitate Marcus, who was heir to the principality; and likewise it would have been utterly destructive to Caracalla, Commodus, and Maximinus to have imitated Severus, they not having sufficient valour to enable them to tread in his footsteps. Therefore a prince, new to the principality, cannot imitate the actions of Marcus, nor, again, is it necessary to follow those of Severus, but he ought to take from Severus those parts which are necessary to found his state, and from Marcus those which are proper and glorious to keep a state that may already be stable and firm.

CHAPTER XX — ARE FORTRESSES, AND MANY OTHER THINGS TO WHICH PRINCES OFTEN RESORT, ADVANTAGEOUS OR HURTFUL?

1. Some princes, so as to hold securely the state, have disarmed their subjects; others have kept their subject towns distracted by factions; others have fostered enmities against themselves; others have laid themselves out to gain over those whom they distrusted in the beginning of their governments; some have built fortresses; some have overthrown and destroyed them. And although one cannot give a final judgment on all of these things unless one possesses the particulars of those states in which a decision has to be made, nevertheless I will speak as comprehensively as the matter of itself will admit.

2. There never was a new prince who has disarmed his subjects; rather when he has found them disarmed he has always armed them, because, by arming them, those arms become yours, those men who were distrusted become faithful, and those who were faithful are kept so, and your subjects become your adherents. And whereas all subjects cannot be armed, yet when those whom you do arm are benefited, the others can be handled more freely, and this difference in their treatment, which they quite understand, makes the former your dependents, and the latter, considering it to be necessary that those who have the most danger and service should have the most reward, excuse you. But when you disarm them, you at once offend them by showing that you distrust them, either for cowardice or for want of loyalty, and either of these opinions breeds hatred against you. And because you cannot remain unarmed, it follows that you turn to mercenaries, which are of the character already shown; even if they should be good they would not be sufficient to defend you against powerful enemies and distrusted subjects. Therefore, as I have said, a new prince in a new principality has always distributed arms. Histories are full of examples. But when a prince acquires a new state, which he adds as a province to his old one, then it is necessary to disarm the men of that state, except those who have been his adherents in acquiring it; and these again, with time and opportunity, should be rendered soft and effeminate; and matters should be managed in such a way that all the armed men in the state shall be your own soldiers who in your old state were living near you.

3. Our forefathers, and those who were reckoned wise, were accustomed to say that it was necessary to hold Pistoia by factions and Pisa by fortresses; and with this idea they fostered quarrels in some of their tributary towns so as to keep possession of them the more easily. This may have been well enough in those times when Italy was in a way balanced, but I do not believe that it can be accepted as a precept for to-day, because I do not believe that factions can ever be of use; rather it is certain that when the enemy comes upon you in divided cities you are quickly lost, because the weakest party will always assist the outside forces and the other will not be able to resist. The Venetians, moved, as I believe, by the above reasons, fostered the Guelph and Ghibelline factions in their tributary cities; and although they never allowed them to come to bloodshed, yet they nursed these disputes amongst them, so that the citizens, distracted by their differences, should not unite against them. Which, as we saw, did not afterwards turn out as expected, because, after the rout at Vaila, one party at once took courage and seized the state. Such methods argue, therefore, weakness in the

prince, because these factions will never be permitted in a vigorous principality; such methods for enabling one the more easily to manage subjects are only useful in times of peace, but if war comes this policy proves fallacious.

4. Without doubt princes become great when they overcome the difficulties and obstacles by which they are confronted, and therefore fortune, especially when she desires to make a new prince great, who has a greater necessity to earn renown than an hereditary one, causes enemies to arise and form designs against him, in order that he may have the opportunity of overcoming them, and by them to mount higher, as by a ladder which his enemies have raised. For this reason many consider that a wise prince, when he has the opportunity, ought with craft to foster some animosity against himself, so that, having crushed it, his renown may rise higher.

5. Princes, especially new ones, have found more fidelity and assistance in those men who in the beginning of their rule were distrusted than among those who in the beginning were trusted. Pandolfo Petrucci, Prince of Siena, ruled his state more by those who had been distrusted than by others. But on this question one cannot speak generally, for it varies so much with the individual; I will only say this, that those men who at the commencement of a princedom have been hostile, if they are of a description to need assistance to support themselves, can always be gained over with the greatest ease, and they will be tightly held to serve the prince with fidelity, inasmuch as they know it to be very necessary for them to cancel by deeds the bad impression which he had formed of them; and thus the prince always extracts more profit from them than from those who, serving him in too much security, may neglect his affairs. And since the matter demands it, I must not fail to warn a prince, who by means of secret favours has acquired a new state, that he must well consider the reasons which induced those to favour him who did so; and if it be not a natural affection towards him, but only discontent with their government, then he will only keep them friendly with great trouble and difficulty, for it will be impossible to satisfy them. And weighing well the reasons for this in those examples which can be taken from ancient and modern affairs, we shall find that it is easier for the prince to make friends of those men who were contented under the former government, and are therefore his enemies, than of those who, being discontented with it, were favourable to him and encouraged him to seize it.

6. It has been a custom with princes, in order to hold their states more securely, to build fortresses that may serve as a bridle and bit to those who might design to work against them, and as a place of refuge from a first attack. I praise this system because it has been made use of formerly. Notwithstanding that, Messer Nicolo Vitelli in our times has been seen to demolish two fortresses in Citta di Castello so that he might keep that state; Guido Ubaldo, Duke of Urbino, on returning to his dominion, whence he had been driven by Cesare Borgia, razed to the foundations all the fortresses in that province, and considered that without them it would be more difficult to lose it; the Bentivogli returning to Bologna came to a similar decision. Fortresses, therefore, are useful or not according to circumstances; if they do you good in one way they injure you in another. And this question can be reasoned thus: the prince who has more to fear from the people than from foreigners ought to build fortresses, but he who has more to fear from foreigners than from the people ought to leave them alone. The castle of Milan, built by Francesco Sforza, has made, and will make, more trouble for the house of Sforza than any other disorder in the state. For this reason the best possible fortress is—not to be hated by the people, because, although you may hold the fortresses, yet they will not save you if the people hate you, for there will never be wanting foreigners to assist a people who have taken arms against you. It has not been seen in our times that such fortresses have been of use to any prince, unless to the Countess of Forli[43], when the Count Girolamo, her consort, was killed; for by that means she was able to withstand the

---

43 Catherine Sforza, a daughter of Galeazzo Sforza and Lucrezia Landriani, born 1463, died 1509. It was to the Countess of Forli that Machiavelli was sent as envoy on 1499. A letter from Fortunati to the countess announces the

popular attack and wait for assistance from Milan, and thus recover her state; and the posture of affairs was such at that time that the foreigners could not assist the people. But fortresses were of little value to her afterwards when Cesare Borgia attacked her, and when the people, her enemy, were allied with foreigners. Therefore, it would have been safer for her, both then and before, not to have been hated by the people than to have had the fortresses. All these things considered then, I shall praise him who builds fortresses as well as him who does not, and I shall blame whoever, trusting in them, cares little about being hated by the people.

CHAPTER XXI — HOW A PRINCE SHOULD CONDUCT HIMSELF SO AS TO GAIN RENOWN

Nothing makes a prince so much esteemed as great enterprises and setting a fine example. We have in our time Ferdinand of Aragon, the present King of Spain. He can almost be called a new prince, because he has risen, by fame and glory, from being an insignificant king to be the foremost king in Christendom; and if you will consider his deeds you will find them all great and some of them extraordinary. In the beginning of his reign he attacked Granada, and this enterprise was the foundation of his dominions. He did this quietly at first and without any fear of hindrance, for he held the minds of the barons of Castile occupied in thinking of the war and not anticipating any innovations; thus they did not perceive that by these means he was acquiring power and authority over them. He was able with the money of the Church and of the people to sustain his armies, and by that long war to lay the foundation for the military skill which has since distinguished him. Further, always using religion as a plea, so as to undertake greater schemes, he devoted himself with pious cruelty to driving out and clearing his kingdom of the Moors; nor could there be a more admirable example, nor one more rare. Under this same cloak he assailed Africa, he came down on Italy, he has finally attacked France; and thus his achievements and designs have always been great, and have kept the minds of his people in suspense and admiration and occupied with the issue of them. And his actions have arisen in such a way, one out of the other, that men have never been given time to work steadily against him.

Again, it much assists a prince to set unusual examples in internal affairs, similar to those which are related of Messer Bernabo da Milano, who, when he had the opportunity, by any one in civil life doing some extraordinary thing, either good or bad, would take some method of rewarding or punishing him, which would be much spoken about. And a prince ought, above all things, always endeavour in every action to gain for himself the reputation of being a great and remarkable man.

A prince is also respected when he is either a true friend or a downright enemy, that is to say, when, without any reservation, he declares himself in favour of one party against the other; which course will always be more advantageous than standing neutral; because if two of your powerful neighbours come to blows, they are of such a character that, if one of them conquers, you have either to fear him or not. In either case it will always be more advantageous for you to declare yourself and to make war strenuously; because, in the first case, if you do not declare yourself, you will invariably fall a prey to the conqueror, to the pleasure and satisfaction of him who has been conquered, and you will have no reasons to offer, nor anything to protect or to shelter you. Because he who conquers does not want doubtful friends who will not aid him in the time of trial; and he who loses will not harbour you because you did not willingly, sword in hand, court his fate.

Antiochus went into Greece, being sent for by the Aetolians to drive out the Romans. He sent envoys to the Achaeans, who were friends of the Romans, exhorting them to remain neutral; and on the other hand the

---

appointment: "I have been with the signori," wrote Fortunati, "to learn whom they would send and when. They tell me that Nicolo Machiavelli, a learned young Florentine noble, secretary to my Lords of the Ten, is to leave with me at once." Cf. "Catherine Sforza," by Count Pasolini, translated by P. Sylvester, 1898.

Romans urged them to take up arms. This question came to be discussed in the council of the Achaeans, where the legate of Antiochus urged them to stand neutral. To this the Roman legate answered: "As for that which has been said, that it is better and more advantageous for your state not to interfere in our war, nothing can be more erroneous; because by not interfering you will be left, without favour or consideration, the guerdon of the conqueror." Thus it will always happen that he who is not your friend will demand your neutrality, whilst he who is your friend will entreat you to declare yourself with arms. And irresolute princes, to avoid present dangers, generally follow the neutral path, and are generally ruined. But when a prince declares himself gallantly in favour of one side, if the party with whom he allies himself conquers, although the victor may be powerful and may have him at his mercy, yet he is indebted to him, and there is established a bond of amity; and men are never so shameless as to become a monument of ingratitude by oppressing you. Victories after all are never so complete that the victor must not show some regard, especially to justice. But if he with whom you ally yourself loses, you may be sheltered by him, and whilst he is able he may aid you, and you become companions on a fortune that may rise again.

In the second case, when those who fight are of such a character that you have no anxiety as to who may conquer, so much the more is it greater prudence to be allied, because you assist at the destruction of one by the aid of another who, if he had been wise, would have saved him; and conquering, as it is impossible that he should not do with your assistance, he remains at your discretion. And here it is to be noted that a prince ought to take care never to make an alliance with one more powerful than himself for the purposes of attacking others, unless necessity compels him, as is said above; because if he conquers you are at his discretion, and princes ought to avoid as much as possible being at the discretion of any one. The Venetians joined with France against the Duke of Milan, and this alliance, which caused their ruin, could have been avoided. But when it cannot be avoided, as happened to the Florentines when the Pope and Spain sent armies to attack Lombardy, then in such a case, for the above reasons, the prince ought to favour one of the parties.

Never let any Government imagine that it can choose perfectly safe courses; rather let it expect to have to take very doubtful ones, because it is found in ordinary affairs that one never seeks to avoid one trouble without running into another; but prudence consists in knowing how to distinguish the character of troubles, and for choice to take the lesser evil.

A prince ought also to show himself a patron of ability, and to honour the proficient in every art. At the same time he should encourage his citizens to practise their callings peaceably, both in commerce and agriculture, and in every other following, so that the one should not be deterred from improving his possessions for fear lest they be taken away from him or another from opening up trade for fear of taxes; but the prince ought to offer rewards to whoever wishes to do these things and designs in any way to honour his city or state.

Further, he ought to entertain the people with festivals and spectacles at convenient seasons of the year; and as every city is divided into guilds or into societies[44], he ought to hold such bodies in esteem, and associate with them sometimes, and show himself an example of courtesy and liberality; nevertheless, always

---

44 "Guilds or societies," "in arti o in tribu." "Arti" were craft or trade guilds, cf. Florio: "Arte . . . a whole company of any trade in any city or corporation town." The guilds of Florence are most admirably described by Mr Edgcumbe Staley in his work on the subject (Methuen, 1906). Institutions of a somewhat similar character, called "artel," exist in Russia to-day, cf. Sir Mackenzie Wallace's "Russia," ed. 1905: "The sons . . . were always during the working season members of an artel. In some of the larger towns there are artels of a much more complex kind— permanent associations, possessing large capital, and pecuniarily responsible for the acts of the individual members." The word "artel," despite its apparent similarity, has, Mr Aylmer Maude assures me, no connection with "ars" or "arte." Its root is that of the verb "rotisya," to bind oneself by an oath; and it is generally admitted to be only another form of "rota," which now signifies a "regimental company." In both words the underlying idea is that of a body of men united by an oath. "Tribu" were possibly gentile groups, united by common descent, and included individuals connected by marriage. Perhaps our words "sects" or "clans" would be most appropriate.

maintaining the majesty of his rank, for this he must never consent to abate in anything.

CHAPTER XXII — CONCERNING THE SECRETARIES OF PRINCES

The choice of servants is of no little importance to a prince, and they are good or not according to the discrimination of the prince. And the first opinion which one forms of a prince, and of his understanding, is by observing the men he has around him; and when they are capable and faithful he may always be considered wise, because he has known how to recognize the capable and to keep them faithful. But when they are otherwise one cannot form a good opinion of him, for the prime error which he made was in choosing them.

There were none who knew Messer Antonio da Venafro as the servant of Pandolfo Petrucci, Prince of Siena, who would not consider Pandolfo to be a very clever man in having Venafro for his servant. Because there are three classes of intellects: one which comprehends by itself; another which appreciates what others comprehended; and a third which neither comprehends by itself nor by the showing of others; the first is the most excellent, the second is good, the third is useless. Therefore, it follows necessarily that, if Pandolfo was not in the first rank, he was in the second, for whenever one has judgment to know good and bad when it is said and done, although he himself may not have the initiative, yet he can recognize the good and the bad in his servant, and the one he can praise and the other correct; thus the servant cannot hope to deceive him, and is kept honest.

But to enable a prince to form an opinion of his servant there is one test which never fails; when you see the servant thinking more of his own interests than of yours, and seeking inwardly his own profit in everything, such a man will never make a good servant, nor will you ever be able to trust him; because he who has the state of another in his hands ought never to think of himself, but always of his prince, and never pay any attention to matters in which the prince is not concerned.

On the other hand, to keep his servant honest the prince ought to study him, honouring him, enriching him, doing him kindnesses, sharing with him the honours and cares; and at the same time let him see that he cannot stand alone, so that many honours may not make him desire more, many riches make him wish for more, and that many cares may make him dread chances. When, therefore, servants, and princes towards servants, are thus disposed, they can trust each other, but when it is otherwise, the end will always be disastrous for either one or the other.

CHAPTER XXIII — HOW FLATTERERS SHOULD BE AVOIDED

I do not wish to leave out an important branch of this subject, for it is a danger from which princes are with difficulty preserved, unless they are very careful and discriminating. It is that of flatterers, of whom courts are full, because men are so self-complacent in their own affairs, and in a way so deceived in them, that they are preserved with difficulty from this pest, and if they wish to defend themselves they run the danger of falling into contempt. Because there is no other way of guarding oneself from flatterers except letting men understand that to tell you the truth does not offend you; but when every one may tell you the truth, respect for you abates.

Therefore a wise prince ought to hold a third course by choosing the wise men in his state, and giving to them only the liberty of speaking the truth to him, and then only of those things of which he inquires, and of none others; but he ought to question them upon everything, and listen to their opinions, and afterwards form his own conclusions. With these councilors, separately and collectively, he ought to carry himself in such a way that each of them should know that, the more freely he shall speak, the more he shall be preferred; outside of these, he should listen to no one, pursue the thing resolved on, and be steadfast in his resolutions. He who does otherwise is either overthrown by flatterers, or is so often changed by varying opinions that he falls into contempt.

I wish on this subject to adduce a modern example. Fra Luca, the man of affairs to Maximilian[45], the present emperor, speaking of his majesty, said: He consulted with no one, yet never got his own way in anything. This arose because of his following a practice the opposite to the above; for the emperor is a secretive man—he does not communicate his designs to any one, nor does he receive opinions on them. But as in carrying them into effect they become revealed and known, they are at once obstructed by those men whom he has around him, and he, being pliant, is diverted from them. Hence it follows that those things he does one day he undoes the next, and no one ever understands what he wishes or intends to do, and no one can rely on his resolutions.

A prince, therefore, ought always to take counsel, but only when he wishes and not when others wish; he ought rather to discourage every one from offering advice unless he asks it; but, however, he ought to be a constant inquirer, and afterwards a patient listener concerning the things of which he inquired; also, on learning that any one, on any consideration, has not told him the truth, he should let his anger be felt.

And if there are some who think that a prince who conveys an impression of his wisdom is not so through his own ability, but through the good advisers that he has around him, beyond doubt they are deceived, because this is an axiom which never fails: that a prince who is not wise himself will never take good advice, unless by chance he has yielded his affairs entirely to one person who happens to be a very prudent man. In this case indeed he may be well governed, but it would not be for long, because such a governor would in a short time take away his state from him.

But if a prince who is not inexperienced should take counsel from more than one he will never get united counsels, nor will he know how to unite them. Each of the counselors will think of his own interests, and the prince will not know how to control them or to see through them. And they are not to found otherwise, because men will always prove untrue to you unless they are kept honest by constraint. Therefore it must be inferred that good counsels, whence soever they come, are born of the wisdom of the prince, and not the wisdom of the prince from good counsels.

CHAPTER XXIV — WHY THE PRINCES OF ITALY HAVE LOST THEIR STATES

The previous suggestions, carefully observed, will enable a new prince to appear well established, and render him at once more secure and fixed in the state than if he had been long seated there. For the actions of a new prince are more narrowly observed than those of an hereditary one, and when they are seen to be able they gain more men and bind far tighter than ancient blood; because men are attracted more by the present than by the past, and when they find the present good they enjoy it and seek no further; they will also make the utmost defence of a prince if he fails them not in other things. Thus it will be a double glory for him to have established a new principality, and adorned and strengthened it with good laws, good arms, good allies, and with a good example; so will it be a double disgrace to him who, born a prince, shall lose his state by want of wisdom.

And if those seigniors are considered who have lost their states in Italy in our times, such as the King of Naples, the Duke of Milan, and others, there will be found in them, firstly, one common defect in regard to arms from the causes which have been discussed at length; in the next place, some one of them will be seen, either to have had the people hostile, or if he has had the people friendly, he has not known how to secure the

---

45 Maximilian I, born in 1459, died 1519, Emperor of the Holy Roman Empire. He married, first, Mary, daughter of Charles the Bold; after her death, Bianca Sforza; and thus became involved in Italian politics.

nobles. In the absence of these defects states that have power enough to keep an army in the field cannot be lost.

Philip of Macedon, not the father of Alexander the Great, but he who was conquered by Titus Quintius, had not much territory compared to the greatness of the Romans and of Greece who attacked him, yet being a warlike man who knew how to attract the people and secure the nobles, he sustained the war against his enemies for many years, and if in the end he lost the dominion of some cities, nevertheless he retained the kingdom.

Therefore, do not let our princes accuse fortune for the loss of their principalities after so many years' possession, but rather their own sloth, because in quiet times they never thought there could be a change (it is a common defect in man not to make any provision in the calm against the tempest), and when afterwards the bad times came they thought of flight and not of defending themselves, and they hoped that the people, disgusted with the insolence of the conquerors, would recall them. This course, when others fail, may be good, but it is very bad to have neglected all other expedients for that, since you would never wish to fall because you trusted to be able to find someone later on to restore you. This again either does not happen, or, if it does, it will not be for your security, because that deliverance is of no avail which does not depend upon yourself; those only are reliable, certain, and durable that depend on yourself and your valour.

CHAPTER XXV — WHAT FORTUNE CAN EFFECT IN HUMAN AFFAIRS AND HOW TO WITHSTAND HER

It is not unknown to me how many men have had, and still have, the opinion that the affairs of the world are in such wise governed by fortune and by God that men with their wisdom cannot direct them and that no one can even help them; and because of this they would have us believe that it is not necessary to labour much in affairs, but to let chance govern them. This opinion has been more credited in our times because of the great changes in affairs which have been seen, and may still be seen, every day, beyond all human conjecture. Sometimes pondering over this, I am in some degree inclined to their opinion. Nevertheless, not to extinguish our free will, I hold it to be true that Fortune is the arbiter of one-half of our actions[46], but that she still leaves us to direct the other half, or perhaps a little less.

I compare her to one of those raging rivers, which when in flood overflows the plains, sweeping away trees and buildings, bearing away the soil from place to place; everything flies before it, all yield to its violence, without being able in any way to withstand it; and yet, though its nature be such, it does not follow therefore that men, when the weather becomes fair, shall not make provision, both with defences and barriers, in such a manner that, rising again, the waters may pass away by canal, and their force be neither so unrestrained nor so dangerous. So it happens with fortune, who shows her power where valour has not prepared to resist her, and thither she turns her forces where she knows that barriers and defences have not been raised to constrain her.

And if you will consider Italy, which is the seat of these changes, and which has given to them their impulse, you will see it to be an open country without barriers and without any defence. For if it had been defended by proper valour, as are Germany, Spain, and France, either this invasion would not have made the great changes it has made or it would not have come at all. And this I consider enough to say concerning resistance to fortune in general.

But confining myself more to the particular, I say that a prince may be seen happy to-day and ruined to-morrow without having shown any change of disposition or character. This, I believe, arises firstly from causes that have already been discussed at length, namely, that the prince who relies entirely on fortune is lost

---

46 Frederick the Great was accustomed to say: "The older one gets the more convinced one becomes that his Majesty King Chance does three-quarters of the business of this miserable universe." Sorel's "Eastern Question."

when it changes. I believe also that he will be successful who directs his actions according to the spirit of the times, and that he whose actions do not accord with the times will not be successful. Because men are seen, in affairs that lead to the end which every man has before him, namely, glory and riches, to get there by various methods; one with caution, another with haste; one by force, another by skill; one by patience, another by its opposite; and each one succeeds in reaching the goal by a different method. One can also see of two cautious men the one attain his end, the other fail; and similarly, two men by different observances are equally successful, the one being cautious, the other impetuous; all this arises from nothing else than whether or not they conform in their methods to the spirit of the times. This follows from what I have said, that two men working differently bring about the same effect, and of two working similarly, one attains his object and the other does not.

Changes in estate also issue from this, for if, to one who governs himself with caution and patience, times and affairs converge in such a way that his administration is successful, his fortune is made; but if times and affairs change, he is ruined if he does not change his course of action. But a man is not often found sufficiently circumspect to know how to accommodate himself to the change, both because he cannot deviate from what nature inclines him to do, and also because, having always prospered by acting in one way, he cannot be persuaded that it is well to leave it; and, therefore, the cautious man, when it is time to turn adventurous, does not know how to do it, hence he is ruined; but had he changed his conduct with the times fortune would not have changed.

Pope Julius the Second went to work impetuously in all his affairs, and found the times and circumstances conform so well to that line of action that he always met with success. Consider his first enterprise against Bologna, Messer Giovanni Bentivogli being still alive. The Venetians were not agreeable to it, nor was the King of Spain, and he had the enterprise still under discussion with the King of France; nevertheless he personally entered upon the expedition with his accustomed boldness and energy, a move which made Spain and the Venetians stand irresolute and passive, the latter from fear, the former from desire to recover the kingdom of Naples; on the other hand, he drew after him the King of France, because that king, having observed the movement, and desiring to make the Pope his friend so as to humble the Venetians, found it impossible to refuse him. Therefore Julius with his impetuous action accomplished what no other pontiff with simple human wisdom could have done; for if he had waited in Rome until he could get away, with his plans arranged and everything fixed, as any other pontiff would have done, he would never have succeeded. Because the King of France would have made a thousand excuses, and the others would have raised a thousand fears.

I will leave his other actions alone, as they were all alike, and they all succeeded, for the shortness of his life did not let him experience the contrary; but if circumstances had arisen which required him to go cautiously, his ruin would have followed, because he would never have deviated from those ways to which nature inclined him.

I conclude, therefore that, fortune being changeful and mankind steadfast in their ways, so long as the two are in agreement men are successful, but unsuccessful when they fall out. For my part I consider that it is better to be adventurous than cautious, because fortune is a woman, and if you wish to keep her under it is necessary to beat and ill-use her; and it is seen that she allows herself to be mastered by the adventurous rather than by those who go to work more coldly. She is, therefore, always, woman-like, a lover of young men, because they are less cautious, more violent, and with more audacity command her.

CHAPTER XXVI — AN EXHORTATION TO LIBERATE ITALY FROM THE BARBARIANS

Having carefully considered the subject of the above discourses, and wondering within myself whether the present times were propitious to a new prince, and whether there were elements that would give an opportunity to a wise and virtuous one to introduce a new order of things which would do honour to him and good to the people of this country, it appears to me that so many things concur to favour a new prince that I never knew a time more fit than the present.

And if, as I said, it was necessary that the people of Israel should be captive so as to make manifest the ability of Moses; that the Persians should be oppressed by the Medes so as to discover the greatness of the soul of Cyrus; and that the Athenians should be dispersed to illustrate the capabilities of Theseus: then at the present time, in order to discover the virtue of an Italian spirit, it was necessary that Italy should be reduced to the extremity that she is now in, that she should be more enslaved than the Hebrews, more oppressed than the Persians, more scattered than the Athenians; without head, without order, beaten, despoiled, torn, overrun; and to have endured every kind of desolation.

Although lately some spark may have been shown by one, which made us think he was ordained by God for our redemption, nevertheless it was afterwards seen, in the height of his career, that fortune rejected him; so that Italy, left as without life, waits for him who shall yet heal her wounds and put an end to the ravaging and plundering of Lombardy, to the swindling and taxing of the kingdom and of Tuscany, and cleanse those sores that for long have festered. It is seen how she entreats God to send someone who shall deliver her from these wrongs and barbarous insolences. It is seen also that she is ready and willing to follow a banner if only someone will raise it.

Nor is there to be seen at present one in whom she can place more hope than in your illustrious house[47], with its valour and fortune, favoured by God and by the Church of which it is now the chief, and which could be made the head of this redemption. This will not be difficult if you will recall to yourself the actions and lives of the men I have named. And although they were great and wonderful men, yet they were men, and each one of them had no more opportunity than the present offers, for their enterprises were neither more just nor easier than this, nor was God more their friend than He is yours.

With us there is great justice, because that war is just which is necessary, and arms are hallowed when there is no other hope but in them. Here there is the greatest willingness, and where the willingness is great the difficulties cannot be great if you will only follow those men to whom I have directed your attention. Further than this, how extraordinarily the ways of God have been manifested beyond example: the sea is divided, a cloud has led the way, the rock has poured forth water, it has rained manna, everything has contributed to your greatness; you ought to do the rest. God is not willing to do everything, and thus take away our free will and that share of glory which belongs to us.

And it is not to be wondered at if none of the above-named Italians have been able to accomplish all that is expected from your illustrious house; and if in so many revolutions in Italy, and in so many campaigns, it has always appeared as if military virtue were exhausted, this has happened because the old order of things was not good, and none of us have known how to find a new one. And nothing honours a man more than to establish new laws and new ordinances when he himself was newly risen. Such things when they are well founded and dignified will make him revered and admired, and in Italy there are not wanting opportunities to bring such into use in every form.

Here there is great valour in the limbs whilst it fails in the head. Look attentively at the duels and the hand-to-hand combats, how superior the Italians are in strength, dexterity, and subtlety. But when it comes to armies

---

47 Giuliano de Medici. He had just been created a cardinal by Leo X. In 1523 Giuliano was elected Pope, and took the title of Clement VII.

they do not bear comparison, and this springs entirely from the insufficiency of the leaders, since those who are capable are not obedient, and each one seems to himself to know, there having never been any one so distinguished above the rest, either by valour or fortune, that others would yield to him. Hence it is that for so long a time, and during so much fighting in the past twenty years, whenever there has been an army wholly Italian, it has always given a poor account of itself; the first witness to this is Il Taro, afterwards Allesandria, Capua, Genoa, Vaila, Bologna, Mestri[48].

If, therefore, your illustrious house wishes to follow these remarkable men who have redeemed their country, it is necessary before all things, as a true foundation for every enterprise, to be provided with your own forces, because there can be no more faithful, truer, or better soldiers. And although singly they are good, altogether they will be much better when they find themselves commanded by their prince, honoured by him, and maintained at his expense. Therefore it is necessary to be prepared with such arms, so that you can be defended against foreigners by Italian valour.

And although Swiss and Spanish infantry may be considered very formidable, nevertheless there is a defect in both, by reason of which a third order would not only be able to oppose them, but might be relied upon to overthrow them. For the Spaniards cannot resist cavalry, and the Switzers are afraid of infantry whenever they encounter them in close combat. Owing to this, as has been and may again be seen, the Spaniards are unable to resist French cavalry, and the Switzers are overthrown by Spanish infantry. And although a complete proof of this latter cannot be shown, nevertheless there was some evidence of it at the battle of Ravenna, when the Spanish infantry were confronted by German battalions, who follow the same tactics as the Swiss; when the Spaniards, by agility of body and with the aid of their shields, got in under the pikes of the Germans and stood out of danger, able to attack, while the Germans stood helpless, and, if the cavalry had not dashed up, all would have been over with them. It is possible, therefore, knowing the defects of both these infantries, to invent a new one, which will resist cavalry and not be afraid of infantry; this need not create a new order of arms, but a variation upon the old. And these are the kind of improvements which confer reputation and power upon a new prince.

This opportunity, therefore, ought not to be allowed to pass for letting Italy at last see her liberator appear. Nor can one express the love with which he would be received in all those provinces which have suffered so much from these foreign scourings, with what thirst for revenge, with what stubborn faith, with what devotion, with what tears. What door would be closed to him? Who would refuse obedience to him? What envy would hinder him? What Italian would refuse him homage? To all of us this barbarous dominion stinks. Let, therefore, your illustrious house take up this charge with that courage and hope with which all just enterprises are undertaken, so that under its standard our native country may be ennobled, and under its auspices may be verified that saying of Petrarch:

Virtu contro al Furore
Prendera l'arme, e fia il combatter corto:
Che l'antico valore
Negli italici cuor non e ancor morto.

Virtue against fury shall advance the fight,
And it i' th' combat soon shall put to flight:
For the old Roman valour is not dead,
Nor in th' Italians' brests extinguished.

---

48 The battles of Il Taro, 1495; Alessandria, 1499; Capua, 1501; Genoa, 1507; Vaila, 1509; Bologna, 1511; Mestri, 1513.

Edward Dacre, 1640.

DESCRIPTION OF THE METHODS ADOPTED BY THE DUKE VALENTINO WHEN MURDERING VITELLOZZO VITELLI, OLIVEROTTO DA FERMO, THE SIGNOR PAGOLO, AND THE DUKE DI GRAVINA ORSINI BY NICOLO MACHIAVELLI

The Duke Valentino had returned from Lombardy, where he had been to clear himself with the King of France from the calumnies which had been raised against him by the Florentines concerning the rebellion of Arezzo and other towns in the Val di Chiana, and had arrived at Imola, whence he intended with his army to enter upon the campaign against Giovanni Bentivogli, the tyrant of Bologna: for he intended to bring that city under his domination, and to make it the head of his Romagnian duchy.

These matters coming to the knowledge of the Vitelli and Orsini and their following, it appeared to them that the duke would become too powerful, and it was feared that, having seized Bologna, he would seek to destroy them in order that he might become supreme in Italy. Upon this a meeting was called at Magione in the district of Perugia, to which came the cardinal, Pagolo, and the Duke di Gravina Orsini, Vitellozzo Vitelli, Oliverotto da Fermo, Gianpagolo Baglioni, the tyrant of Perugia, and Messer Antonio da Venafro, sent by Pandolfo Petrucci, the Prince of Siena. Here were discussed the power and courage of the duke and the necessity of curbing his ambitions, which might otherwise bring danger to the rest of being ruined. And they decided not to abandon the Bentivogli, but to strive to win over the Florentines; and they send their men to one place and another, promising to one party assistance and to another encouragement to unite with them against the common enemy. This meeting was at once reported throughout all Italy, and those who were discontented under the duke, among whom were the people of Urbino, took hope of effecting a revolution.

Thus it arose that, men's minds being thus unsettled, it was decided by certain men of Urbino to seize the fortress of San Leo, which was held for the duke, and which they captured by the following means. The castellan was fortifying the rock and causing timber to be taken there; so the conspirators watched, and when certain beams which were being carried to the rock were upon the bridge, so that it was prevented from being drawn up by those inside, they took the opportunity of leaping upon the bridge and thence into the fortress. Upon this capture being effected, the whole state rebelled and recalled the old duke, being encouraged in this, not so much by the capture of the fort, as by the Diet at Magione, from whom they expected to get assistance. Those who heard of the rebellion at Urbino thought they would not lose the opportunity, and at once assembled their men so as to take any town, should any remain in the hands of the duke in that state; and they sent again to Florence to beg that republic to join with them in destroying the common firebrand, showing that the risk was lessened and that they ought not to wait for another opportunity.

But the Florentines, from hatred, for sundry reasons, of the Vitelli and Orsini, not only would not ally themselves, but sent Nicolo Machiavelli, their secretary, to offer shelter and assistance to the duke against his enemies. The duke was found full of fear at Imola, because, against everybody's expectation, his soldiers had at once gone over to the enemy and he found himself disarmed and war at his door. But recovering courage from the offers of the Florentines, he decided to temporize before fighting with the few soldiers that remained to him, and to negotiate for a reconciliation, and also to get assistance. This latter he obtained in two ways, by sending to the King of France for men and by enlisting men-at-arms and others whom he turned into cavalry of a sort: to all he gave money.

Notwithstanding this, his enemies drew near to him, and approached Fossombrone, where they encountered some men of the duke and, with the aid of the Orsini and Vitelli, routed them. When this happened, the duke resolved at once to see if he could not close the trouble with offers of reconciliation, and being a most perfect

THE PRINCE
DESCRIPTION OF THE METHODS ADOPTED BY THE DUKE VALENTINO WHEN MURDERING VITELLOZZO VITELLI, OLIVEROTTO DA FERMO, THE SIGNOR PAGOLO, AND THE DUKE DI GRAVINA ORSINI BY NICOLO MACHIAVELLI

dissembler he did not fail in any practices to make the insurgents understand that he wished every man who had acquired anything to keep it, as it was enough for him to have the title of prince, whilst others might have the principality.

And the duke succeeded so well in this that they sent Signor Pagolo to him to negotiate for a reconciliation, and they brought their army to a standstill. But the duke did not stop his preparations, and took every care to provide himself with cavalry and infantry, and that such preparations might not be apparent to the others, he sent his troops in separate parties to every part of the Romagna. In the meanwhile there came also to him five hundred French lancers, and although he found himself sufficiently strong to take vengeance on his enemies in open war, he considered that it would be safer and more advantageous to outwit them, and for this reason he did not stop the work of reconciliation.

And that this might be effected the duke concluded a peace with them in which he confirmed their former covenants; he gave them four thousand ducats at once; he promised not to injure the Bentivogli; and he formed an alliance with Giovanni; and moreover he would not force them to come personally into his presence unless it pleased them to do so. On the other hand, they promised to restore to him the duchy of Urbino and other places seized by them, to serve him in all his expeditions, and not to make war against or ally themselves with any one without his permission.

This reconciliation being completed, Guido Ubaldo, the Duke of Urbino, again fled to Venice, having first destroyed all the fortresses in his state; because, trusting in the people, he did not wish that the fortresses, which he did not think he could defend, should be held by the enemy, since by these means a check would be kept upon his friends. But the Duke Valentino, having completed this convention, and dispersed his men throughout the Romagna, set out for Imola at the end of November together with his French men-at-arms: thence he went to Cesena, where he stayed some time to negotiate with the envoys of the Vitelli and Orsini, who had assembled with their men in the duchy of Urbino, as to the enterprise in which they should now take part; but nothing being concluded, Oliverotto da Fermo was sent to propose that if the duke wished to undertake an expedition against Tuscany they were ready; if he did not wish it, then they would besiege Sinigalia. To this the duke replied that he did not wish to enter into war with Tuscany, and thus become hostile to the Florentines, but that he was very willing to proceed against Sinigalia.

It happened that not long afterwards the town surrendered, but the fortress would not yield to them because the castellan would not give it up to any one but the duke in person; therefore they exhorted him to come there. This appeared a good opportunity to the duke, as, being invited by them, and not going of his own will, he would awaken no suspicions. And the more to reassure them, he allowed all the French men-at-arms who were with him in Lombardy to depart, except the hundred lancers under Mons. di Candales, his brother-in-law. He left Cesena about the middle of December, and went to Fano, and with the utmost cunning and cleverness he persuaded the Vitelli and Orsini to wait for him at Sinigalia, pointing out to them that any lack of compliance would cast a doubt upon the sincerity and permanency of the reconciliation, and that he was a man who wished to make use of the arms and councils of his friends. But Vitellozzo remained very stubborn, for the death of his brother warned him that he should not offend a prince and afterwards trust him; nevertheless, persuaded by Pagolo Orsini, whom the duke had corrupted with gifts and promises, he agreed to wait.

Upon this the duke, before his departure from Fano, which was to be on 30th December 1502, communicated his designs to eight of his most trusted followers, among whom were Don Michele and the Monsignor d'Euna, who was afterwards cardinal; and he ordered that, as soon as Vitellozzo, Pagolo Orsini, the Duke di Gravina, and Oliverotto should arrive, his followers in pairs should take them one by one, entrusting certain

DESCRIPTION OF THE METHODS ADOPTED BY THE DUKE VALENTINO WHEN MURDERING VITELLOZZO VITELLI, OLIVEROTTO DA FERMO, THE SIGNOR PAGOLO, AND THE DUKE DI GRAVINA ORSINI BY NICOLO MACHIAVELLI

men to certain pairs, who should entertain them until they reached Sinigalia; nor should they be permitted to leave until they came to the duke's quarters, where they should be seized.

The duke afterwards ordered all his horsemen and infantry, of which there were more than two thousand cavalry and ten thousand footmen, to assemble by daybreak at the Metauro, a river five miles distant from Fano, and await him there. He found himself, therefore, on the last day of December at the Metauro with his men, and having sent a cavalcade of about two hundred horsemen before him, he then moved forward the infantry, whom he accompanied with the rest of the men-at-arms.

Fano and Sinigalia are two cities of La Marca situate on the shore of the Adriatic Sea, fifteen miles distant from each other, so that he who goes towards Sinigalia has the mountains on his right hand, the bases of which are touched by the sea in some places. The city of Sinigalia is distant from the foot of the mountains a little more than a bowshot and from the shore about a mile. On the side opposite to the city runs a little river which bathes that part of the walls looking towards Fano, facing the high road. Thus he who draws near to Sinigalia comes for a good space by road along the mountains, and reaches the river which passes by Sinigalia. If he turns to his left hand along the bank of it, and goes for the distance of a bowshot, he arrives at a bridge which crosses the river; he is then almost abreast of the gate that leads into Sinigalia, not by a straight line, but transversely. Before this gate there stands a collection of houses with a square to which the bank of the river forms one side.

The Vitelli and Orsini having received orders to wait for the duke, and to honour him in person, sent away their men to several castles distant from Sinigalia about six miles, so that room could be made for the men of the duke; and they left in Sinigalia only Oliverotto and his band, which consisted of one thousand infantry and one hundred and fifty horsemen, who were quartered in the suburb mentioned above. Matters having been thus arranged, the Duke Valentino left for Sinigalia, and when the leaders of the cavalry reached the bridge they did not pass over, but having opened it, one portion wheeled towards the river and the other towards the country, and a way was left in the middle through which the infantry passed, without stopping, into the town.

Vitellozzo, Pagolo, and the Duke di Gravina on mules, accompanied by a few horsemen, went towards the duke; Vitellozo, unarmed and wearing a cape lined with green, appeared very dejected, as if conscious of his approaching death—a circumstance which, in view of the ability of the man and his former fortune, caused some amazement. And it is said that when he parted from his men before setting out for Sinigalia to meet the duke he acted as if it were his last parting from them. He recommended his house and its fortunes to his captains, and advised his nephews that it was not the fortune of their house, but the virtues of their fathers that should be kept in mind. These three, therefore, came before the duke and saluted him respectfully, and were received by him with goodwill; they were at once placed between those who were commissioned to look after them.

But the duke noticing that Oliverotto, who had remained with his band in Sinigalia, was missing—for Oliverotto was waiting in the square before his quarters near the river, keeping his men in order and drilling them—signalled with his eye to Don Michelle, to whom the care of Oliverotto had been committed, that he should take measures that Oliverotto should not escape. Therefore Don Michele rode off and joined Oliverotto, telling him that it was not right to keep his men out of their quarters, because these might be taken up by the men of the duke; and he advised him to send them at once to their quarters and to come himself to meet the duke. And Oliverotto, having taken this advice, came before the duke, who, when he saw him, called to him; and Oliverotto, having made his obeisance, joined the others.

So the whole party entered Sinigalia, dismounted at the duke's quarters, and went with him into a secret

THE PRINCE

DESCRIPTION OF THE METHODS ADOPTED BY THE DUKE VALENTINO WHEN MURDERING VITELLOZZO VITELLI, OLIVEROTTO DA FERMO, THE SIGNOR PAGOLO, AND THE DUKE DI GRAVINA ORSINI BY NICOLO MACHIAVELLI

chamber, where the duke made them prisoners; he then mounted on horseback, and issued orders that the men of Oliverotto and the Orsini should be stripped of their arms. Those of Oliverotto, being at hand, were quickly settled, but those of the Orsini and Vitelli, being at a distance, and having a presentiment of the destruction of their masters, had time to prepare themselves, and bearing in mind the valour and discipline of the Orsinian and Vitellian houses, they stood together against the hostile forces of the country and saved themselves.

But the duke's soldiers, not being content with having pillaged the men of Oliverotto, began to sack Sinigalia, and if the duke had not repressed this outrage by killing some of them they would have completely sacked it. Night having come and the tumult being silenced, the duke prepared to kill Vitellozzo and Oliverotto; he led them into a room and caused them to be strangled. Neither of them used words in keeping with their past lives: Vitellozzo prayed that he might ask of the pope full pardon for his sins; Oliverotto cringed and laid the blame for all injuries against the duke on Vitellozzo. Pagolo and the Duke di Gravina Orsini were kept alive until the duke heard from Rome that the pope had taken the Cardinal Orsino, the Archbishop of Florence, and Messer Jacopo da Santa Croce. After which news, on 18th January 1502, in the castle of Pieve, they also were strangled in the same way.

THE LIFE OF CASTRUCCIO CASTRACANI OF LUCCA WRITTEN BY NICOLO MACHIAVELLI

And sent to his friends ZANOBI BUONDELMONTI And LUIGI ALAMANNI

CASTRUCCIO CASTRACANI 1284-1328

It appears, dearest Zanobi and Luigi, a wonderful thing to those who have considered the matter, that all men, or the larger number of them, who have performed great deeds in the world, and excelled all others in their day, have had their birth and beginning in baseness and obscurity; or have been aggrieved by Fortune in some outrageous way. They have either been exposed to the mercy of wild beasts, or they have had so mean a parentage that in shame they have given themselves out to be sons of Jove or of some other deity. It would be wearisome to relate who these persons may have been because they are well known to everybody, and, as such tales would not be particularly edifying to those who read them, they are omitted. I believe that these lowly beginnings of great men occur because Fortune is desirous of showing to the world that such men owe much to her and little to wisdom, because she begins to show her hand when wisdom can really take no part in their career: thus all success must be attributed to her. Castruccio Castracani of Lucca was one of those men who did great deeds, if he is measured by the times in which he lived and the city in which he was born; but, like many others, he was neither fortunate nor distinguished in his birth, as the course of this history will show. It appeared to be desirable to recall his memory, because I have discerned in him such indications of valour and fortune as should make him a great exemplar to men. I think also that I ought to call your attention to his actions, because you of all men I know delight most in noble deeds.

The family of Castracani was formerly numbered among the noble families of Lucca, but in the days of which I speak it had somewhat fallen in estate, as so often happens in this world. To this family was born a son Antonio, who became a priest of the order of San Michele of Lucca, and for this reason was honoured with the title of Messer Antonio. He had an only sister, who had been married to Buonaccorso Cenami, but Buonaccorso dying she became a widow, and not wishing to marry again went to live with her brother. Messer Antonio had a vineyard behind the house where he resided, and as it was bounded on all sides by gardens, any person could have access to it without difficulty. One morning, shortly after sunrise, Madonna Dianora, as the sister of Messer Antonio was called, had occasion to go into the vineyard as usual to gather herbs for seasoning the dinner, and hearing a slight rustling among the leaves of a vine she turned her eyes in that direction, and heard something resembling the cry of an infant. Whereupon she went towards it, and saw the hands and face of a baby who was lying enveloped in the leaves and who seemed to be crying for its mother. Partly wondering and partly fearing, yet full of compassion, she lifted it up and carried it to the house, where she washed it and clothed it with clean linen as is customary, and showed it to Messer Antonio when he returned home. When he heard what had happened and saw the child he was not less surprised or compassionate than his sister. They discussed between themselves what should be done, and seeing that he was priest and that she had no children, they finally determined to bring it up. They had a nurse for it, and it was reared and loved as if it were their own child. They baptized it, and gave it the name of Castruccio after their father. As the years passed Castruccio grew very handsome, and gave evidence of wit and discretion, and learnt with a quickness beyond his years those lessons which Messer Antonio imparted to him. Messer Antonio intended to make a priest of him, and in time would have inducted him into his canonry and other benefices, and all his instruction was given with this object; but Antonio discovered that the character of Castruccio was quite unfitted for the priesthood. As soon as Castruccio reached the age of fourteen he began to take less notice of the chiding of Messer Antonio and Madonna Dianora and no longer to fear them; he left off reading ecclesiastical books, and turned to playing with arms, delighting in nothing so much as in learning their uses, and in running, leaping, and wrestling with other boys. In all exercises he far excelled his companions in courage and bodily strength, and if at any time he did turn to books, only those pleased him which told of wars and the mighty deeds of men. Messer Antonio beheld all this with vexation and sorrow.

There lived in the city of Lucca a gentleman of the Guinigi family, named Messer Francesco, whose profession was arms and who in riches, bodily strength, and valour excelled all other men in Lucca. He had often fought under the command of the Visconti of Milan, and as a Ghibelline was the valued leader of that party in Lucca. This gentleman resided in Lucca and was accustomed to assemble with others most mornings and evenings under the balcony of the Podesta, which is at the top of the square of San Michele, the finest square in Lucca, and he had often seen Castruccio taking part with other children of the street in those games of which I have spoken. Noticing that Castruccio far excelled the other boys, and that he appeared to exercise a royal authority over them, and that they loved and obeyed him, Messer Francesco became greatly desirous of learning who he was. Being informed of the circumstances of the bringing up of Castruccio he felt a greater desire to have him near to him. Therefore he called him one day and asked him whether he would more willingly live in the house of a gentleman, where he would learn to ride horses and use arms, or in the house of a priest, where he would learn nothing but masses and the services of the Church. Messer Francesco could see that it pleased Castruccio greatly to hear horses and arms spoken of, even though he stood silent, blushing modestly; but being encouraged by Messer Francesco to speak, he answered that, if his master were agreeable, nothing would please him more than to give up his priestly studies and take up those of a soldier. This reply delighted Messer Francesco, and in a very short time he obtained the consent of Messer Antonio, who was driven to yield by his knowledge of the nature of the lad, and the fear that he would not be able to hold him much longer.

Thus Castruccio passed from the house of Messer Antonio the priest to the house of Messer Francesco Guinigi the soldier, and it was astonishing to find that in a very short time he manifested all that virtue and bearing which we are accustomed to associate with a true gentleman. In the first place he became an accomplished horseman, and could manage with ease the most fiery charger, and in all jousts and tournaments, although still a youth, he was observed beyond all others, and he excelled in all exercises of strength and dexterity. But what enhanced so much the charm of these accomplishments, was the delightful modesty which enabled him to avoid offence in either act or word to others, for he was deferential to the great men, modest with his equals, and courteous to his inferiors. These gifts made him beloved, not only by all the Guinigi family, but by all Lucca. When Castruccio had reached his eighteenth year, the Ghibellines were driven from Pavia by the Guelphs, and Messer Francesco was sent by the Visconti to assist the Ghibellines, and with him went Castruccio, in charge of his forces. Castruccio gave ample proof of his prudence and courage in this expedition, acquiring greater reputation than any other captain, and his name and fame were known, not only in Pavia but throughout all Lombardy.

Castruccio, having returned to Lucca in far higher estimation that he left it, did not omit to use all the means in his power to gain as many friends as he could, neglecting none of those arts which are necessary for that purpose. About this time Messer Francesco died, leaving a son thirteen years of age named Pagolo, and having appointed Castruccio to be his son's tutor and administrator of his estate. Before he died Francesco called Castruccio to him, and prayed him to show Pagolo that goodwill which he (Francesco) had always shown to him, and to render to the son the gratitude which he had not been able to repay to the father. Upon the death of Francesco, Castruccio became the governor and tutor of Pagolo, which increased enormously his power and position, and created a certain amount of envy against him in Lucca in place of the former universal goodwill, for many men suspected him of harbouring tyrannical intentions. Among these the leading man was Giorgio degli Opizi, the head of the Guelph party. This man hoped after the death of Messer

THE PRINCE
THE LIFE OF CASTRUCCIO CASTRACANI OF LUCCA WRITTEN BY NICOLO MACHIAVELLI

Francesco to become the chief man in Lucca, but it seemed to him that Castruccio, with the great abilities which he already showed, and holding the position of governor, deprived him of his opportunity; therefore he began to sow those seeds which should rob Castruccio of his eminence. Castruccio at first treated this with scorn, but afterwards he grew alarmed, thinking that Messer Giorgio might be able to bring him into disgrace with the deputy of King Ruberto of Naples and have him driven out of Lucca.

The Lord of Pisa at that time was Uguccione of the Faggiuola of Arezzo, who being in the first place elected their captain afterwards became their lord. There resided in Paris some exiled Ghibellines from Lucca, with whom Castruccio held communications with the object of effecting their restoration by the help of Uguccione. Castruccio also brought into his plans friends from Lucca who would not endure the authority of the Opizi. Having fixed upon a plan to be followed, Castruccio cautiously fortified the tower of the Onesti, filling it with supplies and munitions of war, in order that it might stand a siege for a few days in case of need. When the night came which had been agreed upon with Uguccione, who had occupied the plain between the mountains and Pisa with many men, the signal was given, and without being observed Uguccione approached the gate of San Piero and set fire to the portcullis. Castruccio raised a great uproar within the city, calling the people to arms and forcing open the gate from his side. Uguccione entered with his men, poured through the town, and killed Messer Giorgio with all his family and many of his friends and supporters. The governor was driven out, and the government reformed according to the wishes of Uguccione, to the detriment of the city, because it was found that more than one hundred families were exiled at that time. Of those who fled, part went to Florence and part to Pistoia, which city was the headquarters of the Guelph party, and for this reason it became most hostile to Uguccione and the Lucchese.

As it now appeared to the Florentines and others of the Guelph party that the Ghibellines absorbed too much power in Tuscany, they determined to restore the exiled Guelphs to Lucca. They assembled a large army in the Val di Nievole, and seized Montecatini; from thence they marched to Montecarlo, in order to secure the free passage into Lucca. Upon this Uguccione assembled his Pisan and Lucchese forces, and with a number of German cavalry which he drew out of Lombardy, he moved against the quarters of the Florentines, who upon the appearance of the enemy withdrew from Montecarlo, and posted themselves between Montecatini and Pescia. Uguccione now took up a position near to Montecarlo, and within about two miles of the enemy, and slight skirmishes between the horse of both parties were of daily occurrence. Owing to the illness of Uguccione, the Pisans and Lucchese delayed coming to battle with the enemy. Uguccione, finding himself growing worse, went to Montecarlo to be cured, and left the command of the army in the hands of Castruccio. This change brought about the ruin of the Guelphs, who, thinking that the hostile army having lost its captain had lost its head, grew over-confident. Castruccio observed this, and allowed some days to pass in order to encourage this belief; he also showed signs of fear, and did not allow any of the munitions of the camp to be used. On the other side, the Guelphs grew more insolent the more they saw these evidences of fear, and every day they drew out in the order of battle in front of the army of Castruccio. Presently, deeming that the enemy was sufficiently emboldened, and having mastered their tactics, he decided to join battle with them. First he spoke a few words of encouragement to his soldiers, and pointed out to them the certainty of victory if they would but obey his commands. Castruccio had noticed how the enemy had placed all his best troops in the centre of the line of battle, and his less reliable men on the wings of the army; whereupon he did exactly the opposite, putting his most valiant men on the flanks, while those on whom he could not so strongly rely he moved to the centre. Observing this order of battle, he drew out of his lines and quickly came in sight of the hostile army, who, as usual, had come in their insolence to defy him. He then commanded his centre squadrons to march slowly, whilst he moved rapidly forward those on the wings. Thus, when they came into contact with the enemy, only the wings of the two armies became engaged, whilst the center battalions remained out of action, for these two portions of the line of battle were separated from each other by a long interval and thus unable to reach each other. By this expedient the more valiant part of Castruccio's men were opposed to the weaker part of the enemy's troops, and the most efficient men of the enemy were disengaged; and thus the Florentines were unable to fight with those who were arrayed opposite to them, or to give any assistance to their own flanks. So, without much difficulty, Castruccio put the enemy to flight on both flanks, and the centre battalions took to flight when they found themselves exposed to attack, without having a chance of displaying their valour. The defeat was complete, and the loss in men very heavy, there being more than ten thousand men killed with many officers and knights of the Guelph party in Tuscany, and also many princes who had come to help them, among whom were Piero, the brother of King Ruberto, and Carlo, his nephew, and Filippo, the lord of Taranto. On the part of Castruccio the loss did not amount to more than three hundred men, among whom was Francesco, the son of Uguccione, who, being young and rash, was killed in the first onset.

This victory so greatly increased the reputation of Castruccio that Uguccione conceived some jealousy and suspicion of him, because it appeared to Uguccione that this victory had given him no increase of power, but rather than diminished it. Being of this mind, he only waited for an opportunity to give effect to it. This occurred on the death of Pier Agnolo Micheli, a man of great repute and abilities in Lucca, the murderer of whom fled to the house of Castruccio for refuge. On the sergeants of the captain going to arrest the murderer, they were driven off by Castruccio, and the murderer escaped. This affair coming to the knowledge of Uguccione, who was than at Pisa, it appeared to him a proper opportunity to punish Castruccio. He therefore sent for his son Neri, who was the governor of Lucca, and commissioned him to take Castruccio prisoner at a banquet and put him to death. Castruccio, fearing no evil, went to the governor in a friendly way, was entertained at supper, and then thrown into prison. But Neri, fearing to put him to death lest the people should be incensed, kept him alive, in order to hear further from his father concerning his intentions. Ugucionne cursed the hesitation and cowardice of his son, and at once set out from Pisa to Lucca with four hundred horsemen to finish the business in his own way; but he had not yet reached the baths when the Pisans rebelled and put his deputy to death and created Count Gaddo della Gherardesca their lord. Before Uguccione reached Lucca he heard of the occurrences at Pisa, but it did not appear wise to him to turn back, lest the Lucchese with the example of Pisa before them should close their gates against him. But the Lucchese, having heard of what had happened at Pisa, availed themselves of this opportunity to demand the liberation of Castruccio, notwithstanding that Uguccione had arrived in their city. They first began to speak of it in private circles, afterwards openly in the squares and streets; then they raised a tumult, and with arms in their hands went to Uguccione and demanded that Castruccio should be set at liberty. Uguccione, fearing that worse might happen, released him from prison. Whereupon Castruccio gathered his friends around him, and with the help of the people attacked Uguccione; who, finding he had no resource but in flight, rode away with his friends to Lombardy, to the lords of Scale, where he died in poverty.

But Castruccio from being a prisoner became almost a prince in Lucca, and he carried himself so discreetly with his friends and the people that they appointed him captain of their army for one year. Having obtained this, and wishing to gain renown in war, he planned the recovery of the many towns which had rebelled after the departure of Uguccione, and with the help of the Pisans, with whom he had concluded a treaty, he marched to Serezzana. To capture this place he constructed a fort against it, which is called to-day Zerezzanello; in the course of two months Castruccio captured the town. With the reputation gained at that siege, he rapidly seized Massa, Carrara, and Lavenza, and in a short time had overrun the whole of Lunigiana. In order to close the pass which leads from Lombardy to Lunigiana, he besieged Pontremoli and wrested it from the hands of Messer Anastagio Palavicini, who was the lord of it. After this victory he returned to Lucca, and was welcomed by the whole people. And now Castruccio, deeming it imprudent any longer to defer making himself a prince, got himself created the lord of Lucca by the help of Pazzino del Poggio,

Puccinello dal Portico, Francesco Boccansacchi, and Cecco Guinigi, all of whom he had corrupted; and he was afterwards solemnly and deliberately elected prince by the people. At this time Frederick of Bavaria, the King of the Romans, came into Italy to assume the Imperial crown, and Castruccio, in order that he might make friends with him, met him at the head of five hundred horsemen. Castruccio had left as his deputy in Lucca, Pagolo Guinigi, who was held in high estimation, because of the people's love for the memory of his father. Castruccio was received in great honour by Frederick, and many privileges were conferred upon him, and he was appointed the emperor's lieutenant in Tuscany. At this time the Pisans were in great fear of Gaddo della Gherardesca, whom they had driven out of Pisa, and they had recourse for assistance to Frederick. Frederick created Castruccio the lord of Pisa, and the Pisans, in dread of the Guelph party, and particularly of the Florentines, were constrained to accept him as their lord.

Frederick, having appointed a governor in Rome to watch his Italian affairs, returned to Germany. All the Tuscan and Lombardian Ghibellines, who followed the imperial lead, had recourse to Castruccio for help and counsel, and all promised him the governorship of his country, if enabled to recover it with his assistance. Among these exiles were Matteo Guidi, Nardo Scolari, Lapo Uberti, Gerozzo Nardi, and Piero Buonaccorsi, all exiled Florentines and Ghibellines. Castruccio had the secret intention of becoming the master of all Tuscany by the aid of these men and of his own forces; and in order to gain greater weight in affairs, he entered into a league with Messer Matteo Visconti, the Prince of Milan, and organized for him the forces of his city and the country districts. As Lucca had five gates, he divided his own country districts into five parts, which he supplied with arms, and enrolled the men under captains and ensigns, so that he could quickly bring into the field twenty thousand soldiers, without those whom he could summon to his assistance from Pisa. While he surrounded himself with these forces and allies, it happened at Messer Matteo Visconti was attacked by the Guelphs of Piacenza, who had driven out the Ghibellines with the assistance of a Florentine army and the King Ruberto. Messer Matteo called upon Castruccio to invade the Florentines in their own territories, so that, being attacked at home, they should be compelled to draw their army out of Lombardy in order to defend themselves. Castruccio invaded the Valdarno, and seized Fucecchio and San Miniato, inflicting immense damage upon the country. Whereupon the Florentines recalled their army, which had scarcely reached Tuscany, when Castruccio was forced by other necessities to return to Lucca.

There resided in the city of Lucca the Poggio family, who were so powerful that they could not only elevate Castruccio, but even advance him to the dignity of prince; and it appearing to them they had not received such rewards for their services as they deserved, they incited other families to rebel and to drive Castruccio out of Lucca. They found their opportunity one morning, and arming themselves, they set upon the lieutenant whom Castruccio had left to maintain order and killed him. They endeavoured to raise the people in revolt, but Stefano di Poggio, a peaceable old man who had taken no hand in the rebellion, intervened and compelled them by his authority to lay down their arms; and he offered to be their mediator with Castruccio to obtain from him what they desired. Therefore they laid down their arms with no greater intelligence than they had taken them up. Castruccio, having heard the news of what had happened at Lucca, at once put Pagolo Guinigi in command of the army, and with a troop of cavalry set out for home. Contrary to his expectations, he found the rebellion at an end, yet he posted his men in the most advantageous places throughout the city. As it appeared to Stefano that Castruccio ought to be very much obliged to him, he sought him out, and without saying anything on his own behalf, for he did not recognize any need for doing so, he begged Castruccio to pardon the other members of his family by reason of their youth, their former friendships, and the obligations which Castruccio was under to their house. To this Castruccio graciously responded, and begged Stefano to reassure himself, declaring that it gave him more pleasure to find the tumult at an end than it had ever caused him anxiety to hear of its inception. He encouraged Stefano to bring his family to him, saying that he thanked God for having given him the opportunity of showing his clemency and liberality. Upon the word of Stefano and Castruccio they surrendered, and with Stefano were immediately thrown into prison and put to death. Meanwhile the Florentines had recovered San Miniato, whereupon it seemed advisable to Castruccio to make peace, as it did not appear to him that he was sufficiently secure at Lucca to leave him. He approached the Florentines with the proposal of a truce, which they readily entertained, for they were weary of the war, and desirous of getting rid of the expenses of it. A treaty was concluded with them for two years, by which both parties agreed to keep the conquests they had made. Castruccio thus released from this trouble, turned his attention to affairs in Lucca, and in order that he should not again be subject to the perils from which he had just escaped, he, under various pretences and reasons, first wiped out all those who by their ambition might aspire to the principality; not sparing one of them, but depriving them of country and property, and those whom he had in his hands of life also, stating that he had found by experience that none of them were to be trusted. Then for his further security he raised a fortress in Lucca with the stones of the towers of those whom he had killed or hunted out of the state.

Whilst Castruccio made peace with the Florentines, and strengthened his position in Lucca, he neglected no opportunity, short of open war, of increasing his importance elsewhere. It appeared to him that if he could get possession of Pistoia, he would have one foot in Florence, which was his great desire. He, therefore, in various ways made friends with the mountaineers, and worked matters so in Pistoia that both parties confided their secrets to him. Pistoia was divided, as it always had been, into the Bianchi and Neri parties; the head of the Bianchi was Bastiano di Possente, and of the Neri, Jacopo da Gia. Each of these men held secret communications with Castruccio, and each desired to drive the other out of the city; and, after many threatenings, they came to blows. Jacopo fortified himself at the Florentine gate, Bastiano at that of the Lucchese side of the city; both trusted more in Castruccio than in the Florentines, because they believed that Castruccio was far more ready and willing to fight than the Florentines, and they both sent to him for assistance. He gave promises to both, saying to Bastiano that he would come in person, and to Jacopo that he would send his pupil, Pagolo Guinigi. At the appointed time he sent forward Pagolo by way of Pisa, and went himself direct to Pistoia; at midnight both of them met outside the city, and both were admitted as friends. Thus the two leaders entered, and at a signal given by Castruccio, one killed Jacopo da Gia, and the other Bastiano di Possente, and both took prisoners or killed the partisans of either faction. Without further opposition Pistoia passed into the hands of Castruccio, who, having forced the Signoria to leave the palace, compelled the people to yield obedience to him, making them many promises and remitting their old debts. The countryside flocked to the city to see the new prince, and all were filled with hope and quickly settled down, influenced in a great measure by his great valour.

About this time great disturbances arose in Rome, owing to the dearness of living which was caused by the absence of the pontiff at Avignon. The German governor, Enrico, was much blamed for what happened—murders and tumults following each other daily, without his being able to put an end to them. This caused Enrico much anxiety lest the Romans should call in Ruberto, the King of Naples, who would drive the Germans out of the city, and bring back the Pope. Having no nearer friend to whom he could apply for help than Castruccio, he sent to him, begging him not only to give him assistance, but also to come in person to Rome. Castruccio considered that he ought not to hesitate to render the emperor this service, because he believed that he himself would not be safe if at any time the emperor ceased to hold Rome. Leaving Pagolo Guinigi in command at Lucca, Castruccio set out for Rome with six hundred horsemen, where he was received by Enrico with the greatest distinction. In a short time the presence of Castruccio obtained such respect for the emperor that, without bloodshed or violence, good order was restored, chiefly by reason of Castruccio having sent by sea from the country round Pisa large quantities of corn, and thus removed the source of the trouble. When he had chastised some of the Roman leaders, and admonished others, voluntary obedience was rendered to Enrico. Castruccio received many honours, and was made a Roman senator. This dignity was assumed with the greatest pomp, Castruccio being clothed in a brocaded toga, which had the following words embroidered on its front: "I am what God wills." Whilst on the back was: "What God desires shall be."

During this time the Florentines, who were much enraged that Castruccio should have seized Pistoia during the truce, considered how they could tempt the city to rebel, to do which they thought would not be difficult in his absence. Among the exiled Pistoians in Florence were Baldo Cecchi and Jacopo Baldini, both men of leading and ready to face danger. These men kept up communications with their friends in Pistoia, and with the aid of the Florentines entered the city by night, and after driving out some of Castruccio's officials and partisans, and killing others, they restored the city to its freedom. The news of this greatly angered Castruccio, and taking leave of Enrico, he pressed on in great haste to Pistoia. When the Florentines heard of his return, knowing that he would lose no time, they decided to intercept him with their forces in the Val di Nievole, under the belief that by doing so they would cut off his road to Pistoia. Assembling a great army of the supporters of the Guelph cause, the Florentines entered the Pistoian territories. On the other hand, Castruccio reached Montecarlo with his army; and having heard where the Florentines' lay, he decided not to encounter it in the plains of Pistoia, nor to await it in the plains of Pescia, but, as far as he possibly could, to attack it boldly in the Pass of Serravalle. He believed that if he succeeded in this design, victory was assured, although he was informed that the Florentines had thirty thousand men, whilst he had only twelve thousand. Although he had every confidence in his own abilities and the valour of his troops, yet he hesitated to attack his enemy in the open lest he should be overwhelmed by numbers. Serravalle is a castle between Pescia and Pistoia, situated on a hill which blocks the Val di Nievole, not in the exact pass, but about a bowshot beyond; the pass itself is in places narrow and steep, whilst in general it ascends gently, but is still narrow, especially at the summit where the waters divide, so that twenty men side by side could hold it. The lord of Serravalle was Manfred, a German, who, before Castruccio became lord of Pistoia, had been allowed to remain in possession of the castle, it being common to the Lucchese and the Pistoians, and unclaimed by either— neither of them wishing to displace Manfred as long as he kept his promise of neutrality, and came under obligations to no one. For these reasons, and also because the castle was well fortified, he had always been able to maintain his position. It was here that Castruccio had determined to fall upon his enemy, for here his few men would have the advantage, and there was no fear lest, seeing the large masses of the hostile force before they became engaged, they should not stand. As soon as this trouble with Florence arose, Castruccio saw the immense advantage which possession of this castle would give him, and having an intimate friendship with a resident in the castle, he managed matters so with him that four hundred of his men were to be admitted into the castle the night before the attack on the Florentines, and the castellan put to death.

Castruccio, having prepared everything, had now to encourage the Florentines to persist in their desire to carry the seat of war away from Pistoia into the Val di Nievole, therefore he did not move his army from Montecarlo. Thus the Florentines hurried on until they reached their encampment under Serravalle, intending to cross the hill on the following morning. In the meantime, Castruccio had seized the castle at night, had also moved his army from Montecarlo, and marching from thence at midnight in dead silence, had reached the foot of Serravalle: thus he and the Florentines commenced the ascent of the hill at the same time in the morning. Castruccio sent forward his infantry by the main road, and a troop of four hundred horsemen by a path on the left towards the castle. The Florentines sent forward four hundred cavalry ahead of their army which was following, never expecting to find Castruccio in possession of the hill, nor were they aware of his having seized the castle. Thus it happened that the Florentine horsemen mounting the hill were completely taken by surprise when they discovered the infantry of Castruccio, and so close were they upon it they had scarcely time to pull down their visors. It was a case of unready soldiers being attacked by ready, and they were assailed with such vigour that with difficulty they could hold their own, although some few of them got through. When the noise of the fighting reached the Florentine camp below, it was filled with confusion. The cavalry and infantry became inextricably mixed: the captains were unable to get their men either backward or forward, owing to the narrowness of the pass, and amid all this tumult no one knew what ought to be done or what could be done. In a short time the cavalry who were engaged with the enemy's infantry were scattered or killed without having made any effective defence because of their unfortunate position, although in sheer desperation they had offered a stout resistance. Retreat had been impossible, with the mountains on both flanks, whilst in front were their enemies, and in the rear their friends. When Castruccio saw that his men were unable to strike a decisive blow at the enemy and put them to flight, he sent one thousand infantrymen round by the castle, with orders to join the four hundred horsemen he had previously dispatched there, and commanded the whole force to fall upon the flank of the enemy. These orders they carried out with such fury that the Florentines could not sustain the attack, but gave way, and were soon in full retreat—conquered more by their unfortunate position than by the valour of their enemy. Those in the rear turned towards Pistoia, and spread through the plains, each man seeking only his own safety. The defeat was complete and very sanguinary. Many captains were taken prisoners, among whom were Bandini dei Rossi, Francesco Brunelleschi, and Giovanni della Tosa, all Florentine noblemen, with many Tuscans and Neapolitans who fought on the Florentine side, having been sent by King Ruberto to assist the Guelphs. Immediately the Pistoians heard of this defeat they drove out the friends of the Guelphs, and surrendered to Castruccio. He was not content with occupying Prato and all the castles on the plains on both sides of the Arno, but marched his army into the plain of Peretola, about two miles from Florence. Here he remained many days, dividing the spoils, and celebrating his victory with feasts and games, holding horse races, and foot races for men and women. He also struck medals in commemoration of the defeat of the Florentines. He endeavoured to corrupt some of the citizens of Florence, who were to open the city gates at night; but the conspiracy was discovered, and the participators in it taken and beheaded, among whom were Tommaso Lupacci and Lambertuccio Frescobaldi. This defeat caused the Florentines great anxiety, and despairing of preserving their liberty, they sent envoys to King Ruberto of Naples, offering him the dominion of their city; and he, knowing of what immense importance the maintenance of the Guelph cause was to him, accepted it. He agreed with the Florentines to receive from them a yearly tribute of two hundred thousand florins, and he send his son Carlo to Florence with four thousand horsemen.

Shortly after this the Florentines were relieved in some degree of the pressure of Castruccio's army, owing to his being compelled to leave his positions before Florence and march on Pisa, in order to suppress a conspiracy that had been raised against him by Benedetto Lanfranchi, one of the first men in Pisa, who could not endure that his fatherland should be under the dominion of the Lucchese. He had formed this conspiracy, intending to seize the citadel, kill the partisans of Castruccio, and drive out the garrison. As, however, in a conspiracy paucity of numbers is essential to secrecy, so for its execution a few are not sufficient, and in seeking more adherents to his conspiracy Lanfranchi encountered a person who revealed the design to Castruccio. This betrayal cannot be passed by without severe reproach to Bonifacio Cerchi and Giovanni Guidi, two Florentine exiles who were suffering their banishment in Pisa. Thereupon Castruccio seized Benedetto and put him to death, and beheaded many other noble citizens, and drove their families into exile. It now appeared to Castruccio that both Pisa and Pistoia were thoroughly disaffected; he employed much thought and energy upon securing his position there, and this gave the Florentines their opportunity to reorganize their army, and to await the coming of Carlo, the son of the King of Naples. When Carlo arrived they decided to lose no more time, and assembled a great army of more than thirty thousand infantry and ten thousand cavalry—having called to their aid every Guelph there was in Italy. They consulted whether they should attack Pistoia or Pisa first, and decided that it would be better to march on the latter—a course, owing to the recent conspiracy, more likely to succeed, and of more advantage to them, because they believed that the surrender of Pistoia would follow the acquisition of Pisa.

In the early part of May 1328, the Florentines put in motion this army and quickly occupied Lastra, Signa, Montelupo, and Empoli, passing from thence on to San Miniato. When Castruccio heard of the enormous army which the Florentines were sending against him, he was in no degree alarmed, believing that the time had now arrived when Fortune would deliver the empire of Tuscany into his hands, for he had no reason to think that his enemy would make a better fight, or had better prospects of success, than at Pisa or Serravalle. He assembled twenty thousand foot soldiers and four thousand horsemen, and with this army went to Fucecchio, whilst he sent Pagolo Guinigi to Pisa with five thousand infantry. Fucecchio has a stronger position than any other town in the Pisan district, owing to its situation between the rivers Arno and Gusciana and its slight elevation above the surrounding plain. Moreover, the enemy could not hinder its being victualled unless they divided their forces, nor could they approach it either from the direction of Lucca or Pisa, nor could they get through to Pisa, or attack Castruccio's forces except at a disadvantage. In one case they would find themselves placed between his two armies, the one under his own command and the other under Pagolo, and in the other case they would have to cross the Arno to get to close quarters with the enemy, an undertaking of great hazard. In order to tempt the Florentines to take this latter course, Castruccio withdrew his men from the banks of the river and placed them under the walls of Fucecchio, leaving a wide expanse of land between them and the river.

The Florentines, having occupied San Miniato, held a council of war to decide whether they should attack Pisa or the army of Castruccio, and, having weighed the difficulties of both courses, they decided upon the latter. The river Arno was at that time low enough to be fordable, yet the water reached to the shoulders of the infantrymen and to the saddles of the horsemen. On the morning of 10 June 1328, the Florentines commenced the battle by ordering forward a number of cavalry and ten thousand infantry. Castruccio, whose plan of action was fixed, and who well knew what to do, at once attacked the Florentines with five thousand infantry and three thousand horsemen, not allowing them to issue from the river before he charged them; he also sent one thousand light infantry up the river bank, and the same number down the Arno. The infantry of the Florentines were so much impeded by their arms and the water that they were not able to mount the banks of the river, whilst the cavalry had made the passage of the river more difficult for the others, by reason of the few who had crossed having broken up the bed of the river, and this being deep with mud, many of the horses rolled over with their riders and many of them had stuck so fast that they could not move. When the Florentine captains saw the difficulties their men were meeting, they withdrew them and moved higher up the river, hoping to find the riverbed less treacherous and the banks more adapted for landing. These men were met at the bank by the forces which Castruccio had already sent forward, who, being light armed with bucklers and javelins in their hands, let fly with tremendous shouts into the faces and bodies of the cavalry. The horses, alarmed by the noise and the wounds, would not move forward, and trampled each other in great confusion. The fight between the men of Castruccio and those of the enemy who succeeded in crossing was sharp and terrible; both sides fought with the utmost desperation and neither would yield. The soldiers of Castruccio fought to drive the others back into the river, whilst the Florentines strove to get a footing on land in order to make room for the others pressing forward, who if they could but get out of the water would be able to fight, and in this obstinate conflict they were urged on by their captains. Castruccio shouted to his men that these were the same enemies whom they had before conquered at Serravalle, whilst the Florentines reproached each other that the many should be overcome by the few. At length Castruccio, seeing how long the battle had lasted, and that both his men and the enemy were utterly exhausted, and that both sides had many killed and wounded, pushed forward another body of infantry to take up a position at the rear of those who were fighting; he then commanded these latter to open their ranks as if they intended to retreat, and one part of them to turn to the right and another to the left. This cleared a space of which the Florentines at once took advantage, and thus gained possession of a portion of the battlefield. But when these tired soldiers found themselves at close quarters with Castruccio's reserves they could not stand against them and at once fell back into the river. The cavalry of either side had not as yet gained any decisive advantage over the other, because Castruccio, knowing his inferiority in this arm, had commanded his leaders only to stand on the defensive against the attacks of their adversaries, as he hoped that when he had overcome the infantry he would be able to make short work of the cavalry. This fell out as he had hoped, for when he saw the Florentine army driven back across the river he ordered the remainder of his infantry to attack the cavalry of the enemy. This they did with lance and javelin, and, joined by their own cavalry, fell upon the enemy with the greatest fury and soon put him to flight. The Florentine captains, having seen the difficulty their cavalry had met with in crossing the river, had attempted to make their infantry cross lower down the river, in order to attack the flanks of Castruccio's army. But here, also, the banks were steep and already lined by the men of Castruccio, and this movement was quite useless. Thus the Florentines were so completely defeated at all points that scarcely a third of them escaped, and Castruccio was again covered with glory. Many captains were taken prisoners, and Carlo, the son of King Ruberto, with Michelagnolo Falconi and Taddeo degli Albizzi, the Florentine commissioners, fled to Empoli. If the spoils were great, the slaughter was infinitely greater, as might be expected in such a battle. Of the Florentines there fell twenty thousand two hundred and thirty-one men, whilst Castruccio lost one thousand five hundred and seventy men.

But Fortune growing envious of the glory of Castruccio took away his life just at the time when she should have preserved it, and thus ruined all those plans which for so long a time he had worked to carry into effect, and in the successful prosecution of which nothing but death could have stopped him. Castruccio was in the thick of the battle the whole of the day; and when the end of it came, although fatigued and overheated, he stood at the gate of Fucecchio to welcome his men on their return from victory and personally thank them. He was also on the watch for any attempt of the enemy to retrieve the fortunes of the day; he being of the opinion that it was the duty of a good general to be the first man in the saddle and the last out of it. Here Castruccio stood exposed to a wind which often rises at midday on the banks of the Arno, and which is often very unhealthy; from this he took a chill, of which he thought nothing, as he was accustomed to such troubles; but it was the cause of his death. On the following night he was attacked with high fever, which increased so rapidly that the doctors saw it must prove fatal. Castruccio, therefore, called Pagolo Guinigi to him, and addressed him as follows:

"If I could have believed that Fortune would have cut me off in the midst of the career which was leading to that glory which all my successes promised, I should have laboured less, and I should have left thee, if a smaller state, at least with fewer enemies and perils, because I should have been content with the governorships of Lucca and Pisa. I should neither have subjugated the Pistoians, nor outraged the Florentines with so many injuries. But I would have made both these peoples my friends, and I should have lived, if no longer, at least more peacefully, and have left you a state without a doubt smaller, but one more secure and established on a surer foundation. But Fortune, who insists upon having the arbitrament of human affairs, did not endow me with sufficient judgment to recognize this from the first, nor the time to surmount it. Thou hast heard, for many have told thee, and I have never concealed it, how I entered the house of thy father whilst yet a boy—a stranger to all those ambitions which every generous soul should feel—and how I was brought up by him, and loved as though I had been born of his blood; how under his governance I learned to be valiant and capable of availing myself of all that fortune, of which thou hast been witness. When thy good father came to die, he committed thee and all his possessions to my care, and I have brought thee up with that love, and increased thy estate with that care, which I was bound to show. And in order that thou shouldst not only possess the estate which thy father left, but also that which my fortune and abilities have gained, I have never married, so that the love of children should never deflect my mind from that gratitude which I owed to the children of thy father. Thus I leave thee a vast estate, of which I am well content, but I am deeply concerned, inasmuch as I leave it thee unsettled and insecure. Thou hast the city of Lucca on thy hands, which will never rest contented under they government. Thou hast also Pisa, where the men are of nature changeable and unreliable, who, although they may be sometimes held in subjection, yet they will ever disdain to serve under a Lucchese. Pistoia is also disloyal to thee, she being eaten up with factions and deeply incensed against thy family by reason of the wrongs recently inflicted upon them. Thou hast for neighbours the offended Florentines, injured by us in a thousand ways, but not utterly destroyed, who will hail the news of my death with more delight than they would the acquisition of all Tuscany. In the Emperor and in the princes of Milan thou canst place no reliance, for they are far distant, slow, and their help is very long in coming. Therefore, thou hast no hope in anything but in thine own abilities, and in the memory of my valour, and in the prestige which this latest victory has brought thee; which, as thou knowest how to use it with prudence, will assist thee to come to terms with the Florentines, who, as they are suffering under this great defeat, should be inclined to listen to thee. And whereas I have sought to make them my enemies, because I believed that war with them would conduce to my power and glory, thou hast every inducement to make friends of them, because their alliance will bring thee advantages and security. It is of the greatest important in this world that a man should know himself, and the measure of his own strength and means; and he who knows that he has not a genius for fighting must learn how to govern by the arts of peace. And it will be well for thee to rule they conduct by my counsel, and to learn in this way to enjoy what my life-work and dangers have gained; and in this thou wilt easily succeed when thou hast learnt to believe that what I have told thee is true. And thou wilt be doubly indebted to me, in that I have left thee this realm and have taught thee how to keep it."

After this there came to Castruccio those citizens of Pisa, Pistoia, and Lucca, who had been fighting at his side, and whilst recommending Pagolo to them, and making them swear obedience to him as his successor, he died. He left a happy memory to those who had known him, and no prince of those times was ever loved with such devotion as he was. His obsequies were celebrated with every sign of mourning, and he was buried in San Francesco at Lucca. Fortune was not so friendly to Pagolo Guinigi as she had been to Castruccio, for he had not the abilities. Not long after the death of Castruccio, Pagolo lost Pisa, and then Pistoia, and only with difficulty held on to Lucca. This latter city continued in the family of Guinigi until the time of the great-grandson of Pagolo.

From what has been related here it will be seen that Castruccio was a man of exceptional abilities, not only measured by men of his own time, but also by those of an earlier date. In stature he was above the ordinary height, and perfectly proportioned. He was of a gracious presence, and he welcomed men with such urbanity that those who spoke with him rarely left him displeased. His hair was inclined to be red, and he wore it cut short above the ears, and, whether it rained or snowed, he always went without a hat. He was delightful among friends, but terrible to his enemies; just to his subjects; ready to play false with the unfaithful, and willing to overcome by fraud those whom he desired to subdue, because he was wont to say that it was the victory that brought the glory, not the methods of achieving it. No one was bolder in facing danger, none more prudent in extricating himself. He was accustomed to say that men ought to attempt everything and fear nothing; that God is a lover of strong men, because one always sees that the weak are chastised by the strong. He was also wonderfully sharp or biting though courteous in his answers; and as he did not look for any indulgence in this way of speaking from others, so he was not angered with others did not show it to him. It has often happened that he has listened quietly when others have spoken sharply to him, as on the following occasions. He had caused a ducat to be given for a partridge, and was taken to task for doing so by a friend, to whom Castruccio had said: "You would not have given more than a penny." "That is true," answered the friend. Then said Castruccio to him: "A ducat is much less to me." Having about him a flatterer on whom he had spat to show that he scorned him, the flatterer said to him: "Fisherman are willing to let the waters of the sea saturate them in order that they make take a few little fishes, and I allow myself to be wetted by spittle that I may catch a whale"; and this was not only heard by Castruccio with patience but rewarded. When told by a priest that it was wicked for him to live so sumptuously, Castruccio said: "If that be a vice than you should not fare so splendidly at the feasts of our saints." Passing through a street he saw a young man as he came out of a house of ill fame blush at being seen by Castruccio, and said to him: "Thou shouldst not be ashamed when thou comest out, but when thou goest into such places." A friend gave him a very curiously tied knot to undo and was told: "Fool, do you think that I wish to untie a thing which gave so much trouble to fasten." Castruccio said to one who professed to be a philosopher: "You are like the dogs who always run after those who will give them the best to eat," and was answered: "We are rather like the doctors who go to the houses of those who have the greatest need of them." Going by water from Pisa to Leghorn, Castruccio was much disturbed by a dangerous storm that sprang up, and was reproached for cowardice by one of those with him, who said that he did not fear anything. Castruccio answered that he did not wonder at that, since every man valued his soul for what is was worth. Being asked by one what he ought to do to gain estimation, he said: "When thou goest to a banquet take care that thou dost not seat one piece of wood upon another." To a person who was boasting that he had read many things, Castruccio said: "He knows better than to boast of remembering many things." Someone bragged that he could drink much without becoming intoxicated. Castruccio replied: "An ox does the same." Castruccio was acquainted with a girl with whom he had intimate relations, and being blamed by a friend who told him that it was undignified for him to be taken in by a woman, he said: "She has not taken me in, I have taken her." Being also blamed for eating very dainty foods, he answered: "Thou dost not spend as much as I do?" and being told that it was true, he continued: "Then thou art more avaricious than I am gluttonous." Being invited by Taddeo Bernardi, a very rich and splendid citizen of Luca, to supper, he went to the house and was shown by Taddeo into a chamber hung with silk and paved with fine stones representing flowers and foliage of the most beautiful colouring. Castruccio gathered some saliva in his mouth and spat it out upon Taddeo, and seeing him much disturbed by this, said to him: "I knew not where to spit in order to offend thee less." Being asked how Caesar died he said: "God willing I will die as he did." Being one night in the house of one of his gentlemen where many ladies were assembled, he was reproved by one of his friends for dancing and amusing himself with them more than was usual in one of his station, so he said: "He who is considered wise by day will not be considered a fool at night." A person came to demand a favour of Castruccio, and thinking he was not listening to his plea threw himself on his knees to the ground, and being sharply reproved by Castruccio, said: "Thou art the reason of my acting thus for thou hast thy ears in thy feet," whereupon he obtained double the favour he had asked. Castruccio used to say that the way to hell was an easy one, seeing that it was in a downward direction and you travelled blindfolded. Being asked a favour by one who used many superfluous words, he said to him: "When you have another request to make, send someone else to make it." Having been wearied by a similar man with a long oration who wound up by saying: "Perhaps I have fatigued you by speaking so long," Castruccio said: "You have not, because I have not listened to a word you said." He used to say of one who had been a beautiful child and who afterwards became a fine man, that he was dangerous, because he first took the husbands from the wives and now he took the wives from their husbands. To an envious man who laughed, he said: "Do you laugh because you are successful or because another is unfortunate?" Whilst he was still in the charge of Messer Francesco Guinigi, one of his companions said to him: "What shall I give you if you will let me give you a blow on the nose?" Castruccio answered: "A helmet." Having put to death a citizen of Lucca who had been instrumental in raising him to power, and being told that he had done wrong to kill one of his old friends, he answered that people deceived themselves; he had only killed a new enemy. Castruccio praised greatly those men who intended to take a wife and then did not do so, saying that they were like men who said they would go to sea, and then refused when the time came. He said that it always struck him with surprise that whilst men in buying an earthen or glass vase would sound it first to learn if it were good, yet in choosing a wife they were content with only looking at her. He was once asked in what manner he would wish to be buried when he died, and answered: "With the face turned downwards, for I know when I am gone this country will be turned upside down." On being asked if it had ever occurred to him to become a friar in order to save his soul, he answered that it had not, because it appeared strange to him that Fra Lazerone should go to Paradise and Uguccione della Faggiuola to the Inferno. He was once asked when should a man eat to preserve his health, and replied: "If the man be rich let him eat when he is hungry; if he be poor, then when he can." Seeing on of his gentlemen make a member of his family lace him up, he said to him: "I pray God that you will let him feed you also." Seeing that someone had written upon his house in Latin the words: "May God preserve this house from the wicked," he said, "The owner must never go in." Passing through one of the streets he saw a small house with a very large door, and remarked: "That house will fly through the door." He was having a discussion with the ambassador of the King of Naples concerning the property of some banished nobles, when a dispute arose between them, and the ambassador asked him if he had no fear of the king. "Is this king of yours a bad man or a good one?" asked Castruccio, and was told that he was a good one, whereupon he said, "Why should you suggest that I should be afraid of a good man?"

I could recount many other stories of his sayings both witty and weighty, but I think that the above will be sufficient testimony to his high qualities. He lived forty-four years, and was in every way a prince. And as he was surrounded by many evidences of his good fortune, so he also desired to have near him some memorials of his bad fortune; therefore the manacles with which he was chained in prison are to be seen to this day fixed up in the tower of his residence, where they were placed by him to testify for ever to his days of adversity. As in his life he was inferior neither to Philip of Macedon, the father of Alexander, nor to Scipio of Rome, so he died in the same year of his age as they did, and he would doubtless have excelled both of them had Fortune decreed that he should be born, not in Lucca, but in Macedonia or Rome.

www.bnpublishing.com

CPSIA information can be obtained
at www.ICGtesting.com
Printed in the USA
LVOW03s2248070116

469670LV00009B/276/P